GLOBAL PATENTS

Global Patents

LIMITS OF TRANSNATIONAL ENFORCEMENT

Marketa Trimble

OXFORD
UNIVERSITY PRESS

OXFORD
UNIVERSITY PRESS

Oxford University Press, Inc., publishes works that further Oxford University's objective of excellence in research, scholarship, and education.

Oxford New York
Auckland Cape Town Dar es Salaam Hong Kong Karachi Kuala Lumpur Madrid Melbourne Mexico City Nairobi New Delhi Shanghai Taipei Toronto

With offices in
Argentina Austria Brazil Chile Czech Republic France Greece Guatemala Hungary Italy Japan Poland Portugal Singapore South Korea Switzerland Thailand Turkey Ukraine Vietnam

Published by Oxford University Press, Inc.
198 Madison Avenue, New York, New York 10016

Library of Congress Cataloging-in-Publication Data

Trimble, Marketa.
Global patents : limits of transnational enforcement / Marketa Trimble.
p. cm.
Includes bibliographical references and index.
ISBN 978-0-19-984068-7 (hardback)
1. Patent laws and legislation. 2. Intellectual property. I. Title.
K1505.T75 2012
346.04'86—dc23 2011031496

1 2 3 4 5 6 7 8 9

Printed in the United States of America on acid-free paper

Note to Readers
This publication is designed to provide accurate and authoritative information in regard to the subject matter covered. It is based upon sources believed to be accurate and reliable and is intended to be current as of the time it was written. It is sold with the understanding that the publisher is not engaged in rendering legal, accounting, or other professional services. If legal advice or other expert assistance is required, the services of a competent professional person should be sought. Also, to confirm that the information has not been affected or changed by recent developments, traditional legal research techniques should be used, including checking primary sources where appropriate.

(Based on the Declaration of Principles jointly adopted by a Committee of the American Bar Association and a Committee of Publishers and Associations.)

Contents

Preface

AS THE TITLE suggests, this book discusses patents from the global or international perspective. The book is intended primarily for an academic audience; however, it will also be of interest to legal practitioners working in the area of intellectual property law, particularly patents, whether in patent prosecution, patent litigation, patent licensing, or other transactional work involving patents. Inventors, investors, and businesses will find this book useful for learning about the challenges they will face when they encounter patent-related issues that cross national borders. With increasing globalization, such encounters are likely to become more frequent than they have been before, and advance knowledge of the landscape will be essential for operating successfully in a globalized economy.

This book is not the first publication concerning international intellectual property law, or the intersection of intellectual property law and private international law, also referred to as "conflict of laws" in common law countries. Numerous studies exist on the topic of international intellectual property law, the body of law that has developed through international treaties—treaties that specifically address intellectual property issues, and treaties that cover such issues together with other topics, for example, trade-related treaties and agreements.

As compared to the tradition of studies in international intellectual property law, the history of the literature discussing the interplay between intellectual property law and private international law is relatively recent. But in this area several important works have already been written as well, including a major treatise by

James Fawcett and Paul Torremans, *Intellectual Property and Private International Law*, originally published by Oxford University Press in 1998, now in its second edition from 2011.

As opposed to other monographies that analyze issues of private international law and intellectual property law by considering all types of intellectual property, this book focuses solely on patents. This focus might be surprising to readers who are aware of the functioning of national patent systems, which are known for being strictly territorially limited, and affording rights only in the country in which the patent was granted. At first glance it appears that the functioning of patent systems rules out any cross-border problems by definition, but this book points out the wide variety of cross-border issues that are associated with the enforcement of patents.

This book addresses cross-border patent problems in a comprehensive manner; it does this through the view of an inventor or other prospective patent applicant who wishes to protect an invention globally, or at least in as many countries as possible, and who strives to enforce his rights regardless of where acts of infringement occur, or where infringers or their assets happen to be located. The book provides not only new perspectives, such as a comparative analysis of U.S. and German rules on enforcement of national patents beyond national borders, and recent statistical data, such as original statistics on U.S. patent cases, but it also advances topics that have been discussed in other studies, such as the history of patent law internationalization. By covering a large scope of cross-border patent enforcement issues, the book enriches readers' knowledge of the history of patent law internationalization, the development, current state, and possible future trajectory of international patent law, the extraterritoriality of national patent laws, and problems at the intersection of private international law and patent law.

This book is the result of a multiple-year project that could not have been undertaken without the invaluable support of many members of the Stanford Law School community and others who contributed their advice and guidance. My special thanks go to Professor Paul Goldstein; Professor Deborah Hensler, the Associate Dean for Graduate Studies; Professor Amalia Kessler; and Professor Mark Lemley of Stanford Law School. My work benefited greatly from the assistance of the staff of the Robert Crown Law Library at Stanford Law School. Particularly, I would like to express my gratitude to Paul Lomio, the Director of the Library; Sonia Moss; and Sergio Stone. I could not have conducted this research without the Stanford IP Litigation Clearinghouse database, later Lex Machina, Inc.; I would like to thank Professor Mark Lemley and Joshua Walker, the CEO of Lex Machina, Inc., for arranging for me to have early access to the database.

My research for this book was supported by the Ewing Marion Kauffman Foundation and Stanford Law School. My knowledge of the European legal landscape and particularly German law was greatly enhanced by a research stay at the Max Planck Institute for Intellectual Property and Competition Law, which was made possible by dissertation research funding from Stanford Law School. I am grateful to Professor Paul Goldstein; Professor Joseph Straus, a Director Emeritus of the Institute; Professor Josef Drexl, the current Co-Director of the Institute; and Dr. Peter Weber, the Director of the Institute's Library.

There are a number of other individuals who assisted me with my research for this book; they provided advice, interviews, comments on various drafts, and encouragement. From among the many I would like to mention Professor Barton Beebe, Matthew L. Cutler, Professor Graeme Dinwoodie, Professor Rochelle Dreyfuss, Professor Branislav Hazucha, Blair Jacobs, Philippe de Jong, Judge Thomas Kaess of the München Landgericht, Professor Annette Kur of the Max Planck Institute for Intellectual Property and Competition Law, Michael S. Nadel, WIPO Deputy Director General for Patents James Pooley, and Judge Paul Springer of the Siegen Amtsgericht.

I would like to thank my family for their support, without which my achievements would not be possible. I could not have progressed to this point without the loving support of my husband, Gary A. Trimble. To him I owe many thanks for his patience during countless discussions about my research and for his superb editing advice and many substantive comments.

The text of this book reflects the state of the law as of June 1, 2011.

Introduction

THERE IS CURRENTLY no "global patent" that would protect novel, non-obvious, and useful inventions in all countries of the world; instead, patent protection remains fragmented, as it has been since systems for protecting inventions first emerged. This fragmentation means that inventions are protected only in those countries where an inventor[1] has filed a patent application and where a patent has been granted (a "protecting country"); outside protecting countries inventions may be freely exploited by anyone, and no license needs to be granted by the patent holder. Theoretically, an inventor could achieve global protection for his invention by applying for a patent in every single country in the world; however, it should be readily apparent that applying for patents all over the world is an option feasible only to the wealthiest and most sophisticated of inventors.[2]

[1] A patent application does not have to be filed only by an inventor, and a patent does not need to be held only by an inventor, either; however, for simplification this book speaks of an "inventor" when it refers to any prospective patent applicant or patent holder. *E.g.*, in the United States, 35 U.S.C. §118 ("Filing by other than inventor") and 35 U.S.C. §261 ("Ownership; assignment").

[2] In some instances, patenting in every country of the world may also be impossible because of differences in standards of patentability that persist notwithstanding the international treaties that aim to align countries'

The fact that a global patent does not exist might be surprising, given the integration of the world economy in the twenty-first century. The existing fragmented patent systems rest on the principle of territoriality, which made sense when the world functioned on a country-by-country basis; countries' individual patent laws reflected their perceptions of policies that were necessary for promoting local inventing activity that would benefit their economies. However, a number of phenomena run counter to the arguments for maintaining the strict territoriality of patents: First, industrialization has now spread to all corners of the world; it is no longer confined to only a small number of countries. Second, the world is much more interconnected; trade crosses borders not only with regularity but also with great volume and speed. The Internet provides an enhanced and instant connectivity that not only facilitates exchange of information but also offers a platform for development of new inventions and business opportunities. Third, policy making is gradually departing from a strictly territorial framework. When setting their policies, countries now must more carefully consider the global context of their actions, and the global aspect of policy making is highlighted by the fact that nongovernmental actors are increasingly globalized as well; businesses, not-for-profit organizations, and other stakeholders in policy making are linked across national borders and represent their common interests in multiple countries with a significant degree of uniformity.

Although the march of globalization in the twenty-first century has increased the need for a global approach to patent policy, the history of the internationalization of patent law, which shows countries' awareness of cross-border patent problems in patent law and policy, began about 140 years ago when a number of countries recognized that the promotion of inventing activity would require countries to facilitate the patenting of inventions in multiple countries. During those 140 years countries undertook significant and important steps to overcome their initial nationalistic approaches to patenting and build the system that we take for granted today. The compromises that countries accepted allowed for the development of the body of international patent law that brought multiple important achievements, including mechanisms that make it easier for patent applicants to apply for and obtain patents in multiple countries. However, the fragmentation of the system of patenting in individual countries persists and presents challenges in the globalized world.

When an inventor made an invention 140 years ago, or even a few decades ago, it was easy to determine where the invention should be patented. It was easier in some

---

patent laws. *See* Chapter 1, Section 1.2, for a discussion of countries' resistance to uniform standards of patentability.

industries than in others, but in general it was possible to predict in which countries the necessary industrial capacity existed—or was likely to develop during the lifespan of the patent—to practice the invention. Even potential markets for the invention, although perhaps more difficult to predict than industrial capacity, were identifiable. Today the situation is vastly different; with isolated exceptions, it is difficult to predict which parts of the world, if any, will *not* be able to amass the necessary industrial capacity or the market power to practice or utilize an invention.

The fragmented patent system exposes inventors to the risk that their inventions will be exploited in countries where they have not obtained a patent, and this risk is potentially detrimental to the disclosure incentive that the patent systems are designed to provide.[3] By requiring that a patent applicant disclose his invention in exchange for a government-granted time-limited monopoly on practicing the invention, society safeguards the benefits of the disclosure of inventions. The disclosure requirement assures that the invention will be fully revealed and available to society, and can spark further innovation built on the knowledge of the invention. Without the incentive of a monopoly, inventors may decide not to disclose their inventions, or refrain from inventing.

The fact that an invention is exploited freely in countries where it is not protected by a patent may be considered a natural by-product of operating in an interconnected world. The patent monopoly in protecting countries helps the inventor to recover his research and development costs, and as long as the markets in those countries generate sufficient returns on his investment during the term of the patent monopoly, he should not have to be concerned if his invention is exploited outside any protecting countries. A market analysis should reveal the countries in which the inventor needs to patent his invention, in order for the inventor to properly allocate his investment costs to those countries. However, policy makers should take into account additional considerations when evaluating patent incentives: it is advantageous to society if the inventor can allocate his costs to as many markets as possible. Additionally, if deemed relevant by legislators, moral rights considerations may dictate that the invention be attributed to a particular inventor without regard to the place of exploitation, and a natural rights perspective will call for the inventor to be remunerated for his inventing activity regardless of where benefits arise.

Because inventors seek global protection for their inventions, they wish to have not only access to global patenting but also effective patent enforcement; for enforcement to be effective, it must be supported by functioning and accessible enforcement mechanisms. As is the patenting process, enforcement is not without difficulties;

[3] *See* Chapter 1, Section 1.1, for a discussion about incentives that patent systems ought to provide.

in addition to general deficiencies in the enforcement capacities of individual countries that complicate enforcement of any rights in those countries, patent right enforcement also suffers from fragmentation. When patents are issued in multiple countries to cover a single invention—even when they are granted based on a single international application[4]—patent holders must enforce the resulting individual national patents country by country. For now, there is no single world patent court, or even a regional patent court, to adjudicate infringements of patents in multiple countries, and existing national courts, with narrow exceptions, refrain from deciding cases in which a foreign patent is at issue. Fragmented enforcement is complex and costly, which means that out of the few inventors who actually secure patents in multiple countries, many still lack effective protection because they cannot pursue enforcement of their rights in all these countries.

This book analyzes the various challenges extant in both obtaining and enforcing patents in multiple protecting countries, and pursuing enforcement against those who exploit inventions outside protecting countries. Chapter 1 begins by explaining the principle of territoriality, exploring the impact that the principle has on patent law, and discussing the clash of territoriality of the patent monopoly with the global consequences of disclosure of an invention. Building on this foundation, Chapter 1 explains why no world patent exists, and reviews various versions of and substitutes for a world patent that have been proposed since 1909 when the term "world patent" seems to have appeared for the first time. Although countries have agreed on a number of features to harmonize their patent systems, they have been unable to advance harmonization to the point of creating one unitary patent system. To retain national patent system identities while facilitating as territorially wide patenting as possible, countries consented to the creation of a patent application system that streamlined the process of applying for patents in multiple countries simultaneously. Although the system has greatly assisted patent applicants by enabling them to adopt a patent strategy with wide territorial impact, statistics show that significant hurdles persist for those wishing to patent in multiple countries, and that most patent applicants continue to be unable to take advantage of the system.

Chapter 2 explores another significant obstacle to obtaining and maintaining patents in multiple countries—fragmentation of enforcement. The negative impact of fragmentation on maintaining patents is not only direct, it is also indirect because it negatively affects the process of obtaining patents—the high costs associated with

[4] International applications are applications submitted under the Patent Cooperation Treaty, the European Patent Convention, or under other regional instruments. *See* Chapter 1, Section 1.3.2, for a discussion of these instruments.

litigating severally in multiple countries deter applicants from filing for patents in multiple countries. Chapter 2 analyzes the mechanisms that have been used or have been proposed to address the fragmentation of patent litigation; drafters of the mechanisms search for ways to concentrate patent litigation in one national, regional, or supranational court. The only mechanism tested so far, the "Brussels regime"[5] in the European Union,[6] has suffered from a number of problems, and Chapter 2 reviews both the problems and the attempted solutions to the problems. The experience with the Brussels regime has provided important lessons for the development of other mechanisms to address patent litigation fragmentation, and Chapter 2 covers two major proposals for such mechanisms that have been drafted specifically for intellectual property litigation; additionally, it explains a patent-specific mechanism that has been in development in Europe for a number of years. Despite the interest of numerous academics and practitioners in solving fragmentation problems, the proposals remain in either nonbinding principles or draft agreements, and the Brussels regime has been curtailed by judicial interpretation. Therefore, with isolated exceptions,[7] concentration of patent litigation remains unavailable.

Because of the costs associated with simultaneous multicountry litigation, or because of the limited availability of patent protection or substantive or procedural law advantages, patent holders often choose to litigate in only one protecting country. Using the extraterritorial reach of the patent laws of a protecting country, patent holders can sometimes reach activities that adversely affect their economic interests even when the activities occur outside a protecting country. Chapter 3 analyzes the laws and legal doctrines that patent holders have used to reach conduct outside protecting countries. Chapter 3 offers a comparative analysis using the United States and Germany, which have two of the three largest volumes of patent litigation in the world, and shows that German patent law not only meets U.S. patent law in its extraterritorial reach, but in some respects exceeds it.[8] Regardless of the extraterritorial ambitions of any particular country's patent laws, natural limitations arise when the laws are applied against parties that are outside the jurisdiction's enforcement power. If enforcement of a court decision against foreign parties becomes necessary, a court

---

[5] *See* Chapter 2, Section 2.1.1, for an explanation of the term and a discussion of the regime.

[6] For simplification, this book uses the term "European Union" even when references are made to the time when only the "European Communities" existed (prior to the Maastricht Treaty) or had legal personality (prior to the Treaty of Lisbon). Similarly, this book uses the term "Court of Justice of the European Union" (CJEU) even when it refers to the time when the title of the court was "Court of Justice of the European Communities."

[7] *See* Chapter 2, Sections 2.1.1, 2.1.2, 2.1.3, and 2.1.6, on the limited possibilities of concentration of patent litigation.

[8] Certain procedural differences may still make U.S. courts more desirable for patent litigation than German courts. *See* Chapter 3, Section 3.7, for examples of such differences.

in a protecting country must rely on the cooperation of a foreign court—a court in the country where the parties are domiciled or assets are located—to recognize and enforce any decision.

Chapter 4 shows the recognition and enforcement difficulties that arise when a party seeks to enforce a court decision in a foreign country. It begins by presenting an original empirical project that studied all patent cases filed in U.S. federal district courts in 2004 and 2009, in order to observe the involvement of foreign defendants in patent cases filed in those years. The involvement of foreign defendants suggests a potential for cross-border enforcement difficulties when courts issue decisions against those defendants. In addition to providing a statistical picture of the possible magnitude of the problem, the project also identified the types of injunctions that have been issued against foreign defendants; the difficulties associated with the enforcement of these injunctions are also analyzed in Chapter 4. Additionally, Chapter 4 discusses obstacles associated with the enforcement of monetary relief; although less problematic than enforcement of injunctions, enforcement of monetary relief can also raise complex issues. While some of the enforcement problems discussed are of a general nature and arise in any cross-border case, particular enforcement problems may be either patent-law specific or likely to be exacerbated in the context of a patent case; these particular problems are also identified in Chapter 4.

The mechanisms that have been proposed to solve the patent litigation fragmentation problem have resulted from attempts to improve the current system of obtaining and enforcing multiple patents, but they have not addressed the contentious issue of deeper patent law harmonization. Based on a thorough analysis of cross-border enforcement problems concerning patents, this book argues that, while the proposed mechanisms appear to fit into the overall trend of the evolution of patent law internationalization, they will function only if countries accept the inevitability of harmonization. Even if harmonization is not achieved through a substantive patent law treaty, it will occur through private international law solutions; these solutions, whether they rely on concentration in a national, regional, or supranational court, necessarily lead to harmonization through converging judicial interpretations arising from concentrated proceedings concerning the patents of multiple countries. With this prospect in mind the question arises as to whether it would be prudent to proceed with substantive harmonization, or perhaps even with the creation of a unitary patent that could initially be limited in scope by territory and subject matter.

The fact that this book proposes that substantive harmonization or unification might be unavoidable does not mean that it advocates that patent rights be expanded in such a manner so as to broaden the rights of patent holders throughout the world; it does not. The book does not advocate a particular level of patent protection, nor does it analyze what level of protection would be suitable for a harmonized framework. Identifying the appropriate level of protection should be the goal of the process of harmonization, which should also entail a careful consideration of the availability of and the conditions for exceptions to patent protection and compulsory licensing; exceptions and compulsory licensing are included in the existing intellectual property treaties, and they should remain available to facilitate particular solutions for individual countries according to their specific economic and social situations.

Finally, a note on what this book does not cover: This book focuses on cross-border enforcement through civil litigation, and either leaves aside or mentions only briefly other forms of enforcement of patent rights. For example, Chapter 3 discusses only briefly enforcement through border measures that are effectuated by customs authorities, and arbitration is not discussed in the book at all. Arbitration is used primarily in situations where a preexisting contractual relationship, such as a licensing agreement, exists, which is typically not the case in patent infringement cases, as has been confirmed by available statistics showing that intellectual property infringements are rarely arbitrated.[9] Arbitration would rely on the same substantive patent laws that are analyzed in Chapter 3 and would face some (although not all) of the same enforcement difficulties that are explored in Chapter 4.[10] Given the limited applicability of arbitration in cases of infringements, arbitration is not covered in this book.

---

[9] Daniel Schimmel & Ila Kapoor, *Resolving International Intellectual Property Disputes in Arbitration*, INTELL. PROP. & TECH L. J., at 5, 5 (February 2009).

[10] Cross-border enforcement of remedies is easier in arbitration than in civil litigation because as opposed to court decisions, arbitration awards are recognized and enforced based on a widely supported and long-established international convention on cross-border recognition and enforcement of such awards. Convention on the Recognition and Enforcement of Foreign Arbitral Awards, 1958. There are currently 146 parties to the Convention. For the current signatories, see information by UNCITRAL, *available at* http://www.uncitral.org/uncitral/en/uncitral_texts/arbitration/NYConvention_status.html (last visited Sept. 2, 2011). However, the process suffers from some of the same enforcement problems that civil litigation does, such as the difficulty of enforcement of injunctions where the infringer raises a design-around argument. *See* Chapter 4, Section 4.2.3, for challenges associated with enforcement of injunctions.

1 Global Protection for Inventions

UNDER THE CURRENT patent systems, inventors who want global patent protection for their inventions must patent their inventions in every country in the world; however, it is uncommon for inventors to do this. In most instances patent holders cannot afford to patent an invention everywhere, and therefore will hold patents for their inventions in only one or a few countries, the "protecting countries."[1] This chapter explains why even in the twenty-first century, when trade is globalized and information spreads instantly to most parts of the world, inventors must still rely on single-country patents to protect their inventions. Because they secure patent protection in only one or a small number of countries inventors expose their inventions to possible exploitation outside a few protecting countries and relinquish part—perhaps a significant part—of the income that they could have generated from licensing their inventions in all countries of the world.

A global patent would solve the problem of territorially limited protection for inventions because it would give patentees rights everywhere and with these rights the possibility of litigating where enforcement is necessary; however, there is no

[1] *See* Introduction, note 2 for an additional reason for which patenting in all countries may be impossible.

global patent. The current "global patent system," which consists of individual national systems, is fragmented and has never offered a unitary global protection. Although countries have tried to compensate for the shortcomings of the global system by making protection in multiple countries easily accessible, the result suffers from a major defect: it is too costly[2] and fragmented to serve as a viable option for the great majority of inventors, particularly noncorporate inventors and small or medium-sized enterprises (SMEs). As a result, notwithstanding the 140 years of achievements in patent law internationalization, which are detailed in this chapter, most inventions are protected in only one or in a very small number of countries; according to recent statistics, 90 percent of inventions for which patents have been issued in multiple countries are patented in fewer than four countries.[3]

Using as a background the territorial limitations that still exist under the current patent system (outlined in Section 1.1 below), this chapter discusses how countries around the world have attempted to address these limitations. Section 1.2 reviews the most obvious solution, the creation of a world patent, and explains why this option has failed to gain ground and why countries now rely on a network of national patents, which are issued for the same invention; these are so-called "parallel patents," and they offer national protection in each country where the patent holder secures them. For this network of national patents to develop it was first necessary

---

[2] According to one study co-authored by a former European Patent Office chief economist, in 2003 the estimated costs of prosecuting and maintaining patents in the thirteen most often designated countries of the European Patent Organization and the United States and Japan were more than €500,000. The authors used an "average patent" for the analysis, meaning a patent with an average number of claims, time to grant, and type of firm. Bruno van Pottelsberghe de la Potterie & Didier Francois, *The Cost Factor in Patent Systems*, CEB Working Paper No. 06/002, *available at* http://ideas.repec.org/p/sol/wpaper/06-002.html (last visited Sept. 2, 2011), 14. For data per claim, see *id.*, 31. Since the study was undertaken, the costs of obtaining European patents have been reduced. *See* Bruno van Pottelsberghe de la Potterie & Malwina Mejer, *The London Agreement and the Cost of Patenting in Europe*, Bruegel Working Paper No. 2008/05, *available at* http://ideas.repec.org/p/cpr/ceprdp/7033.html (last visited Sept. 2, 2011). On the correlation of decisions by patent applicants to validate European patents and postgrant fees related to validation, see Dietmar Harhoff, Karin Hoisl, & Bruno van Pottelsberghe de la Potterie, *Languages, Fees and the International Scope of Patenting*, Discussion Paper 2009-06, *available at* http://ideas.repec.org/p/cpr/ceprdp/7241.html (last visited Sept. 2, 2011). For information on fees associated with the grant and the maintenance of a patent in selected countries, see, for instance, Gaétan de Rassenfosse & Bruno van Pottelsberghe, *The Role of Fees in Patent Systems: Theory and Evidence*, Intellectual Property Research Institute of Australia, Working Paper No. 7/10, November 2010, 26.

[3] According to WIPO statistics, only "around 10% of all patent families include filings at four or more patent offices." "Patent families" are defined as "a set of patent applications interrelated by either priority claims or PCT national phase entries." World Intellectual Property Indicators 2009, WIPO, *available at* http://www.wipo.int/freepublications/en/intproperty/941/wipo_pub_941.pdf (last visited Sept. 2, 2011). According to a survey conducted by *inovia*, a company that lists itself as a "foreign filing platform," while "45% of respondents filed more than half of their patent applications overseas in 2010, [. . .] they only filed into an average of 5.9 countries." The U.S. 2011 Global Patent & IP Trends Indicator, inovia, February 2001, *available at* http://www.inovia.com/survey/inovia_2011_US_IP_Trends_Report.pdf (last visited Sept. 2, 2011).

for countries to abandon their strict nationalistic views of their own patent systems, which shaped the systems until the second half of the nineteenth century, and to allow, first, their own nationals to obtain patents abroad, and second, foreigners to obtain patents under the same conditions as their own nationals. These developments are covered in Section 1.3.1, while Section 1.3.2 surveys the various mechanisms that were created to help patentees achieve territorially wide protection for their inventions. Available data show[4] that such mechanisms are indeed utilized by patentees seeking territorially broad protection, with the limiting factor being that the high costs associated with patenting in multiple countries still cause many patentees to apply for patents in only one or a small number of countries. Therefore, even under the international conventions and within the institutional cooperative frameworks that were created as a result of internationalization efforts, the "global patent system" remains far short of offering effective global protection for all inventors, as explained in Section 1.4.

1.1 The Territorial Limitations of Patent Protection

The patent system was born to create cross-border problems. We tend today to attribute the existence of such problems to massively increased globalization,[5] which involves extensive cross-border trade and the rapid exchange of an unprecedented volume of information facilitated by the Internet. However, the patent system was predestined to generate these problems—problems that have been observed for more than a century, and certainly long before the words "Internet" and "globalization" were ever known.[6] As a result, the entire history of international patent law is

---

[4] *See infra* Section 1.3 for statistics concerning the use of the mechanisms.

[5] *E.g.*, Rochelle C. Dreyfuss, *Resolving Patent Disputes in a Global Economy*, *in* PATENT LAW AND THEORY: A HANDBOOK OF CONTEMPORARY RESEARCH (Toshiko Takenaka & Rainer Moufang eds., 2007), *available at* http://papers.ssrn.com/sol3/papers.cfm?abstract_id=1226562 (last visited Sept. 2, 2011), 1; Timothy R. Holbrook, *Territoriality Waning? Patent Infringement for Offering in the United States to Sell an Invention Abroad*, 37 U.C. DAVIS L. REV. 701, 703 (2003–2004). Christian Osterrieth and Klaus Haft point out that given the common market and the lack of trade barriers in Europe "the purely national patent infringement proceedings look like relics from a long time ago." Christian Osterrieth & Klaus Haft, *Grenzüberschreitende Patentverletzungsverfahren in Europa*, *in* FESTSCHRIFT ZU 50 JAHRE VPP 372 (Rolf W. Einsele & Erich R. Franke eds., 2005); Matthias Rößler, *The Court of Jurisdiction for Joint Parties in International Patent Disputes*, 38 IIC 380, 381 (2007).

[6] For an overview of early attempts to solve cross-border problems of patent law, see, for instance, Alois Troller, *Europäisierung des Patentrechts und Gerichtsstand*, 1955 GRUR INT. 529; Richard Spencer, *A European Patent: An Old and Vexing Problem*, 42 J. PAT. OFF. SOC'Y 371 (1960). In 1931 Eduard Reimer noted that "[w]ith the many modes of transportation of all kinds one reaches the borders of Germany very quickly even from the very center of the country." Eduard Reimer, *Patentverletzung durch Lieferung ins Ausland*, 31 MITTEILUNGEN VOM

replete with attempts to find solutions to mitigate cross-border problems. It is useful to first explain the territoriality problem inherent in the patent system before reviewing the history and current state of internationalization of the system.

The patent system is unfit for a global economy because it functions territorially, on a one-country, one-patent principle. For an invention to be protected in a country a patent must be obtained in that specific country, and for an invention to be protected in multiple countries, patents must be obtained in each of the countries individually. There exists no patent that covers the entire world; the Patent Cooperation Treaty (PCT), signed by most of the countries of the world, and the only treaty to offer the opportunity to file one application for patents in so many signatory countries, does not result in one patent covering all the signatory countries—it helps only in obtaining patents in each designated PCT country individually.[7] The term "world patent" serves—at least for now—only as a catch phrase used in the marketing world.[8]

The core of the territoriality problem in the patent system is simple: The system is built on the principle that a time-limited monopoly on practicing an invention will be granted in exchange for disclosure of the invention. However, the protection provided by a country's patent is limited to the territory of that particular country, while the disclosure is by definition global—once the invention is disclosed, there are no limits as to how far the information will spread.[9] And unless the potential patent holder files for patents in every country where he wishes his invention to be protected, his global disclosure is rewarded with a mere one-country monopoly.

Determining the countries in which inventors should seek patent protection is often difficult; for most inventors it is impracticable to obtain patents even in multiple selected countries. To decide where it is necessary or desirable to file for patents, inventors have to ask, "In what countries around the world during the term of patent protection will industries exist that are or will be capable of practicing the

VERBAND DEUTSCHER PATENTANWÄLTE 85, 85 (1931). *See also* Jean-Marc Mousseron, Jacques Raynard, & Pierre Véron, *Cross-Border Injunctions—A French Perspective*, 29 IIC 884, 884 (1998); Graeme B. Dinwoodie, *Developing a Private International Intellectual Property Law: The Demise of Territoriality?*, 51 WM. & MARY L. REV. 713, 713 (2009).

[7] *See infra* Section 1.3.2 for more on the PCT, including associated cost savings.

[8] *See infra* Section 1.2 on the proposal for a world patent.

[9] As du Bois-Reymond noted in 1909, "[i]n the development of the economic value that is to be extracted from an invention, the exploitation of foreign markets has an important position." A. du Bois-Reymond, *Das Weltpatent*, *in* STUDIEN ZUR FÖRDERUNG DES GEWERBLICHEN RECHTSSCHUTZES 465, 468 (1909). For a discussion of the requirement of disclosure in the patent system, see Alan Devlin, *The Misunderstood Function of Disclosure in Patent Law*, 23 HARV. J.L. & TECH. 401 (2010).

invention, and where will important markets for the invention arise?" Rarely will the question lead to only one country; industrial capability or market power is rarely concentrated in only one country.

It is true that for some inventions the potential to practice the invention will arise in only a few countries, and consequently potential patent holders can obtain effective protection by filing for patents in only those selected countries. Approaching patent protection in such a territorially limited manner will still be costly but probably manageable for patent holders who are active in the kinds of industries that are so exclusive and specialized that they exist only in a few countries. The aerospace industry is one such industry.

Ironically, inventors not backed by a wealthy industry and thus not likely to be capable of patenting in multiple countries are those in nonexclusive industries who, in order to protect their inventions adequately, *should* file for patents in many if not all countries of the world.[10] The rapid progress of industrialization may soon render most if not all industries nonexclusive, which means that there might soon be very few inventions that during their twenty-year term of patent protection[11] can be practiced in only one or a few countries. All other inventions will have the potential to be exploited globally, and to protect them adequately patent holders should seek global protection by obtaining patents in all countries.

Given that global disclosure is a by-product of obtaining a patent in even one country,[12] it is not surprising that patent holders wish to capture the worldwide value of their disclosure. There is at least one significant reason why all countries should help patent holders to do so:[13] Allowing an inventor to collect the reward for his invention worldwide is vital to maintaining at least one of the incentives that the patent system was designed to provide—not necessarily the incentive to innovate

---

[10] According to the 2008 WIPO World Patent Report, "[n]on-resident patent filings originate from a relatively small number of countries, led by the United States of America (21.9% of non-resident filings worldwide)." World Patent Report, WIPO, 2008, *available at* http://www.wipo.int/export/sites/www/ipstats/en/statistics/patents/pdf/wipo_pub_931.pdf (last visited Sept. 2, 2011), 7. The fields of technology with "an above-average concentration" of filings by foreign applicants vary by country but are generally concentrated in the areas of biotechnology, pharmaceuticals, medical technology, telecommunications, information technology, and semiconductors. *Id.*, 43.

[11] TRIPs, *infra* note 19, Article 33.

[12] Disclosure can also occur de facto when practicing the invention if the technology can be reverse-engineered. If the product that embeds the invention provides enough details about the invention so that others can replicate the invention, putting the product on the market will give away the invention and cause its disclosure.

[13] *See* Conclusions chapter in this book for other considerations.

(the correlation between the patent system and this incentive is subject to great debate)[14]—but the incentive to disclose information.[15]

It is important that potential patent holders not be discouraged from disclosing their inventions simply because they can afford to patent in only one country, while their invention will be practiced worldwide. If they are concerned about their inventions being practiced in countries where they cannot secure a patent, they may be reluctant to disclose the invention in any country; instead of applying for a patent, they may opt to rely on trade secrets to protect their invention, thereby depriving society of the disclosure of the invention. However, another outcome may be even more detrimental to society: the inventor may refuse to disclose or practice the invention entirely or not to invent at all. For some inventions protection through trade secrets is not an option; the practicing of an invention can amount to de facto disclosure if the invention can be reverse-engineered.[16] Without any protection for their inventions that would provide at least a temporary monopoly, inventors may be unable to recover their research and development costs. If inventors are subject to the risk of reverse-engineering and cannot secure effective patent protection, they may decide to forego altogether the disclosure and practice of their inventions.

---

[14] Andrew W. Torrance & Bill Tomlinson, *Patents and the Regress of Useful Arts*, 10 COLUM. SCI. & TECH. L. REV. 130 (2009). On a patent's decreased impact on innovation in cases of certain types of inventions, see Alan Devlin & Neel Sukhatme, *Self-Realizing Inventions and the Utilitarian Foundation of Patent Law*, 51 WM. & MARY L. REV. 897 (2009) ("[E]ven enormously useful inventions should not receive patent protection if sufficient alternative incentives to innovate and commercialize exist outside of the patent system."); in various industries, see Dan L. Burk & Mark A. Lemley, *Policy Levers in Patent Law*, 89 VA. L. REV. 1575 (2003); in a university setting, see Mark A. Lemley, *Are Universities Patent Trolls?*, 18 FORDHAM INTELL. PROP. MEDIA & ENT. L. J. 611, 621 (2008) ("[T]he contribution of patents to university incentives to innovate seems smaller than in profit-driven companies."). The criticism is supported by the fact that practice has shown that the patent system does not unequivocally lead to the support of domestic industries and may even retard industrial progress and reduce innovation. Among the phenomena related to these problems are the existence of non-practicing entities (some of them referred to as "patent trolls") and practices that these entities employ, and patent thicket or patent crowding. *See, e.g.*, Knut Blind, Katrin Cremers, & Elisabeth Mueller, *The Influence of Strategic Patenting on Companies' Patent Portfolios*, Centre for European Economic Research, Discussion Paper No. 07-013, *available at* ftp://ftp.zew.de/pub/zew-docs/dp/dp07013.pdf (last visited Sept. 2, 2011) (noting that in the 1990s "[p]atents gained a strategic importance that exceeded their traditional role of appropriating direct returns from R&D. Patenting has been motivated by the desire to block competitors in their research activities.").

[15] On the concept of an inventor as the "teacher of the nation" and the connection of the concept to the term of patent protection under the English Statute of Monopolies of 1623, see FELIX DAMME, DAS DEUTSCHE PATENTRECHT 8 (1906). *See also infra* Section 1.3.1. Damme explained that "[t]he *disclosure* of the invention is the reason for the protection and by itself an important one. The fact that the exclusive right appears to be a reward for the intellectual work of the inventor is only a side effect." *Id.*, 15–16. For theories explaining the existence of patent law, see, e.g., RUDOLF KRASSER, PATENTRECHT 34–35 (2004).

[16] *See* Devlin, *supra* note 9.

The global disclosure phenomenon is not new; it has always been present in patent systems. However, when the first patent systems were created, language and access to information and inventions were sufficient barriers to lock the information about the invention within one country; later, industrial capabilities limited the number of countries where an invention could be practiced. Today these limitations have disappeared and the incentive to disclose has become more and more dependent on the ability of holders to enforce their patents globally.[17]

1.2 A World Patent

One possible solution to the problem of territoriality in patent protection would be a single world patent that would protect an invention in all the countries of the world. With one application potential patent holders would submit their invention to one examination and obtain one patent covering the planet. An alternative approach to a world patent was outlined at the beginning of the twentieth century by a Berlin patent attorney, A. du Bois-Reymond; in his 1909 article "Das Weltpatent" he proposed that patents continue to be granted by individual countries but subsequently be recognized by other countries. This system would have effectively led to a world patent.[18] Whatever the procedural details might be, however, the idea of the world patent is constrained by two major obstacles that make its application impracticable for now and very unlikely in the near future.

The first obstacle to a world patent is the problem of substantive patent law harmonization. A world patent would require that all countries adopt a uniform standard of patentability; however, the countries of the world actually disagree on what should be patentable. Despite the substantive harmonization provisions of the PCT and the Agreement on Trade-Related Aspects of Intellectual Property Rights (TRIPs Agreement),[19] and despite the similarities in national provisions on patentability, the content given to the provisions by court interpretations makes them very different.[20] Ideas about patentability are often deeply embedded in the social and

[17] Another reason why patent holders should be rewarded globally for their disclosure is the following: If we accept the premise that the patent system should enable patent holders to recover their research and development costs, rewarding them globally for their disclosure will promote an apportionment of the costs of the inventive activity among all the beneficiaries of their invention.

[18] Du Bois-Reymond, *supra* note 9, 465–90.

[19] Agreement on Trade-Related Aspects of Intellectual Property Rights, Annex 1C of the Marrakesh Agreement Establishing the World Trade Organization (Apr. 15, 1994).

[20] In the 1940s Paul Wiegand noted that great differences in patentability persist not because of substantive patent laws but because of the relevant jurisprudence in various countries. Paul Wiegand, *Die europäische*

moral perceptions of societies and cannot easily be changed by international agreements; at the very beginning of the process of patent law internationalization in the 1870s countries agreed to disagree on the issue and relinquished any idea of establishing a world patent.[21]

Although countries today have notions of patentability that might be converging,[22] their ideas are still sufficiently different and unfit for the adoption of a uniform standard.[23]

It is questionable whether a worldwide unification of substantive patent law is desirable at all, at least at present and as concerns all kinds of protectable subject matter. Among the reasons for not harmonizing patent laws are the significant divergences in national policies that underlie patent laws[24] and the absence of a consensus at even a national level of what an ideal patent system should be.[25] Jerome Reichman and Rochelle C. Dreyfuss oppose even "a deep harmonization" that would stop short of unifying national patents into one global patent, since they view that development as being a step toward the creation of a de facto world patent; they suggest that patent practice should facilitate "legal experimentation" in different jurisdictions as individual countries strive to solve new legal challenges that arise out of the emergence of new players and technologies.[26] Reichman and Dreyfuss emphasize that recent efforts to achieve a substantial harmonization have the potential not only

---

Vereinheitlichung auf dem Gebiet der Rechtsprechung in Patentangelegenheiten, 1942 GRUR 468, 479. *See also* Assessment of the Impact of the European Patent Litigation Agreement (EPLA) on Litigation of European Patents (European Patent Office 2006), *available at* http://www.eplaw.org/Downloads/EPLA_Impact_Assessment_2006_.pdf (last visited Sept. 2, 2011), 3.

[21] Spencer, *supra* note 6, 372.

[22] On converging "approaches to various aspects of intellectual property law," see Intellectual Property: Principles Governing Jurisdiction, Choice of Law, and Judgments in Transnational Disputes 4–5 (ALI 2008). *See also* Brief for Amici Curiae Law Professors in Support of the Appellee, *Jan K. Voda, M.D. v. Cordis Corporation*, No. 05-1238 (Fed. Cir. July 29, 2005).

[23] The European Commission commented on the "very little support for any (further) harmonization of substantive patent law" in *Communication from the Commission to the European Parliament and the Council—Enhancing the Patent System in Europe*, 8302/07 (Apr. 4, 2007), 3.

[24] Christopher Heath of the European Patent Office notes that "the ideal level of protection is likely to be different for countries at different stages of development, or with different industrial strengths and weaknesses." Christopher Heath, *Harmonisation of International Patent Law?—A Reply to Straus and Klunker*, 39 IIC 210, 214 (2008).

[25] Heath suggests that "harmonization [. . .] remains doubtful where the world's major patent systems in their current form have been called into question." Heath, *Harmonisation*, *supra* note 24, 210.

[26] Jerome H. Reichman & Rochelle Cooper Dreyfuss, *Harmonization without Consensus: Critical Reflections on Drafting a Substantive Patent Law Treaty*, 57 Duke L. J. 85, 92–93 (2007). On legal experimentation, see also John F. Duffy, *Harmony and Diversity in Global Patent Law*, 17 Berkeley Tech. L.J. 685, 707–10 (2002). "A consolidation of existing patent systems into a single monolith would impoverish the field; it would be mass extinction of legal species." *Id.*, 726.

to disadvantage developing countries but also to "boomerang against even its developed country promoters."[27] Similarly, Christopher Heath, who lists a number of reasons for not harmonizing patent laws as they exist today, warns that harmonization should not become "an end in itself" at a time when "there is little evidence to conclude that a uniform patent system [. . .] would benefit developed or developing countries."[28]

The second obstacle to the creation of a world patent is the fact that such a patent could not exist without being uniformly interpreted. World rights (or even regional rights) such as the ones that would be created by a world patent (or by a European Union patent)[29] serve a purpose only if they are consistently applied, and therefore an institutional structure would need to be superimposed over individual countries' judicial systems to secure consistency in enforcement of the rights.[30] Calls for a unified patent court have been voiced several times in history in the context of proposals for regionally limited patent systems; for instance, in 1919 an author suggested that such a court be created in the context of a patent system for the British Empire.[31] For several years a proposal has been discussed that would create a unified patent litigation system in Europe.[32]

So far attempts to create at least a regional unified court structure have failed. The failure may be attributed to the same reasons for which countries resist substantive harmonization of patent laws: countries dislike the idea of a single patent court as much as they dislike the idea of a single substantive standard. The problem is that even if the differences in the substantive patent laws of individual countries were to be preserved by designing a structure that would respect those differences, a common court would very likely steer the interpretation of these laws in a common direction and thus become a "back door" for substantive patent law harmonization.[33]

---

[27] Reichman & Dreyfuss, *supra* note 26, 86. Also *id.*, 93–94 and 102–08.

[28] Heath, *Harmonisation*, *supra* note 24, 214.

[29] *See* Chapter 2, Section 2.2, for a discussion of the proposed European Union patent.

[30] In the United States the desire for uniform enforcement led to the creation of a single appellate court, today the U.S. Court of Appeals for the Federal Circuit.

[31] Theobald, *Englische Gedanken über ein britisches Reichspatent*, 1920 GRUR 29, 30.

[32] *See* Chapter 2, Section 2.2, for a discussion of the proposed patent litigation system. For one of the first European proposals, see F.-K. Beier, *Stand und Aussichten der europäischen Rechtsvereinheitlichung auf dem Gebiete des gewerblichen Rechtsschutzes*, 1969 GRUR INT. 145.

[33] Klaus Grabinski, *Kann und darf die Bestimmung des Schutzbereichs eines europäischen Patents in verschiedenen Ländern zu unterschiedlichen Ergebnissen führen?*, 1998 GRUR 857, 862–63; Paul Edward Geller, *An International Patent Utopia?*, 85 J. PAT. & TRADEMARK OFF. SOC'Y 582, 605–06 (2003). Geller suggested that the crisis of the current patent system be remedied by introduction of an "interim regime" built on a "first-to-post system." *Id.*, 582 and 590 ff. Thomas Borecki suggested that "a convergence of substantive law" can already be observed "as judges around the world are looking to other judges' decisions on substantive law."

The harmonizing potential of a unified court system was recognized as early as the 1940s and 1950s when Paul Wiegand[34] and Eduard Reimer[35] asserted that even absent a single European patent, a single European patent court, if created, would contribute to a gradual unification of patent law.[36] Similarly, the late Justice Laddie foresaw the harmonizing function that a unified court would have when he suggested in 2003 that a unified European patent litigation structure "would emphasize the similarities between national laws and expose as unnecessary the differences."[37] However, with countries resisting substantive unification, the introduction of a single judicial structure for litigating patents granted in multiple countries is likely to be difficult.[38]

1.3 Parallel Patents

When countries determined in the 1870s that the establishment of a world patent was infeasible[39] they decided to focus on ensuring that even in the absence of unitary global protection patent holders could enjoy the most territorially extensive protection possible. This meant, first and foremost, that inventors who held patents in one country should be able to obtain patents in other countries, even if they were not citizens or residents of the other countries or were not incorporated there. It may

Thomas Borecki, *Moving Towards Regional Patent Systems*, *in* RETHINKING INTERNATIONAL INTELLECTUAL PROPERTY: BIODIVERSITY & DEVELOPING COUNTRIES, EXTRATERRITORIAL ENFORCEMENT, THE GRACE PERIOD, AND OTHER ISSUES 58, 60 (Kraig M. Hill, Toshiko Takenaka, & Kevin Takeuchi eds., 2000). Wiegand, *Die europäische Vereinheitlichung*, *supra* note 20, 469.

[34] Wiegand, *Die europäische Vereinheitlichung*, *supra* note 20, 479.

[35] Eduard Reimer, Professor, Director of the Institute for Foreign and International Patent, Trademark and Copyright Law in Munich, President of the German Patent Office. His plans from 1953 and 1954 were reprinted in EDUARD REIMER, EUROPÄISIERUNG DES PATENTRECHTS 259–81 (1955).

[36] Haan criticized Reimer's plan because it suggested that the jurisprudence of national courts and the centralized court could exist side by side; Haan warned that such a solution would in fact destabilize legal certainty. Haan's plan of 1954, reprinted in REIMER, EUROPÄISIERUNG, *supra* note 35, 243–44.

[37] Remco De Ranitz, *Mr. Justice Laddie in Conversation with Remco De Ranitz*, 25 EUR. INTELL. PROP. REV. 528, 535 (2003). Justice Laddie continued: "Furthermore, I cannot see why you need multiple patents. That is what it comes down to." *Id. See also* Jean-François Thony in his opening remarks during the 14th European Patent Judges' Symposium in Bordeaux, September 16–20, 2008. 14th European Patent Judges' Symposium, European Patent Office, O.J. 1/2009, Spec. ed., 2. "Everyone in patents agrees on the need for a unified court system to help harmonise the case law and improve legal certainty." *Id.*

[38] Klaus Grabinski, *Kann und darf*, *supra* note 33, 863. *See* Chapter 2, Section 2.2, for the proposal for a litigation system in Europe. *See also* a description of the history of the proposals for a unitary patent in the European Union in Proposal for a Regulation of the European Parliament and of the Council implementing enhanced cooperation in the area of creation of unitary patent protection, COM(2011) 215/3, 3.

[39] Spencer, *supra* note 6, 371–72.

surprise us today that patenting abroad would be a novel idea, but this idea was quite new in the nineteenth century. Second, once it was made possible to apply for patents abroad, filing for patents on the same invention in multiple countries—parallel patents—needed to be made as simple as possible.

1.3.1 OBTAINING A PATENT ABROAD

That an inventor should be able to file for a patent in multiple countries seems obvious today, but originally countries not only discouraged the practice of applying for patents abroad, they actually tried to prevent it. The rationale that hindered the patenting of the same invention in multiple countries was the belief held by countries that the patent system should support only their own local industries.[40] This notion was inherited from the concept of monopolies, which granted exclusive rights in the hope that the specific object of the monopoly would flourish *domestically* under the care of the monopoly holder.[41] For instance, the preamble to the first patent law of the Austrian Empire, the Act on Privileges to Inventions of 1820, listed among its goals the intention to "positively impact the revival of domestic industry."[42] The rationale had four manifestations.

The first manifestation sounds rather exotic today, and not surprisingly, of the four it was the first to disappear. It was based on the concept of the inventor as the "teacher of the nation,"[43] according to which the inventor was expected to teach his invention to his own nation and had, in fact, no business spreading the knowledge to other countries. This concept influenced the duration of the patent term, which was set in relation to a regular term of trade apprenticeship;[44] additionally, the concept led, in some countries, to a result that appears completely absurd today: The patent laws of France, Holland, and Belgium, for example, stipulated that once a holder of a patent applied for a patent on the same invention in another country,

---

[40] A German author wrote in 1839: "England justifiably views its patent law as a guarantee that no invention [. . .] will be lost for the country, but instead it must contribute—and with all potential of which it is able—to the welfare and progress of the domestic industry. In the recent years [. . .] progressive governments have adopted the same opinion." FRIEDRICH GEORG WIECK, GRUNDSÄTZE DES PATENTWESENS 6 (1839).

[41] CARL THEODOR VON KLEINSCHROD, DIE INTERNATIONALE PATENTGESETZGEBUNG NACH IHREN PRINZIPIEN NEBST VORSCHLÄGEN FÜR EIN KÜNFTIGES GEMEINES DEUTSCHES PATENTRECHT 131–33 (1855).

[42] *Id.*, 133.

[43] *See supra* note 15 for the concept of the "teacher of the nation."

[44] *Id.*

his domestic patent expired.[45] Thus up to a certain time[46] it was impossible for inventors who held patents in these countries to obtain protection in multiple countries without forfeiting their existing domestic patents.

The second manifestation of the support for local industries was that some countries preferred that patents not be granted to foreigners; therefore, the patent statutes of those countries discriminated against foreigners, using various approaches. The most drastic approach was the denial of patent protection to foreigners altogether; such was the case in the United States, where between 1793 and 1836 foreigners could not obtain a patent at all, or only with certain difficulties.[47] In Sweden, the Patent Act of 1834 permitted the granting of patents to foreigners but required that the foreign patentee within one year from the grant either establish residence in Sweden or transfer the patent ownership to a person residing there.[48] The last industrialized country that would not grant patents to foreigners was Prussia;[49] only a citizen of the state or a permanent resident of a municipality could obtain a patent in Prussia.[50] The only exception was made for foreigners who were citizens of other states of the German Customs Union.[51]

The third manifestation of the desire for patents to benefit the development of only domestic industry was that even if patents were granted to foreigners, a working requirement was imposed under penalty of forfeiture to ensure that the inventions

[45] Christian Friedrich Jaeger, Ueber Erfindungs-Patente 35 (1840); Damme, *supra* note 15, 26. For the Belgian law, see Richard Godson, A Practical Treatise on the Law of Patents for Inventions and of Copyright 296 (1840). *But cf.* the Austrian Patent Act of 1852, which provided in §22 explicit authorization for patent holders to seek patent protection for the same invention abroad. Oesterreichisches Patentgesetz, 1852, reprinted in von Kleinschrod, *supra* note 41, 149.

[46] The Belgian law was amended in 1854. Law of May 24, 1854 (Belgium), reprinted in Benjamin Vaughan Abbott, The Patent Laws of All Nations: Algeria–Turkey 42 ff. (2009).

[47] Patent Act of 1793, Section 1, reprinted in Albert Henry Walker, Text-Book of the Patent Laws of the United States of America 591 (1904). Beginning in 1800 patents could be granted to "aliens who at the time of petitioning [for a patent] resided for two years within the United States." Patent Act of 1800, Section 1. *Id.*, 597. The Act of 1832 also enabled an alien to petition for a patent if "at the time of petitioning for a patent [the alien was] resident in the United States, and [. . .] declared his intention, according to law, to become a citizen thereof." Patent Act of July 13, 1832. *Id.*, 601. The limitations were removed by the Patent Act of 1836, Section 6. *Id.*, 604.

[48] Eduard Stolle, Die einheimische und ausländische Patentgesetzgebung zum Shutze gewerblicher Erfindungen 26 (1855).

[49] Stolle, *supra* note 48, 25; Jaeger, *supra* note 45, 34.

[50] Von Kleinschrod, *supra* note 41, 164. According to Kleinschrod, this was one of the aspects that made the Prussian Act different from acts of "the majority of other European states and primarily [of] the most significant industrialized states." *Id.* Jaeger was already describing the arrangement as an anomaly in 1840. Jaeger, *supra* note 45, 34.

[51] Stolle, *supra* note 48, 25.

were practiced domestically.[52] Patent laws did not permit the working requirement to be bypassed by importation of the invention;[53] they conferred exclusive rights to make, use, and sell, but not to import.[54] Recognizing, however, that some inventions could not be practiced domestically but were of such importance that they needed to be imported,[55] countries eventually introduced special patents for importation. The conditions for granting such patents varied; in general, countries required that the invention be patented in the country from which it was imported.[56] The Austrian Patent Act of 1852 added that the importation patent could be granted only to the holder of the respective foreign patent.[57]

The fourth manifestation of the preference for the support of domestic industry was a limitation of the patent term. Some countries limited the patent term if the invention was first patented abroad; in France, Belgium, Italy, the United States, and for some time also in England,[58] if an invention was previously patented abroad,

---

[52] *See, for instance*, §3 of the Austrian Patent Act of 1852. Oesterreichisches Patentgesetz, 1852, reprinted in VON KLEINSCHROD, *supra* note 41, 140–41. *Also*, Article XXIII of the Patent Act of Belgium. Law of May 24, 1854, reprinted in BENJAMIN VAUGHAN ABBOTT, *supra* note 46, 46. *See also* Article 32(2) of the French patent law. Law of July 5, 1844 (France), reprinted in *id.*, 190. *Also* article 58(2) and (3) of the Italian patent law. The Italian Law and Regulations of January 31, 1864, extending the Sardinian Law of October 30, 1859, to the entire Kingdom of Italy, reprinted in *id.*, 294.

[53] For instance, the situation in Belgium was described as follows: "[I]t is not considered sufficient to import the patented articles from abroad and put them on sale in one or more shops or warehouses, even if large numbers were sold in the country by this means. It is not even considered sufficient to have a certain number of the patented articles made and sold in Belgium, the same articles being imported also from abroad and sold in Belgium." *Extracts from a Report of the patent-law of Belgium, by Mr. J. G. Kennedy of the British Legation, published, 1873, in* BENJAMIN VAUGHAN ABBOTT, *supra* note 46, 41.

[54] For instance, the Austrian Patent Act of 1852 conferred the exclusive right to use, make, and sell the invention, license it, transfer the patent itself, and obtain a patent on the same invention abroad (§21 and §22). Oesterreichisches Patentgesetz, 1852, reprinted in VON KLEINSCHROD, *supra* note 41, 149. The 1854 Article IV(a) of the Patent Law of Belgium guaranteed the exclusive rights to make, sell, or license the invention. Law of May 24, 1854, reprinted in BENJAMIN VAUGHAN ABBOTT, *supra* note 46, 43.

[55] For instance, §2 of the Patent Act of Bayern made it a condition for granting an importation patent that the invention have "a generally beneficial impact." Quoted in STOLLE, *supra* note 48, 27.

[56] The 1832 Austrian Patent Act stipulated that importation privileges could be granted only for inventions that were patented abroad. *See also* the 1842 Patent Act of Bayern, the 1836 Act of Württemberg, the 1854 Act of Belgium. STOLLE, *supra* note 48, 27–28; Article XIV of the Law of May 24, 1854 (Belgium), reprinted in BENJAMIN VAUGHAN ABBOTT, *supra* note 46, 44.

[57] *See* §3 of the Oesterreichisches Patentgesetz, 1852, reprinted in VON KLEINSCHROD, *supra* note 41, 140–41. A similar provision was included in the 1853 Patent Regulation of Sachsen but only in relation to other states of the German Union. STOLLE, *supra* note 48, 27. For the list of countries that still issued importation patents in the 1970s and for the proposal to conclude an International Arrangement for Importation Patents and other related proposals, see STEPHEN PERICLES LADAS, PATENTS, TRADEMARKS, AND RELATED RIGHTS 375–77 (1975).

[58] In England, a limitation of the patent term when the invention was first patented abroad existed between 1852 and 1883. WILLIAM MARTIN, THE ENGLISH PATENT SYSTEM 32 (1904).

the term of the domestic patent could not exceed the term of the foreign patent.[59] This approach had two consequences: First, it induced foreign patent holders to seek domestic patent protection as early as possible after they obtained a patent in the foreign country; only if they did so could they enjoy the maximum term of domestic protection. Second, the approach protected the domestic competitors of the inventor and other further innovators because the domestic competitors would otherwise be disadvantaged if their foreign competitors could start freely practicing the invention abroad earlier than domestic competitors could practice the invention domestically; without concurrent domestic and foreign patent terms, the foreign patent protection would otherwise expire before domestic protection would.

The "shell of nationalism" in which national patent systems were encased fell apart in the 1870s. Following a wave of disillusionment with the existing patent regimes and an anti-patent movement in some countries,[60] governments sought to reform their patent systems in a manner that would comply with the needs of internationalization. The Austro-Hungarian Empire spearheaded an initiative for an international patent congress, which took place during the World Exposition in Vienna in 1873.[61] During the Vienna Congress, calls for an international agreement on patent law were voiced,[62] and the Paris Congress, organized during the Paris World Exposition in 1878, launched negotiations that eventually led to the signing of the Convention for the Protection of Industrial Property in Paris in 1883 (Paris Convention).[63]

The Paris Convention introduced several major advances for internationalization: First, it secured national treatment for those applying for patents in foreign countries.[64] This meant not only that foreigners could now apply for patents, but that

---

[59] STOLLE, *supra* note 48, 26; DAMME, *supra* note 15, 26. For the Belgian law, see GODSON, *supra* note 45, 295; Article XIV of the Law of May 24, 1854 (Belgium), reprinted in BENJAMIN VAUGHAN ABBOTT, *supra* note 46, 44. For Article 29 of the French law, see Law of July 5, 1844, reprinted in *id.*, 187. For Article 11 of the Italian patent law, see the Italian Law and Regulations of January 31, 1864, extending the Sardinian Law of October 30, 1859, to the entire Kingdom of Italy, reprinted in *id.*, 285.

[60] ROBERT ANDREW MACFIE, JOHN MACLAURIN DREGHORN, & MICHEL CHEVALIER ET AL., RECENT DISCUSSIONS ON THE ABOLITION OF PATENTS FOR INVENTIONS IN THE UNITED KINGDOM, FRANCE, GERMANY, AND THE NETHERLANDS (1869); RUDOLF KLOSTERMANN, DAS PATENTGESETZ FÜR DAS DEUTSCHE REICH VOM 25. MAI 1877 (1877); Fritz Machlup & Edith Penrose, *The Patent Controversy in the Nineteenth Century*, J. ECON. HIST., May 1950, at 1. In Prussia, the number of patents granted dropped and the term of patent protection was in many cases only three years. KLOSTERMANN, 105–06.

[61] PAUL VON BECK-MANNAGETTA, DAS ÖSTERREICHISCHE PATENTRECHT 53–54 (1893).

[62] On resolutions of the Congress, see VON BECK-MANNAGETTA, *supra* note 61, 54–55.

[63] Paris Convention for the Protection of Industrial Property, Mar. 20, 1883, revised in 1900, 1911, 1925, 1934, 1958, and 1967, and amended in 1979 ("Paris Convention"), Article 2. Spencer, *supra* note 6, 372.

[64] The national treatment was secured for both citizens and residents of the Paris Union countries. Paris Convention, *supra* note 63, Articles 2 and 3.

they would be treated as equals to a country's own nationals. Second, the Convention set forth rules for an international priority;[65] from that time on inventors no longer had to worry that filing for a patent in a country and disclosing their invention would immediately disqualify them from obtaining patents in other countries. Third, the Convention set forth a rule that importation by a patentee would not lead to a forfeiture of the patent.[66]

Subsequent revisions of the Paris Convention—in 1900, 1911, 1925, 1934, 1958, and 1967[67]—further improved the situation of foreign patentees; for instance, the 1911 revision added inter alia a provision prohibiting countries from requiring foreign patentees to establish residence.[68] Before 1958 the limitations of the domestic working requirement were gradually relaxed, and in the 1958 revision the Convention stipulated that a nonworking status should preferably be remedied by compulsory licensing rather than forfeiture of the patent.[69] Other revisions included an extension of the international priority from the original six to twelve months,[70] and confirmation of the international priority for cases of subsequent applications filed in the same country[71] and for divided applications.[72] Since its most recent revision in 1967 the Convention has not been revised,[73] which can be explained by a shift in focus of the international community to other fora, such as the World Trade Organization (WTO), to change the international patent system.[74]

An important boost to the internationalization of patent law was accomplished at the WTO through the TRIPs Agreement concluded in 1994.[75] TRIPs incorporated provisions of the Paris Convention[76] and added new provisions that further

---

[65] Paris Convention, *supra* note 63, Article 4.

[66] *Id.*, Article 5.A(1).

[67] Paris Convention for the Protection of Industrial Property, WIPO, *available at* http://www.wipo.int/treaties/en/ip/paris/trtdocs_wo020.html (last visited Sept. 2, 2011). The Convention was also amended in 1979. The absolute majority of the countries that are parties to the Convention are parties to the latest act of revision—the 1967 Stockholm revision.

[68] Paris Convention, *supra* note 63, Article 2(2); Georg Hendrik Christiaan Bodenhausen, Guide to the Application of the Paris Convention for the Protection of Industrial Property as Revised at Stockholm in 1967 31 (WIPO 2004) (1969).

[69] Paris Convention, *supra* note 63, Article 5.A(2) and (3).

[70] Paris Convention, *supra* note 63, Article 4.C(1); Bodenhausen, *supra* note 68, 43.

[71] Paris Convention, *supra* note 63, Article 4.C(4); Bodenhausen, *supra* note 68, 45.

[72] Paris Convention, *supra* note 63, Article 4.G; Bodenhausen, *supra* note 68, 55.

[73] Another revision conference took place in the early 1980s but no revision was adopted by the conference. The Convention was amended in 1979.

[74] On the role of the WTO in lawmaking, see Samuel P. Baumgartner, *Is Transnational Litigation Different?*, 25 U. Pa. J. Int'l Econ. L. 1297 (2004).

[75] TRIPs, *supra* note 19.

[76] *Id.*, Article 2.1.

enhanced the ease with which patents could be sought in multiple countries. First, it adopted the principle of most-favored-nation treatment for foreign patentees, which ensures that they are given all advantages that are extended to nationals of any other country.[77] Second, TRIPs provided for a partial unification of the approaches of various patent systems to patentability, scope of exclusive rights, and term of protection.[78] Third, TRIPs outlined basic minimum standards for enforcement of intellectual property rights, including patent rights, in signatory countries. Additionally, TRIPs enhanced the protections included in the Paris Convention and the protections of its own provisions through the enforcement mechanism of the WTO; the Paris Convention itself had never provided an effective mechanism to force countries to comply with its provisions. The WTO dispute resolution mechanism now includes a means to secure compliance with the provisions of TRIPs and the provisions of the Convention that were incorporated by TRIPs.[79]

Both the Paris Convention and TRIPs have been very successful; as of July 2011, 173 countries were parties to the Paris Convention,[80] and the 153 members of the WTO were bound by TRIPs.[81] The wide adoption of the principles and standards set by the two treaties has been assured because the WTO and the European Union made adherence to the treaties mandatory for countries that seek membership in the WTO and the European Union. Additionally, standards at an increased TRIPs-plus level have been incorporated into free trade and preferential trade agreements, and bilateral investment treaties that the United States and other countries have concluded,[82] and adoption of such elevated standards was also sought when the

---

[77] *Id.*, Article 4. This principle was adopted from other trade treaties.

[78] *Id.*, Section 5.

[79] The enforcement mechanism has its limits, however, because the effectiveness of enforcement within the WTO depends on countries' readiness to enforce the decisions rendered within the dispute resolution mechanism. If countries decide for whatever reason not to proceed with enforcement, decisions will remain unenforced. For an example of an as yet unenforced decision concerning the TRIPs Agreement, see the dispute over Section 110(5) of the U.S. Copyright Act (dispute DS160); the request for consultations was filed by the European Union and its member states on January 26, 1999, and the arbitration report was circulated in 2001. The provision of the U.S. Copyright Act that was found inconsistent with Article 13 of TRIPs remains part of the Act. One problem of subjecting TRIPs to the WTO dispute resolution mechanism is that intellectual property rights may be included in retaliatory measures for noncompliance with WTO rules.

[80] In the last thirty years the number of countries that are parties to the Convention has doubled. Information by the WTO, *available at* http://www.wipo.int/export/sites/www/treaties/en/documents/pdf/paris.pdf and http://www.wipo.int/treaties/en/statistics/StatsResults.jsp?treaty_id=2&lang=en (last visited Sept. 2, 2011).

[81] Information by the WTO, *available at* http://www.wto.org/english/thewto_e/whatis_e/tif_e/org6_e.htm (last visited Sept. 2, 2011). The United Nations had 193 member states as of September 2011. UN at a Glance, *available at* http://www.un.org/en/members/growth.shtml#text (last visited Sept. 2, 2011).

[82] *E.g.*, Assafa Endeshaw, *Free Trade Agreements as Surrogates for TRIPs-Plus*, 28 EUR. INTELL. PROP. REV. 374 (2006); Beatrice Lindstrom, *Scaling Back TRIPs-Plus: An Analysis of Intellectual Property Provisions in Trade*

European Union drafted the European Union Enforcement Directive. The resulting 2004 Directive must be respected by member states and all countries seeking membership in the European Union.[83]

Without doubt the Paris Convention and TRIPs have positively impacted the ability of patent holders to seek and obtain patents in foreign countries. Statistical data suggest an increasing trend in the number of patents filed by foreigners. According to World Intellectual Property Organization (WIPO) data the number of nonresident patent filings grew from 30.7 percent of all applications filed in the world in 1985 to 44 percent in 2008;[84] the percentage of nonresident patent filings in the world remained over 40 percent every year in 1998–2008.[85] Similarly, the 2008 Organisation for Economic Co-operation and Development (OECD) Compendium of Patent Statistics noted "an increase in the level of internationalisation,"[86] which it attributed primarily to activities of multinational corporations.

1.3.2 OBTAINING PATENTS IN MULTIPLE COUNTRIES

Once countries had ensured that inventors could file for patents abroad and extend the territorial scope of protection for their inventions by obtaining patents in multiple countries, countries sought a procedure to streamline the multiple application procedure. Applying for patents in each country individually was cumbersome and costly, and providing potential patent holders with a mechanism that would make it

---

Agreements and Implications for Asia and the Pacific, 42 Intl. L. & Politics 917 (2010); Hennig Grosse Ruse-Khan, *Protecting Intellectual Property under BITs, FTAs, and TRIPs: Conflicting Regimes or Mutual Coherence?*, *in* Evolution in Investment Treaty Law and Arbitration (K. Miles & C. Brown eds., Cambridge University Press 2011).

[83] *See, e.g.*, Francisco Rossi, *Free Trade Agreements and TRIPS-Plus Measures*, 1 Int'l J. Intell. Prop. Mgmt. 150 (2006); Directive 2004/48/EC of the European Parliament and of the Council of 29 Apr. 2004 on the enforcement of intellectual property rights, 2004 O.J. (L 157) 45 ("European Union Enforcement Directive"). The original proposal of the Directive was more ambitious but was toned down during the legislative process under pressure from the member states. It was not a coincidence that the Directive was adopted just two days before ten new countries joined the European Union. *See Proposal for a Directive of the European Parliament and of the Council on measures and procedures to ensure the enforcement of intellectual property rights*, COM(2003) 46 final (January 30, 2003).

[84] World Intellectual Property Indicators 2010, WIPO, *available at* http://www.wipo.int/export/sites/www/ipstats/en/statistics/patents/pdf/941_2010.pdf (last visited Sept. 2, 2011). For statistics on resident and nonresident filings in twenty major patent offices in 2008, see *id.*, 40.

[85] World Intellectual Property Indicators 2010, *supra* note 84, 35.

[86] Compendium of Patent Statistics, OECD, 2008, *available at* http://www.oecd.org/dataoecd/5/19/37569377.pdf (last visited Sept. 2, 2011), 4 and 28–31.

easier to pursue patents in multiple countries was essential for establishing the option of a global, or at least as territorially wide as possible, protection for inventions.

Not surprisingly, given the turmoil that the industrialized world faced in the first half of the twentieth century, mechanisms that were attempted in that era did not succeed. As early as 1916 at the economic conference of the allies in Paris it was proposed that an international patent register and an organization for a unified patent examination be established to facilitate a territorially wide patenting. After the international agreement that arose from this conference had failed[87] the idea was reintroduced in different forms by different authors; in 1932 a similar proposal was submitted by Italy at the London Congress,[88] and during the Second World War authors in Germany, Austria, Yugoslavia, and Hungary discussed proposals for a patent system in Europe after the war.[89]

After the Second World War, work on a European solution accelerated and eventually led to the creation of the European Patent Convention.[90] A French Senate member, Henri Longchambon, resuscitated the idea of a regional mechanism for obtaining patents in multiple countries when he presented to the Council of Europe in 1949 a plan for the creation of a European Patent Office.[91] Professor Eduard Reimer also suggested a solution at the European level in 1953; he advocated that national patent offices gradually be abolished and eventually replaced by the European Patent Office.[92] In the 1950s and early 1960s three conventions were concluded within the Council of Europe framework that sought to align processes before the national patent offices and even unify substantive patent law; however, none was ever widely accepted.[93] With the exception of the International Patent

[87] The Paris Agreement of 1921 was signed by a number of countries but never came into force. Additionally, the United States and England did not adhere to the Agreement. Eduard Reimer, *Die europäische Idee im Patentrecht*, 1955 GRUR INT. 473, 476–77; Spencer, *supra* note 6, 373–74.

[88] REIMER, EUROPÄISIERUNG, *supra* note 35, 48.

[89] Von Knieriem, *Europäisches Patent*, 1942 GRUR 449, 449–50; Franz Redies, *Zur Frage der Vereinheitlichung des Patenterteilungsverfahrens*, 1942 GRUR 450; Wiegand, *Die europäische Vereinheitlichung*, *supra* note 20; Dr. Lindenmaier, *Die Vereinheitlichung des Materiellen Europäischen Patentrechts*, 1942 GRUR 485; Reimer, *Die europäische Idee*, *supra* note 87, 479–81.

[90] The European Patent Convention, which was signed in 1973, is discussed *infra* in this section.

[91] Reprinted in REIMER, EUROPÄISIERUNG, *supra* note 35, 227–38.

[92] Plan Reimer (Deutschland) Nr. 1, 1953, reprinted in REIMER, EUROPÄISIERUNG, *supra* note 35, 259–77, and Plan Remier (Deutschland) Nr. 2, 1954, reprinted in *id.*, 279–81.

[93] The 1953 European Convention Relating to Formalities Required for Patent Applications came into force in 1955 and was ratified by twenty-one countries, fifteen of which denounced the Convention before 1980; one country denounced the Convention in 1991. The 1954 European Convention on the International Classification of Patents of Invention was ratified by fifteen countries, fourteen of which denounced the Convention before 1980; one country denounced the Convention in 1998. The 1963 Convention on the Unification of Certain Points of Substantive Law on Patents for Invention did not come into force until 1980 and was ratified by

Institute, which was established in The Hague in 1947 and which conducted only prior art searches,[94] there was no substantial result until the 1970s from efforts to streamline the process of obtaining patents in multiple countries. In the 1970s two systems were finally created that became significant in terms of content and geographical scope—the PCT and the European Patent Convention (EPC).

The Patent Cooperation Treaty of 1970 introduced a mechanism for international patent filings that helps patent applicants obtain patents in multiple countries. By filing an international application in any of the 144 states of the PCT Union,[95] any resident or national of a state of the Union[96] may request an international search by an international searching authority[97] that will prepare an international search report,[98] publish the application,[99] and forward it to the national or regional patent offices designated by the applicant.[100] If the applicant desires, the application may also be subjected to an international preliminary examination by an international preliminary examining authority.[101] The resulting international preliminary examination report[102] further simplifies procedures before the designated national patent offices because it provides an opinion about novelty, nonobviousness, and industrial applicability of the invention.[103]

The statistics show modest success for the PCT as a tool for obtaining patents in multiple countries; today, in the 144 countries that are parties to the PCT[104] the PCT mechanism is used frequently, although not as often as one would expect. According to a WIPO report, in 2008 about 164,000 PCT applications were filed,[105]

---

thirteen countries. Council of Europe, *available at* http://conventions.coe.int/ (last visited Sept. 2, 2011). *See also* Per von Holstein, *International Co-operation in the Field of Patent Law with Special Reference to the Activities of the Council of Europe*, 16 INT'L & COMP. L.Q. 191, 200–02 (1967); Christopher Wadlow, *Strasbourg, the Forgotten Patent Convention, and the Origins of the European Patents Jurisdiction*, 41 IIC 123 (2010).

[94] Von Holstein, *supra* note 93, 196–97.

[95] PCT Contracting Parties, *available at* http://www.wipo.int/treaties/en/ShowResults.jsp?lang=en&treaty_id=6 (last visited Sept. 2, 2011); Patent Cooperation Treaty, June 19, 1970 ("PCT"), Articles 3 and 4.

[96] PCT, *supra* note 95, Article 9.

[97] *Id.*, Articles 15 and 16.

[98] *Id.*, Article 18.

[99] *Id.*, Article 21.

[100] *Id.*, Articles 4.1(ii) and 20.

[101] *Id.*, Articles 31 and 32.

[102] *Id.*, Article 35.

[103] *Id.*, Article 33.

[104] As of July 2011. In the last twenty years the number of countries that are parties to the PCT more than tripled. Information by WIPO, *available at* http://www.wipo.int/treaties/en/SearchForm.jsp?search_what=C and http://www.wipo.int/treaties/en/statistics/StatsResults.jsp?treaty_id=6&lang=en (last visited Sept. 2, 2011).

[105] The International Patent System, Yearly Review, WIPO, 2009, *available at* http://www.wipo.int/export/sites/www/ipstats/en/statistics/pct/pdf/901e_2009.pdf (last visited Sept. 2, 2011), 3.

which is a rather small number compared to the estimated total of 1.91 million patent applications that were filed around the globe that year.[106] Each PCT application can represent filings for multiple national or regional patents; for instance, in 2008 about 464,000 national or regional filings were made via PCT applications.[107] Although this figure represents a significant increase since 1995 in national and regional filings made via PCT applications,[108] it is still much smaller than one might expect.

The relatively small interest in PCT applications may be caused by the costs associated with using the mechanism; unfortunately, unless a patentee is seeking patent protection in approximately fifteen or more countries, he will pay more in fees when using the PCT application than when he files in each country individually.[109] Despite the fees, PCT applications offer other savings that may be relevant even when fewer patents are involved; for example, patentees save resources that they would otherwise have to spend to retain patent representatives or patent attorneys in each country individually for the entire patent prosecution procedure. Also, by filing a PCT application, patent applicants de facto extend the period during which they may decide in which countries they will pursue national patents; this extension of the period for the decision on where to patent is important if applicants need time to secure capital or investigate their options for commercialization.

Even considering the relatively low number of applications, the role of the PCT application in helping patentees obtain patents in multiple countries is important, and WIPO reports that the use of PCT applications to obtain patents in foreign countries is on the rise. According to WIPO, the 164,000 PCT applications that were filed in 2008 represented a 2.3 percent increase over the filings of the previous year.[110] Although in 2009 the number of PCT applications dropped 4.5 percent year-on-year, this decrease was probably an outlier caused by the economic downturn.[111] Until 2001 there was a steady and steep increase in the number of PCT

---

[106] World Intellectual Property Indicators 2010, *supra* note 84, 34.

[107] *Id.*, 56.

[108] *Id.*, 56. "[T]he share of PCT national phase entries in total non-resident patent filings doubled in the past 14 years, from 25% in 1995 to over 52% in 2008." *Id.*

[109] World Patent Report, WIPO, 2008, *supra* note 10, 8, 51. According to the Report, when at least fifteen countries are targeted, the cost of a PCT filing is about $1,000 cheaper than direct filings in individual countries. *Id.*

[110] World Intellectual Property Indicators 2009, *available at* http://www.wipo.int/export/sites/www/ipstats/en/statistics/patents/pdf/wipo_pub_941.pdf (last visited Sept. 2, 2011), 8.

[111] World Intellectual Property Indicators 2010, *supra* note 84, 51; The International Patent System, Yearly Review, WIPO, 2009, *supra* note 105, 8. In 2010, the PCT recorded renewed growth when the number of PCT applications rose 5.7 percent year-on-year. The International Patent System, Yearly Review, WIPO, 2010, *available at* http://www.wipo.int/export/sites/www/pct/en/activity/pct_2010.pdf (last visited Sept. 2, 2011), 11.

applications filed each year; the increase exceeded 10 percent almost every year.[112] The percentage of nonresident filings based on the PCT route increased from 25.4 percent in 1995 to 52 percent in 2008.[113]

In Europe the proposals by Longchambon and Reimer finally materialized when the EPC was signed in 1973.[114] The EPC became another important facilitator for patenting in multiple countries; it contains both substantive law provisions for a European patent[115] and provisions streamlining the application process for multiple national patents and a European patent.[116] An applicant files a European patent application[117] in the European Patent Office or in a national patent office,[118] which forwards the application to the European Patent Office.[119] The application may be filed for all Convention countries and the applicant has until the grant of a European patent to select the designated countries.[120] The European Patent Office conducts an examination as to formal requirements,[121] draws up a European search report, and publishes the application.[122] Upon request by the applicant, the European Patent Office will continue with the examination of the claimed invention as to its compliance with the requirements of the Convention,[123] and if it complies, the European Patent Office will grant and publish a European patent.[124] The European patent is equal to a national patent;[125] it confers the same rights as a national patent, and if needed to be enforced, must be enforced in each country in accordance with that

---

[112] The International Patent System, Yearly Review, WIPO, 2009, *supra* note 105, 13.

[113] World Intellectual Property Indicators 2009, *supra* note 3, 29. Patent applicants from the United States are the most frequent users of the system; in 2008 they filed 30.6 percent of all PCT applications in the world. The International Patent System, Yearly Review, WIPO, 2009, *supra* note 105, 32. Notably, 22 percent of all PCT applications filed in the United States came from inventors from California. Compendium of Patent Statistics, *supra* note 86, 10.

[114] Convention on the Grant of European Patents, October 5, 1973 ("European Patent Convention").

[115] European Patent Convention, *supra* note 114, Part II. A European patent must be distinguished from the proposed "European Union patent," also referred to under the older title "Community patent." The European patent arises under the EPC; the European Union patent does not exist yet and is subject to a proposal by the Commission of the European Union. *See also* Chapter 2, Section 2.2, for the proposed European Union patent.

[116] *Id.*, Part III.

[117] *Id.*, Articles 78–85.

[118] *Id.*, Article 75.1.

[119] *Id.*, Article 77.

[120] *Id.*, Article 79.

[121] *Id.*, Article 90.

[122] *Id.*, Articles 92 and 93.

[123] *Id.*, Article 94.

[124] *Id.*, Articles 97 and 98.

[125] *Id.*, Article 2.

country's national law.[126] Therefore, even if worded identically in all countries, it may be interpreted differently according to the jurisprudence of each country.[127]

The EPC system has been quite successful; it grew from its original sixteen signatory countries to the thirty-eight member countries in the system today,[128] and from the first application filed in 1978 the system logged its millionth EPC application in 1997.[129] In 2010 the European Patent Office received the largest number of patent applications in its history; the 235,000 applications filed in 2010 represented an 11 percent increase over the number of applications filed in 2009.[130] The utility of the EPC system for applying for foreign patents is evidenced by the fact that it also serves well applicants from countries outside the EPC; for instance, U.S. applicants are frequent users of EPC applications. In 2010 U.S. applicants filed 26 percent of all EPC applications—more than applicants from any other country, including countries that are members of the EPC.[131] EPC applications are used frequently by those seeking patents in countries even outside the EPC; according to the 2009 European Patent Office Annual Report, out of all EPC applications received

[126] *Id.*, Article 64.

[127] *See, e.g.*, Düsseldorf Landgericht in *Sonnenblende II*: "Article 69 of the EPC does provide the framework for the extent of the protection; however, it does not regulate definitely how the extent of protection should be determined in detail, instead it gives room for application of national laws." *Sonnenblende II*, Landgericht Düsseldorf, 4 O 377/95, September 22, 1998, 1999 GRUR INT. 458, 460. In *WC-Erfrischer*, the Düsseldorf Landgericht noted the following: "Notwithstanding existing harmonization tendencies, it is [. . .] still the case that the concept of equivalence is determined in each designated country based on different criteria." *WC-Erfrischer*, Landgericht Düsseldorf, 4b O 166/02, June 10, 2003, 3 ENTSCHEIDUNGEN DER INSTANZGERICHTE ZUM RECHT DES GEISTIGEN EIGENTUMS 3, 153, 158–59 (2002). *See also* Assessment of the Impact, *supra* note 20, 3.

[128] Information by the European Patent Office, *available at* http://www.epo.org/about-us/office/history.html (last visited Sept. 2, 2011). Additionally, two countries, Bosnia and Herzegovina and Montenegro, recognize European patents upon request. Member States of the European Patent Organization, *available at* http://www.epo.org/about-us/epo/member-states.html (last visited Sept. 2, 2011).

[129] Information by the European Patent Office, *available at* http://www.epo.org/about-us/office/history.html (last visited Sept. 2, 2011). While the EPC system reached its millionth application in the twenty years of its existence in 1997, the PCT system took eighteen years before it recorded its 250,000th PCT application in 1996 and twenty-two years for its 500,000th application in 2000. Patrick Smith, *Harmonisation, Regional Collaboration and Small Patent Offices, in* INTELLECTUAL PROPERTY HARMONISATION WITHIN ASEAN AND APEC 227, 229 (Christopher Antons, Michael Blakeney, & Christopher Heath eds., 2004). In April 2011 the PCT system logged its two millionth PCT application. *PCT Two Million*, *available at* http://www.wipo.int/pct/en/2million/ (last visited Sept. 2, 2011).

[130] *Number of Patent Applications in Europe Hits All-Time High*, EPO, Apr. 13, 2011, *available at* http://www.epo.org/news-issues/news/2011/20110413.html (last visited Sept. 2, 2011).

[131] European Patent Office Press Conference on Patent Statistics 2010, Apr. 13, 2011, *available at* http://documents.epo.org/projects/babylon/eponot.nsf/0/6be088f728f3e2dcc125787000384641/$FILE/20110413_press_folder_en.pdf (last visited Sept. 2, 2011), 3. Residents of all EPC member countries combined filed 39 percent of all applications in 2010. *Id.*

in 2009, 58 percent were filed as PCT applications.[132] This indicates that they were parts of a patenting strategy that geographically exceeded the territory of the EPC countries.

In addition to the EPC system, there are four other regional patent systems in the world that offer similar regional patents: two in Africa, one in Eurasia, and one in the Middle East.

The African Intellectual Property Organization (AIPO), established in 1977 upon a preexisting system that originated in 1962, covers French-speaking Africa,[133] while sixteen English-speaking African countries are organized into the African Regional Intellectual Property Organization (ARIPO), which was created in 1976. On average, ARIPO receives about 500 patent applications each year and grants about 130 patents.[134] The system is used primarily by foreign applicants; about 98 percent of all applications are filed by applicants from non-ARIPO countries.[135] A large percentage of applications come to ARIPO through the PCT route (about 92 percent), which demonstrates that the ARIPO system is used primarily by applicants who also seek protection in countries outside ARIPO.[136]

The Eurasian Patent Convention was created in 1991 by ten countries of the former Soviet Union as a replacement for the Soviet patent system that came to an end with the collapse of the Soviet Union.[137] The Eurasian patent system is much smaller than the EPC system, not only in the number of countries that it covers, but also in the number of patents; at the end of 2008 a total of 8,079 Eurasian patents were in force in the member states, as opposed to the several hundred thousand European patents in force in EPC member states.[138] The Eurasian patent system is small compared to the EPC system, but even the Eurasian patent shows a growing trend in patentee interest. The annual number of Eurasian patent applications grew from 1,630 in

---

[132] 2009 EPO Annual Report, *available at* http://documents.epo.org/projects/babylon/eponet.nsf/0/afbc07d9e3b95f12c125770d0055a883/$FILE/epo_annual_report_2009.pdf (last visited Sept. 2, 2011), 62–63. An applicant may file a PCT application with the European Patent Office when the applicant wishes to utilize the European Patent Office as the international searching and preliminary examining authority under the PCT.

[133] Unfortunately, no statistics were located for AIPO. Patrick Smith lists AIPO as an example of a fully unified regional system. Smith, *supra* note 129, 234.

[134] The author obtained the statistics from ARIPO in July 2009; the correspondence including the data is on file with the author.

[135] *Id.*

[136] *Id.*

[137] History of the Eurasian patent organization, *available at* http://www.eapo.org/eng/ea/patsys/history.html (last visited Sept. 2, 2011).

[138] Granted Patents, *available at* http://www.epo.org/about-us/statistics/granted-patents.html (last visited Sept. 2, 2011).

2004 to 3,066 in 2008,[139] but in 2009 dropped to 2,801; the decline was likely the result of the impact of the economic downturn.[140] As with other regional patents, the Eurasian patent is an attractive option for foreign applicants; for instance, in 2009 more than one in five Eurasian patent applications were filed by U.S. applicants.[141] The system is used by applicants seeking protection through the PCT; in 2009, 80 percent of Eurasian patent applications were filed as PCT applications.[142]

The Gulf Cooperation Council Patent Office is the youngest of the regional offices; it was established in 1998 by the Cooperation Council for the Arab States of the Gulf.[143] Patents granted by the Office are valid in the six member states of the Council.[144]

Outside the six frameworks presented above—the PCT, the EPC, the AIPO, the ARIPO, the Eurasian Patent Convention, and the Gulf Cooperation Council—patent offices of various countries have cooperated in a number of ways, primarily seeking possibilities for streamlining the prosecution of patents that are filed for the same invention in multiple countries.[145] This cooperation has not necessarily been limited by political geography; the field of patents, as do other technical fields such as technical standardization or official statistics, often overcomes the political divide and unites experts from various countries without regard to countries' political preferences. Thus, cooperative mechanisms such as the International Classification of Patents[146] and the documentation management system of the ICIREPAT (the Committee for International Co-operation in Information Retrieval Among Examining Patent Offices) were adopted not only by democratic countries but also by some countries of the communist bloc.[147]

---

[139] 2008 Annual Report of the Eurasian Patent Organization, *available at* http://www.eapo.org/rus/ea/reports/eapo_2008.pdf (last visited Sept. 2, 2011), 15.

[140] 2009 Annual Report of the Eurasian Patent Organization, *available at* http://www.eapo.org/rus/ea/reports/eapo_2009.pdf (last visited Sept. 2, 2011), 13. In 2010 the number of Eurasian patent applications filed was up again; 3,329 applications were filed in 2010. 2010 Annual Report of the Eurasian Patent Organization, *available at* http://www.eapo.org/rus/ea/reports/eapo_2010.pdf (last visited Sept. 2, 2011), 17.

[141] *Id.*, 15. In 2009 U.S. applicants filed 21 percent of all Eurasian patent applications, followed by German applicants (12 percent) and Russian applicants (8 percent). *Id.*

[142] *Id.*, 15. Patrick Smith lists the Eurasian Patent Convention as an example of a fully unified regional system. Smith, *supra* note 129, 234.

[143] About the GCC Patent Office, *available at* http://www2.gccpo.org/about%20gcc%20patent%20office.htm (last visited Sept. 2, 2011).

[144] *Id.*

[145] *See, e.g., infra* note 153.

[146] *See supra* note 93.

[147] First Czechoslovakia and later the Soviet Union became members of the ICIREPAT. Von Holstein, *supra* note 93, 204; Gordon Asher, *International Patent Cooperation*, 11 J. Chemical Documentation 14, 16 (1971).

The most significant cooperative relationship among patent offices[148] today is the Trilateral Cooperation framework established in 1983 by the European Patent Office, the Japan Patent Office, and the United States Patent and Trademark Office (USPTO).[149] The most notable[150] of the projects being developed within the framework[151] is the Patent Prosecution Highway, which focuses on "optimi[zing] the existing schemes for accelerated prosecution of patent applications [. . .] so that applicants can obtain corresponding patents faster and more efficiently."[152] The offices save labor and expedite prosecution because only the first office has to complete a full patent examination; after that the other two offices need to conduct only an accelerated examination.[153]

Notwithstanding the significant level of patent law harmonization, particularly at the regional levels, the mechanisms designed to facilitate patenting in multiple countries, and the willingness of patent offices to streamline their procedures through mutual cooperation, it remains complex and costly to patent in multiple countries, and proposals for deeper harmonization or creation of a unitary system have not been successful so far. At the European Union level, the project for a single European Union patent was proposed, suffered failures, and is now being redeveloped.[154]

148 There are many examples of bilateral cooperation between patent offices; see, for instance, cooperation between the U.K. and Brazilian patent offices, Press Release by the U.K. Intellectual Property Office from September 21, 2009, *available at* http://www.ipo.gov.uk/about/press/press-release/press-release-2009/press-release-20090921.htm (last visited Sept. 2, 2011); cooperation between the USPTO and ARIPO, Press Release by the USPTO from September 25, 2009, *available at* http://www.uspto.gov/web/offices/com/speeches/09-18.htm (last visited Sept. 2, 2011); cooperation between the Danish and Japanese offices, Hans Christian Thomsen, *Recent Developments in Denmark Since 2006*, 14th European Patent Judges' Symposium, European Patent Office, O.J. 1/2009, Spec. ed., 127. For an initiative on cooperation among patent offices of the European Union member states, see *Towards an Enhanced Partnership between Patent Offices under the Community Patent—European Standard for Searches*, 12342/09 (July 30, 2009).

149 According to the 2007 Trilateral Statistical Report, about 77 percent of all patents currently in force worldwide were granted in the United States, Japan, or the EPC member states. Trilateral Statistical Report, 2007 Edition, *available at* http://www.trilateral.net/statistics/tsr/2007/TSR.pdf (last visited Sept. 2, 2011), 13.

150 For other "significant achievements," see http://www.trilateral.net/about/achievements.html (last visited Sept. 2, 2011).

151 Projects, *available at* http://www.trilateral.net/projects.html (last visited Sept. 2, 2011).

152 2008 EPO Annual Report, *available at* http://www.epo.org/service-support/publications/general-information/annual-reports/2008.html (last visited Oct. 22, 2011), 40.

153 *See also* the Nordic Patent Institute established by the Agreement on the Establishing of the Nordic Patent Institute from July 5, 2006.

154 For an overview of the history, see Impact Assessment, Accompanying Document to the Proposal for a Regulation of the European Parliament and of the Council implementing enhanced cooperation in the area of creation of unitary patent protection, SEC (2011) 482/2, 5–8. For the latest proposal, see Proposal for a Regulation of the European Parliament and of the Council implementing enhanced cooperation in the area of creation of unitary patent protection, COM(2011) 215/3. According to the Proposal, a European Union patent would be a European patent (patent granted by the European Patent Office) "with an identical scope of protection in respect to all participating" countries. *Id.*, Article 3, p. 16.

The 1991 proposal for the Patent Harmonization Treaty[155] stumbled when the United States declined to switch from the first-to-invent to the first-to-file principle.[156] The 2000 Patent Law Treaty,[157] which was the result of discussions held within WIPO between 1995 and 2000, was signed by twenty-eight countries[158] and entered into force in 2005;[159] it aimed to "bring [. . .] national/regional laws [. . .] closer by providing the maximum requirements that the Contracting Parties can require"[160] and focused on procedural formalities instead of harmonization of substantive patent law. A treaty that would address the harmonization of substantive patent rules began being negotiated in 2000; however, the draft Substantive Patent Law Treaty eventually failed in a stalemate.[161] Dreyfuss and Reichman suggested that the proposed Substantive Patent Law Treaty was simply "premature."[162]

In light of all the failures of substantive patent law harmonization in the past two decades it is remarkable that the international community eventually agreed on a set of measures,[163] including an amendment to TRIPs,[164] that altered the obligations of some countries with respect to TRIPs implementation. The amendment resulted

---

[155] Treaty Supplementing the Paris Convention as Far as Patents Are Concerned (Oct. 2, 2000).

[156] Tomoko Miyamoto, *International Treaties and Patent Law Harmonization: Today and Beyond*, *in* PATENT LAW AND THEORY: A HANDBOOK OF CONTEMPORARY RESEARCH 154, 165 (Toshiko Takenaka ed., 2009).

[157] Patent Law Treaty, Geneva, June 1, 2000.

[158] Contracting Parties, Patent Law Treaty, WIPO, *available at* http://www.wipo.int/treaties/en/ShowResults.jsp?lang=en&treaty_id=4 (last visited Sept. 2, 2011).

[159] Summary of the Patent Law Treaty, *available at* http://www.wipo.int/treaties/en/ip/plt/summary_plt.html (last visited Sept. 2, 2011).

[160] Miyamoto, *supra* note 156, 170.

[161] Draft Substantive Patent Law Treaty, WIPO, SCP/10/4, September 30, 2003; Miyamoto, *supra* note 156, 176–80.

[162] Reichman & Dreyfuss, *supra* note 26, 85. In September 2009 the WIPO director general, Francis Gurry, warned that WIPO might lose its rulemaking role. Daniel Pruzin, *WIPO Chief Warns Organization Risks Losing Its IP Rulemaking Role*, BNA, September 24, 2009. For a law and economics analysis of the problem, see Dongwook Chun & Minwook Kang, *Patent Law Harmonization in an Open Economy: How Should the Patent System React in the International Arena?*, 2 ASIAN JOURNAL OF LAW AND ECONOMICS 1 (2010).

[163] Declaration on the TRIPs Agreement and Public Health, WTO, WT/MIN(01)/DEC/2 (November 20, 2001); Extension of the Transition Period under Article 66.1 of the TRIPs Agreement for Least-Developed Country Members for Certain Obligations with Respect to Pharmaceutical Products, Decision of the Council for TRIPs of June 27, 2002, WTO, IP/C/25 (July 1, 2002); Least-Developed Country Members—Obligations under Article 70.9 of the TRIPs Agreement with Respect to Pharmaceutical Products, Decision of July 8, 2002, WTO, WT/L/478 (July 12, 2002); Implementation of Paragraph 6 of the Doha Declaration on the TRIPs Agreement and Public Health, Decision of August 30, 2002, WTO, WT/L/540 (September 2, 2003).

[164] Amendment of the TRIPs Agreement, Decision of 6 December 2005, WTO, WT/L/641 (Dec. 8, 2005).

from the Doha Round of WTO negotiations and was prompted by concerns about whether developing countries were successfully able to fight epidemics.[165]

1.4 Obstacles to Global Protection

As the preceding sections have outlined, great progress has been made in the internationalization of patent law in the last 140 years, even considering the rejection of proposals for a global patent and the resistance to deeper harmonization of substantive patent law. Several important tools were added to provide possibilities for territorially broad patenting; they allow inventors to obtain patent protection in multiple foreign countries under the same conditions as nationals of those countries and to utilize simplified procedures for filing parallel patents through the PCT. Regional mechanisms have been created with the same goal; they offer an easier route to obtain parallel patents in multiple countries of a region, and some, such as the AIPO, go beyond the facilitation of parallel national patents to offer a fully unified patent protection with one patent covering multiple countries of a single region. If a proposal for a European Union patent eventually succeeds, patentees will also be able to benefit from a unitary patent covering this entire regional market.[166]

The fact remains that the process of obtaining parallel patents is still difficult and costly; even if applicants use mechanisms established to help them obtain territorially wide patent protection, they still face the obstacles of expense and decentralization. The mechanisms fail to eliminate the need to hire local patent attorneys (or patent representatives) to aid in prosecuting individual national patents before national patent offices, a problem that is compounded because applicants also face differences in the substantive laws of the various countries where they apply for patents. Translation costs are also significant. In the end, the single most important limitation on the geographical scope of protection is the resources available to a patent applicant for patent prosecution.

The high cost that parallel patenting imposes on small inventors—individual persons and SMEs—means that only large companies can obtain territorially wide patent protection and use it to enhance their position on the global market. SMEs cannot take advantage of the protection of a network of parallel patents because they must limit their patenting activities to one country or a small number

[165] Although perceived as an essential measure, the mechanism that was established—the compulsory licensing system—has not been utilized to the degree expected; research has been conducted to try to explain the underutilization.

[166] *See* Chapter 2, Section 2.2, for a discussion of the proposed European Union patent.

of countries. In China, for example, the discrepancy between the numbers of patent applications filed by Chinese SMEs domestically and internationally is large; Chinese SMEs account for 66 percent of domestic patent applications, but even with the advantage provided by the PCT application mechanism,[167] the activity of these SMEs in patenting abroad is significantly lower.[168] This situation prompted the Chinese government to adopt a program in September 2009 that set aside $14.65 million to assist SMEs in applying for patents abroad.[169] Based on this program, nonstate enterprises may apply for subsidies of up to more than $70,000 to finance patent applications outside of China.[170] The policy of the Chinese government to assist Chinese businesses in obtaining patent protection abroad was reiterated in the *National Patent Development Strategy (2011–2020)*, published in November 2010.[171]

Although the initiative by the Chinese government is logical, it is probably a measure that is insufficient to ensure that Chinese SMEs will be able to obtain and maintain effective patent protection abroad. For protection to be effective, patent holders must also be able to police and enforce their rights; without effective enforcement patents are worthless. Enforcement is extremely costly, particularly when parallel rights are held in multiple countries, and even more so because the current system provides no method that is less costly or less complicated than enforcing each patent individually in the country that granted it.[172] Again, only large companies can afford such enforcement; the burden for an independent inventor or an SME is prohibitive, and therefore, as was recently observed by an official of the European Commission, "the current fragmentation of patent litigation [. . .] hampers access to the patent system for SMEs."[173] The Chinese government has recognized the

---

167 China became a party to the PCT as of January 1, 1994. *Central Government to Subsidize Foreign Patent Applications*, People's Daily Online, October 16, 2009, *available at* http://english.people.com.cn/90001/90778/90862/6782417.html (last visited Sept. 2, 2011).

168 Tu Lei, *MOF to Support Overseas Patents*, Global Times, October 14, 2009, *available at* http://business.globaltimes.cn/china-economy/2009-10/476759.html (last visited Sept. 2, 2011).

169 *Central Government to Subsidize Foreign Patent Applications*, People's Daily Online, October 16, 2009, *available at* http://english.people.com.cn/90001/90778/90862/6782417.html (last visited Sept. 2, 2011); Tu Lei, *MOF to Support Overseas Patents*, Global Times, October 14, 2009, *available at* http://business.globaltimes.cn/china-economy/2009-10/476759.html (last visited Sept. 2, 2011).

170 Tu Lei, *MOF to Support Overseas Patents*, Global Times, October 14, 2009, *available at* http://business.globaltimes.cn/china-economy/2009-10/476759.html (last visited Sept. 2, 2011).

171 National Patent Development Strategy (2011–2020), the State Intellectual Property Office, *available at* http://graphics8.nytimes.com/packages/pdf/business/SIPONatPatentDevStrategy.pdf (last visited Sept. 2, 2011), 10.

172 Possible narrow exceptions to this rule that are available even under the current system are discussed in Chapter 2.

173 Margot Fröhlinger, *Patent Litigation in Europe*, 14th European Patent Judges' Symposium, European Patent Office, O.J. 1/2009, Spec. ed., 31. *See also* Donald Chisum's remark that "[t]he cumulative costs of registering

problem of enforcement of patents abroad: its *National Patent Development Strategy* mentions the need to help businesses resolve their patent disputes in foreign countries.[174]

The next stage of the internationalization of the patent system must address the intractable problem of enforcement of parallel patents; some proposals on the subject have already been developed, and the next chapter discusses these proposals and problems associated with their current or future implementation.

---

and maintaining trademarks and patents internationally threaten to exclude small, independent enterprises, which may be unable to obtain funding and to compete in product and service markets that are heavily dependent on intellectual property protection." Donald S. Chisum, *Normative and Empirical Territoriality in Intellectual Property: Lessons from Patent Law*, 37 VA. J. INT'L L. 603, 618 (1997).

[174] National Patent Development Strategy, *supra* note 171, 10.

2 Enforcing Parallel Patents

CROSS-BORDER ENFORCEMENT PROBLEMS arise when patent holders cannot sue in the country of actual enforcement; although it seems that in cases involving patents the country of infringement and enforcement should be identical because of the territoriality principle of patent protection,[1] there is not necessarily an equivalence. If an infringer does not comply with a court decision voluntarily, the actual enforcement of the court decision has to occur where the infringer or his assets are located, or in other words, where a contempt order or a similar measure may be effectuated, which may not be the country where the infringer infringed the patent. To avoid cross-border enforcement problems, a patent holder should sue instead, or simultaneously, for infringement of a parallel patent that was granted in the country where the infringer or his assets are located, as long as the patentee holds such a parallel patent in that country and the infringer infringed the patent there as well. However, not all patentees hold parallel patents in multiple countries, and even if they do, enforcement of multiple parallel patents is complex and extremely costly. This chapter reviews the various mechanisms that have been developed to deal with

[1] *See* Chapter 1, Section 1.1, for a discussion of the territorial limitations of patent protection.

the issue of enforcement of parallel patents and analyzes the probabilities that the mechanisms will be successful in making parallel patent enforcement feasible.

With narrowly limited exceptions,[2] patent infringements must be litigated in the country in which the infringed patent was issued; when multiple parallel patents need to be enforced, patentees must litigate in all the countries where the patents were infringed. This fragmented patent enforcement has been criticized not only for its cost but also for its inconsistent and unpredictable results;[3] if there is anything predictable about fragmented enforcement, it is that different courts will likely interpret patents differently, even if the patents arise from the same regional patent, as happens in cases involving European patents. There is even a great difference in courts' interpretations of patents within one country; the rate at which the U.S. Court of Appeals for the Federal Circuit reverses U.S. district court decisions on patent claim construction is good evidence of this phenomenon. Not surprisingly, such differences also exist among courts and judges of different countries, and the different interpretations of patents, combined with different procedural rules, easily lead to different results in infringement suits even when parallel patents are litigated.[4] Therefore, in a system in which parallel patents must be enforced before different courts, the one accurate prediction that can be made is that the outcomes of the litigations are likely to be different.

The costs of litigating in many countries simultaneously can overwhelm a non-corporate patent holder or a small or medium-sized enterprise. A study commissioned by the European Commission revealed the estimated costs for a litigant to litigate in the four member states where most patent litigation in the European Union takes place—Germany, France, the United Kingdom, and the Netherlands. The Commission claims that when litigating in these four countries in parallel, a litigant will incur cumulative costs between €310,000 and €1,950,000 in first instance proceedings, and an additional €320,000–€1,390,000 if a first instance decision is reviewed on appeal.[5] This estimate is very rough because it is based on a simple sum of the costs of individual national proceedings in the four countries; the true cost of

---

[2] *See infra* Section 2.1.6 for instances in which courts have agreed to decide cases that concerned foreign patents.

[3] Fröhlinger, Chapter 1, note 173, 34; *Communication from the Commission to the European Parliament and the Council—Enhancing the Patent System in Europe*, 8302/07 (Apr. 4, 2007), 6.

[4] For instances of such varying results, see, for instance, *Data Security Systems v. European Central Bank*, reported in Fröhlinger, Chapter 1, note 173, 33.

[5] *Communication from the Commission to the European Parliament and the Council—Enhancing the Patent System in Europe*, 8302/07 (Apr. 4, 2007), 7 and 22. For additional information on the costs of patent litigation, see, e.g., Assessment of the Impact, Chapter 1, note 20, 10–12; Joachim Bornkamm, *Intellectual Property Litigation under the Civil Law Legal System; Experience in Germany*, WIPO/ACE/2/3 (June 4, 2004), 7; Dietmar Harhoff, Economic Cost-Benefit Analysis of a Unified and Integrated European Patent Litigation System,

enforcement of parallel patents involves more than computing the sum of the costs of the individual national proceedings. On the one hand, some costs may be saved as certain evidence and argumentation may repeat in the parallel litigation; on the other hand, additional expenses will be incurred in coordinating those proceedings because litigating in several countries requires an extensive and sophisticated overall plan.[6] It has been reported, for instance, that some pharmaceutical companies have spent as much as £100,000 per month to maintain special litigation teams solely for the purpose of coordinating the enforcement of their parallel patents.[7] Naturally, this level of expense is something that only a large corporate patent holder can afford, and so far the existing insurance schemes have not offered an affordable solution even for those who might consider insuring themselves against the threat of patent litigation.[8]

Two types of solutions have been discussed to solve the problem of enforcement of parallel patents, and both operate on the same premise: that litigation concerning parallel patents should be concentrated in one court. However, the solutions differ in what they consider the best institution to handle the litigation. The first proposes that litigation take place in one of the existing national courts that would be given jurisdiction to decide disputes over foreign patents. This approach can be labeled the private international law solution because it relies solely on the rules of private international law to achieve the desired result. The second approach would also require some adjustment to the private international law rules; however, it is primarily an institutional solution—it calls for the creation of a multinational court before which proceedings concerning parallel patents would be concentrated.

So far only one version of the private international law solution has been tested; no institutional solution has ever been implemented. It is important to note that the one version tested was not specifically designed to address cross-border problems in the patent system. In fact, it was not even crafted to address intellectual property

---

available at http://ec.europa.eu/internal_market/indprop/docs/patent/studies/litigation_system_en.pdf (last visited Sept. 2, 2011), 32–34.

[6] On the need to lift the burden of extensive coordination, see Robert Blackburn, *Extraterritorial Enforcement: Practical Considerations for Lawyers*, *in* RETHINKING INTERNATIONAL INTELLECTUAL PROPERTY: BIODIVERSITY & DEVELOPING COUNTRIES, EXTRATERRITORIAL ENFORCEMENT, THE GRACE PERIOD, AND OTHER ISSUES 63 (Kraig M. Hill, Toshiko Takenaka, & Kevin Takeuchi eds., 2000); *Recommendation from the Commission to the Council, To Authorise the Commission to Open Negotiations for the Adoption of an Agreement Creating a Unified Patent Litigation System*, SEC (2009) 330 final (Mar. 20, 2009), 2–3.

[7] Fröhlinger, Chapter 1, note 173, 35.

[8] For a discussion of patent litigation insurance and patent enforcement insurance, see J. Rodrigo Fuentes, *Patent Insurance: Towards a More Affordable, Mandatory Scheme?*, 10 COLUM. SCI. & TECH. L. REV. 267 (2009). "[T]he demand [for patent insurance] remains severely limited. [... P]atent insurance is too expensive for businesses and too risky for insurers." *Id.*, 298.

litigation problems; it was adopted as a general private international law convention[9] to set rules of jurisdiction and recognition and enforcement of judgments in a large variety of civil and commercial disputes. Notwithstanding the various difficulties associated with the regime created by the convention, it became a source of inspiration for a number of followers who have promoted the private international law route while in search of solutions to cross-border problems. Several proposals have been discussed and developed for both types of solutions, and both continue to attract the attention of scholars and practitioners who understand that the current state of mechanisms for the enforcement of patents is untenable.

This chapter reviews both the private international law solutions and the institutional solutions to the problem of enforcement of parallel patents and analyzes the hurdles to their implementation. Section 2.1.1 presents the only private international law solution that has been tested—the regime used in Europe that was originally formed under the Brussels and Lugano Conventions—and explains the problems that the regime generated; Section 2.1.2 shows how these problems were or are being mitigated. Sections 2.1.3–2.1.5 discuss the international treaty and two major proposals that were developed as instruments of private international law—The Hague Convention, the American Law Institute Principles, and the Principles drafted by the Group for Conflict of Laws in Intellectual Property (CLIP) organized within the Max Planck Institute for Intellectual Property and Competition Law.[10] Section 2.1.6 analyzes the hurdles to adoption of the private international solutions; specifically, using the situations in the United States and Germany as examples, it examines the reluctance of courts to decide questions of foreign patent validity. Section 2.2 turns to the institutional solutions as they have been discussed in Europe and suggests the reasons for the delay in their adoption. Finally, Section 2.3 summarizes the barriers that exist to the adoption and implementation of both types of solutions at the global level.

[9] Convention of 27 September 1968 on Jurisdiction and the Enforcement of Judgments in Civil and Commercial Matters, 1978 O.J. (L 304) 36 ("the Brussels Convention").

[10] Other proposals have been developed in Japan and Korea. For an analysis of the Japanese Transparency Project, which was presented in October 2009 and is entitled the *Proposal on Jurisdiction, Choice of Law, Recognition and Enforcement of Foreign Judgments in Intellectual Property*, see Shigeki Chaen, Toshiyuki Kono, & Dai Yokomizo, *Jurisdiction in Intellectual Property Cases: The Transparency Proposal*, *in* INTELLECTUAL PROPERTY IN THE GLOBAL ARENA (Jürgen Basedow, Toshiyuki Kono, & Axel Metzger eds., Mohr Siebeck 2010), 77. In Korea, the Korean Private International Law Association approved in March 2010 the *Principles on International Intellectual Property Litigation*. A copy provided by Professor Kyung Han Sohn is on file with the author.

2.1 Private International Law Solutions to the Problem of Enforcement of Parallel Patents[11]

One solution to the difficulty of enforcement of parallel patents is to entrust a court in one country (most likely the court of the infringer's domicile or residence) with the adjudication of cases involving all parallel patents that have been infringed by the same infringer, or by the same group of infringers acting in concert. But as it was a precondition to parallel patents that nations allow patenting abroad and the granting of patents to foreigners, so it is also a precondition to the centralized litigation of parallel patents that countries permit foreign courts to adjudicate and enforce their patents.

The reason why a patent holder cannot enforce his patent through litigation outside the country where the patent was granted, and therefore cannot centralize all infringement proceedings concerning parallel patents in one country, is that courts generally abstain from deciding the validity of foreign patents. This position not only prevents courts from entertaining declaratory judgment suits for foreign patent invalidity, but also makes them reluctant to adjudicate infringement suits involving foreign patents, since the issue of validity of the foreign patent is often raised as a counterclaim or used as a defense in patent infringement suits.[12]

Courts use the act of state doctrine to explain their abstention; the doctrine allows them to decline adjudication of decisions made by foreign governments for fear of interfering with the sovereignty of foreign countries.[13] The doctrine prohibits courts from second-guessing the decisions of foreign authorities; in the words of the U.S. Supreme Court, the doctrine precludes courts from "sit[ting] in judgment on the acts of the government of another done within its own territory."[14] Based on this doctrine, U.S. courts have rejected cases involving actions arising out of harassment by a foreign army[15] or nationalization by a foreign government;[16] for the same reasons they also refuse to adjudicate the validity of foreign patents.[17] In Europe as well,

---

[11] Parts of Section 2.1.1 appeared in Marketa Trimble, *Cross-Border Injunctions in U.S. Patent Cases and Their Enforcement Abroad*, 13 MARQ. INTELL. PROP. L. REV. 331 (2009).

[12] A Belgian court stated that because an invalid patent cannot be infringed, the issue of validity comes up in every infringement suit. *See infra* note 66 and the accompanying text.

[13] On the doctrine in general, see Andrew D. Patterson, *The Act of State Doctrine Is Alive and Well: Why Critics of the Doctrine Are Wrong*, 15 U.C. DAVIS J. INT'L L. & POL'Y 111 (2008).

[14] Underhill v. Hernandez, 168 U.S. 250, 252 (1897).

[15] *Id.*

[16] Banco National De Cuba v. Sabbatino, 376 U.S. 398 (1964).

[17] Jan K. Voda, M.D. v. Cordis Corporation, 476 F.3d 887 (Fed. Cir. 2007).

a grant of a patent has been viewed as "an exercise of national sovereignty"[18] that should not be questioned by the courts of another country.

The application of the doctrine in patent cases has not been without its critics.[19] Some charge that it is merely a relic of the old system of privileges out of which the patent system grew;[20] others warn that its application can lead to a denial of justice in cases where no alternative forum exists or where a foreign judgment from an alternative jurisdiction would not be enforceable against the infringer.[21] Some critics contend that the doctrine should not apply to patents because of the nondiscretionary nature of the act of granting a patent, which makes the grant only a confirmation by the state that the applicant complied with the legal requirements for a grant of a patent.[22] However, the application of the doctrine to patents has survived the criticism to date and continues to shape the approach to litigation in cases of parallel patents.

2.1.1 THE BRUSSELS REGIME

The only private international law solution to the problem of enforcement of parallel patents that has ever been tested is the solution created in Europe by what will be called hereafter the "Brussels regime." The Brussels regime is built on three instruments that provide rules of jurisdiction and recognition and enforcement of judgments; they are the Brussels Convention,[23] its lesser-known but mirror-image companion the Lugano Convention,[24] and the Brussels I Regulation.[25] The oldest instrument, the Brussels Convention, was concluded among the member states of

---

[18] *Report on the Convention on Jurisdiction and the Enforcement of Judgments in Civil and Commercial Matters*, P. Jenard, 1979 O.J. (C 59) 1, 36 ("Jenard Report").

[19] Troller, *Europäisierung*, Chapter 1, note 6, 532; Volkmar Tetzner, *Die Verfolgung der Verletzung ausländischer Patente vor deutschen Gerichten unter Berücksichtigung des EWG-Gerichtsstands und Vollstreckungs-Abkommens*, 1976 GRUR 669, 669.

[20] Troller, *Europäisierung*, Chapter 1, note 6, 532.

[21] Tetzner, *Die Verfolgung*, *supra* note 19, 669.

[22] Brief for Amici Curiae Law Professors in Support of the Appellee, Jan K. Voda, M.D. v. Cordis Corporation, No. 05-1238 (Fed. Cir. July 29, 2005), 23. Alois Troller furthered the same argument in the 1950s; he suggested that the doctrine should not apply if the grant of a patent is only a declaratory (as opposed to a constitutive) act. Troller, *Europäisierung*, Chapter 1, note 6, 532.

[23] The Brussels Convention, *supra* note 9.

[24] Convention of 16 September 1988 on Jurisdiction and the Enforcement of Judgments in Civil and Commercial Matters, 1988 O.J. (L319) 9 ("the Lugano Convention"). The Convention was revised in 2007; Convention on Jurisdiction and the Recognition and Enforcement of Judgments in Civil and Commercial Matters, 2009 O.J. (L 147) 5 ("the Lugano II Convention").

[25] Council Regulation (EC) No 44/2001 of 22 December 2000 on jurisdiction and the recognition and enforcement of judgments in civil and commercial matters, 2001 O.J. (L 12) 1 ("Brussels I Regulation").

the European Union[26] in 1968, and in 2001 it was transformed into a European Union regulation, referred to as the Brussels I Regulation, through which the original Convention's provisions were made directly applicable to the European Union member states.[27] The provisions of the Brussels Convention were mirrored in the 1988 Lugano Convention,[28] which binds the countries of the European Union and the European Economic Area. The Lugano Convention was revised in 2007.[29]

The Brussels regime is far from an ideal solution and deserves specific review because it actually created problems that reveal several weaknesses in this type of solution. The regime has been heavily criticized; for instance, Professor Joseph Straus described "life under the Brussels (and Lugano) Convention" as "thorny"[30] and suggested that the regime not only does not make litigation more efficient but to the contrary manages to complicate matters.[31] He pointed to the words by the late Justice Laddie, who condemned the regime, noting that "[a] less sensible system could not have been dreamt by Kafka."[32]

Two historical observations about the regime are important. First, it was negotiated among countries that were socially, economically, and geographically proximate and that exhibited a strong desire to adopt the regime; the similarities and the desire made agreement possible on common rules of jurisdiction, recognition, and enforcement. Second, the features of the regime, and particularly its projected effect on patent litigation, were negotiated at a time when a number of experts were promoting the idea of centralizing litigation of parallel patents in one forum.[33] The experts

---

[26] *See* Introduction, note 6 on the use of the term "European Union" throughout this book.

[27] The transformation into a binding Regulation was enabled by the Amsterdam Treaty, signed in 1997 and effective since 1999, which moved matters of judicial cooperation in civil and commercial matters from the Third Pillar of the European Union (in which no regulations could have been adopted) into the First Pillar (in which regulations could have been adopted). Treaty Establishing the European Community, Consolidated Version, 2002 O.J. (C 325) 33, Articles 65 and 249.

[28] The Lugano Convention and Lugano II Convention, *supra* note 24.

[29] The Lugano II Convention, *supra* note 24.

[30] Joseph Straus, *Patent Litigation in Europe—A Glimmer of Hope? Present Status and Future Perspectives*, 2 Wash. U. J.L. & Pol'y 403, 408 (2000).

[31] *Id.*, 418.

[32] Sepracor Inc. v. Hoechst Marrion Roussel Ltd. et al., [1999] F.S.R., 352 (Eng.), quoted in Straus, *supra* note 30, 418.

[33] Troller, *Europäisierung*, Chapter 1, note 6, 538; Alois Troller, *Vorschlag für den Abschluß eines Gerichtsstands- und Vollstreckungsabkommens zwischen einzelnen Mitgliedstaaten der PVÜ in Form einer Union restreinte*, 1956 GRUR Int. 521; Friedrich Groß, *Wie mache ich im Inland Ansprüche aus Schutzrechten geltend, deren Verletzung im Ausland erfolgt ist?*, 1957 GRUR Int. 346, 348; Heinz W. Auerswald, *Können Ansprüche wegen Verletzung eines ausländischen Patents vor deutschen Gerichten verfolgt werden?*, *in* Festschrift Werner von Stein 8 (1961). Auerswald mentions Reimer, Riezler, and Raape as being among those who supported the idea of international patent jurisdiction for German courts.

understood the premise that courts should not adjudicate the validity of foreign patents but recognized the high value of centralizing infringement proceedings and therefore proposed that courts be able to decide on the infringement of foreign patents to facilitate the centralization of proceedings. Although the Convention was not tailored to intellectual property cases specifically, it reflected the discussions of the intellectual property experts and their expectations that a new unitary European Union patent would be created with independent rules of jurisdiction.[34]

In general, the Brussels regime's rules on jurisdiction, recognition, and enforcement apply to all cases where the defendant is domiciled in a European Union member state or contracting country (the "Brussels regime countries").[35] Additionally, the rules may also be invoked when parties, at least one of which is domiciled in a Brussels regime country, agree to choose a court in a Brussels regime country.[36] In all cases that remain outside the Brussels regime, countries follow their own national rules on jurisdiction, recognition, and enforcement.[37]

In Brussels regime patent litigation a distinction is made between cases involving patents granted by a Brussels regime country and cases involving patents granted by other countries. Article 22.4,[38] the exclusive jurisdiction provision, grants exclusive jurisdiction "in proceedings concerned with the registration or validity of patents" to "the courts *of the Member State* in which the [. . .] registration has been applied for, has taken place or is under the terms of a Community instrument or an international convention deemed to have taken place."[39] Therefore, if jurisdiction is asserted based on the Brussels regime—for instance against a company from a Brussels regime country in the place of its domicile, such as a German company in Germany[40]—and the case involves infringement of a patent granted by a country of the Brussels regime—such as France—the exclusive jurisdiction provision of Article 22.4 applies. But if the case involves infringement of a patent granted by a country outside the

[34] Jenard Report, *supra* note 18, 36. On the current state of negotiations of the unified European Union patent, see *infra* Section 2.2 and *Conclusions on an Enhanced Patent System in Europe, Council of the European Union* (Dec. 4, 2009), *available at* http://www.consilium.europa.eu/uedocs/cms_data/docs/pressdata/en/intm/111744.pdf (last visited Sept. 2, 2011).

[35] The Brussels Convention, *supra* note 9, Article 3; Jenard Report, *supra* note 18, 13; Brussels I Regulation, *supra* note 25, Article 3.

[36] The Brussels Convention, *supra* note 9, Article 17; Brussels I Regulation, *supra* note 25, Article 23.

[37] Brussels I Regulation, *supra* note 25, Article 4.

[38] Throughout this chapter an article number appearing without a statute refers to the Brussels I Regulation, *supra* note 25.

[39] Brussels I Regulation, *supra* note 25, Article 22.4 (emphasis added).

[40] *Id.*, Article 2.1. On the domicile of "a company or other legal person," see *id.*, Article 60.

Brussels regime—such as the United States—the exclusive jurisdiction provision does not apply.[41]

The Brussels regime thus created a two-track system in which cases follow one track if an infringement is based on a patent granted by a Brussels regime country and another track if the infringement is based on a patent granted elsewhere. It is unclear whether this system was purposefully designed to operate in this manner or whether the result occurred by chance. Neither the Jenard Report on the Brussels Convention[42] nor the Explanatory Report on the 2007 Lugano Convention[43] comment about the limitation of the exclusive jurisdiction provision to patents granted by the Brussels regime countries, or suggest whether courts are expected to apply their own national provisions when the issue of the validity of a patent granted outside the Brussels regime countries is raised. In fact, the absence of any discussion about patents granted by countries that are outside the regime suggests that drafters of the conventions presumed that such patents would not be litigated before the courts of the Brussels regime countries at all. It remains unclear what courts should do when they assert jurisdiction based on the Brussels regime (for instance a German court over a German entity) and invalidity of a patent granted outside the Brussels regime countries is raised (such as a U.S. patent);[44] presumably the courts would for this particular issue apply their own national rules.[45]

Apart from entrusting the courts of the country where the patent was issued with exclusive jurisdiction in "proceedings concerned with the registration or validity of patents,"[46] the regime leaves other patent-related proceedings to courts that have jurisdiction based on other provisions. Such proceedings may take place in the place of defendant's domicile (Article 2), or in the place of the tortious activity—meaning

---

[41] *See* Primus v. Roche, The Hague Court of Appeal, Nov. 30, 2007 (Neth.), reported in Josine Fasseur-van Santen & R. A. Grootoonk, *Court of Appeal of The Hague—Some Recent Developments in Dutch Patent Law*, 14th European Patent Judges' Symposium, European Patent Office, O.J. 1/2009, Spec. ed., 157, 160. "[T]he Supreme Court [of the Netherlands] ruled that Article 16(4) of the Brussels Convention also applied in a case against a defendant which claims nullity as mentioned above and is a foreign company not domiciled in the EU." *Id.*

[42] Jenard Report, *supra* note 18.

[43] *Explanatory Report, Fausto Pocar*, 2009 O.J. (C319) 1, 68–69.

[44] Marko Schauwecker, *Die Entscheidung GAT gegen LuK und drittstaatliche Patente*, 2009 GRUR Int. 187, 187.

[45] Marko Schauwecker suggests four different outcomes based on four possible interpretations: 1) the issue of foreign patent validity would be treated as being analogous to Brussels regime country patent validity on the presumption that Article 22.4 of the Brussels I Regulation was not intended to be limited solely to Brussels regime country patents; 2) the national law of the deciding court (and not the Brussels regime) would govern the issue; 3) an autonomous procedural rule would be developed to govern the issue; or 4) it would be presumed that the Brussels regime includes all applicable rules and therefore raising non-Brussels regime patent invalidity must have no impact on the proceedings. Schauwecker, *Die Entscheidung*, *supra* note 44, 189.

[46] Brussels I Regulation, *supra* note 25, Article 22.4.

the place where the infringing activity or its effects occurred (Article 5.3),[47] or, under certain circumstances, where a co-defendant is domiciled (Article 6.1).[48] Jurisdiction may also be extended over a defendant when the parties agree on the court's jurisdiction or when the defendant enters an appearance before the court (Articles 23 and 24). Additionally, a plaintiff may ask a court in any contracting country to issue provisional measures against a defendant (Article 31).[49]

Predictably, a number of problems arose because of the availability of the multiple grounds of jurisdiction; all of the problems were related to the phenomenon of forum shopping. First, there were doubts about the scope of the exclusive jurisdiction provision of Article 22.4; some argued that the exclusive jurisdiction provision applied only to declaratory judgment suits for invalidity, while others suggested that the provision should also cover infringement proceedings because of the importance of questions of validity in infringement proceedings. Second, commentators have perceived as problematic the fact that some courts used the regime's provisions to grant cross-border relief;[50] the courts issued remedies that covered multiple countries even when they were not the courts of the infringer's domicile. This practice has been criticized as encouraging forum shopping.[51] Finally, the possibility of bringing suits in multiple jurisdictions has prompted some infringers to adopt an aggressive method for fighting patent holders: without waiting for the patent holder to file an infringement suit against them, they file a declaratory judgment suit in a jurisdiction known for its slow pace. Even if the right holder eventually files an infringement suit, the court addressed with such a suit must stay its proceedings pending the decision of the court first seized.[52] Understandably, this infamous practice, well known

---

[47] For the interpretation by the Court of Justice of the European Union ("CJEU") narrowing the scope of the provision see decisions Case C-21/76, Mines de Potasse de l'Alsace, 1976; Case C-220/88, Dumez France and Tracoba, 1990; Case C-189/8, Kalfelis v. Bankhaus Schröder, 1988; and Case C 68/93, Shevill v. Press Alliance, 1995. *See also* Straus, *supra* note 30, 410–11; JOHANN PITZ, PATENTVERLETZUNGSVERFAHREN 224–27 (2003); JENS ADOLPHSEN, EUROPÄISCHES UND INTERNATIONALS ZIVILPROZESSRECHT IN PATENTSACHEN 157–58 (2nd ed. 2009).

[48] For the CJEU interpretation narrowing the scope of the provision, see Case C-189/8, Kalfelis v. Bankhaus Schröder, 1988; Case C-539/03, Roche Nederland BV and Others v. Frederick Primus, Milton Goldenberg, 2006 (the CJEU decision in Roche is further discussed *infra* in Section 2.1.2). *See also* Straus, *supra* note 30, 412–13; Rößler, Chapter 1, note 5, 382–84.

[49] For an explanation of the narrowing interpretation by the CJEU, see Straus, *supra* note 30, 415–16.

[50] De Ranitz, *Mr. Justice Laddie*, Chapter 1, note 37, 530. The late Justice Laddie noted: "[R]unning a legal system is not much different from running a supermarket. If your goods are not good enough, people will go somewhere else." *Id.*, 532.

[51] *Id.*

[52] Brussels I Regulation, *supra* note 25, Article 27.

as the "Italian torpedo" or the "Belgian torpedo," depending on the court used, has also been heavily criticized.

These three phenomena associated with the Brussels regime, which are further discussed in detail below, did not emerge until quite late in the life of the regime. Although the Brussels Convention came into force in 1973, it took the patent litigation community almost two decades to begin exploiting the possibilities of the Convention.[53] Richard Ebbink suggests that the interest in the exploitation was first sparked by developments in the legal culture of the patent litigation bar; he attributes the emergence of cases utilizing the various grounds of jurisdiction to three factors: the natural centralization of patent litigation in a few courts in Europe,[54] exchanges among judges facilitated by international meetings,[55] and the realization of the need for effective patent protection.[56]

2.1.2 MITIGATING THE PROBLEMS CREATED BY THE BRUSSELS REGIME

As it had addressed other ambiguities and problems under the Brussels regime, the Court of Justice of the European Union (CJEU) was expected to solve the three problems described above (the interpretation of Article 22.4 and the problems of cross-border injunctions and torpedoes) and to provide an interpretation binding upon all parties to the regime. At one time it seemed that two cases that were referred

---

[53] Richard Ebbink traces the beginning of interest in the ambiguities and possibilities offered by the Convention to the mid-1980s. Richard Ebbink, *A Fire-Side Chat on Cross-Border Issues (before the ECJ in GAT v. LuK)*, *in* FESTSCHRIFT FÜR JOCHEN PAGENBERG 255, 256–57 (Dietrich Beier, Laurence Brüning-Petit, & Christopher Heath eds., 2006). Professor Joseph Straus puts the "discovery" of the Brussels Convention in the area of patents in the 1970s but notes that "it was not until 1994 that it gained practical importance in that field." Straus, *supra* note 30, 416. Volkmar Tetzner in 1976 noted that the entry into force of the Brussels Convention in 1973 remained "widely unnoticed by the expert world." Tetzner, *Die Verfolgung*, *supra* note 19, 669. The first instance of a cross-border injunction was reported in a 1989 trademark case. Johann Pitz & Wolfgang V. Meibom, *Cross-Border Injunctions in International Patent Infringement Proceedings*, 19 EUR. INTELL. PROP. REV. 469, 469 (1997); Pierre Véron, *Thirty Years of Experience with the Brussels Convention in Patent Infringement Litigation*, 84 J. PAT. & TRADEMARK OFF. SOC'Y 431, 435–36 (2002).

[54] According to the European Commission, as of 2007, more than 90 percent of all patent litigation in the European Union took place before the courts of only four countries (Germany, France, the United Kingdom, and the Netherlands). *Communication from the Commission to the European Parliament and the Council—Enhancing the Patent System in Europe*, 8302/07 (Apr. 4, 2007), 7.

[55] The first European Patent Judges' Symposium took place in October 1982; in September 2008, the 14th Symposium was organized. 14th European Patent Judges' Symposium, European Patent Office, O.J. 1/2009, Spec. ed. The European Patent Lawyers Association was created in 2001, *available at* http://www.eplaw.org/ (last visited Sept. 2, 2011). *See also* remarks by Lord Justice Jacob *in* Robin Jacob, *The Judge's Perspective—A Speech Given at the EPLA Munich Conference*, July 2007.

[56] Ebbink, *A Fire-Side*, *supra* note 53, 256–57.

to the CJEU—*GAT*[57] and *Roche*[58]—would finally offer the right occasion to clarify the rules;[59] however, the impact of the CJEU's decisions in these cases turned out to be limited. Of the three problems outlined above only the problems of interpretation of Article 22.4 and of cross-border injunctions were partially resolved, leaving certain issues of procedure to further debate and uncertainty.

The question of the proper interpretation of Article 22.4 mobilized those who advocated the centralization of infringement proceedings of multiple parallel patents in one court. They argued against application of the provision in cases where invalidity was counterclaimed or raised as a defense because of the high percentage of infringement cases in which such a counterclaim or defense arises. Applying the exclusive jurisdiction provision in these cases would either drastically slow down the proceedings (if courts stayed the infringement proceedings and waited for a decision by a foreign court or foreign patent authority) or defeat the centralization of parallel patent litigation (if courts declined to adjudicate such cases altogether). The latter scenario would turn the exclusive jurisdiction rule de facto into the only jurisdiction rule in all patent cases[60]—a step that Annette Kur described as "a backward roll into the nineteenth century."[61] The Jenard Report on the Brussels Convention seems to back those who interpreted the exclusive jurisdiction provision of Article 22.4 narrowly; the Report states that actions other than those concerned with the validity of patents "including those for infringement of patents, are governed by the general rules of the Convention."[62] An interpretation with the same conclusion was also provided by the CJEU in its 1983 decision in *Duijnstee v. Goderbauer*.[63]

Courts interpreted Article 22.4 and its effects in the context of patent litigation in various ways. Some courts said that once the issue of validity had been raised, the entire proceedings should be dealt with by the court of exclusive jurisdiction—the court of the country where the patent was granted. English courts were among the courts that furthered this view; they took the position that "once the defendant

---

[57] Case C-4/03, Gesellschaft für Antriebstechnik mbH & Co. KG v. Lamellen und Kupplungsbau Beteiligungs KG, 2006 ("GAT").

[58] Case C-539/03, Roche Nederland BV and Others v. Frederick Primus, Milton Goldenberg, 2006 ("Roche").

[59] Other cases were referred to the CJEU, but they all settled before the CJEU could issue a preliminary ruling. *See, e.g.*, case 2 W 60/98 before the Düsseldorf Oberlandesgericht described in Johann Pitz, *Torpedos unter Beschuss*, 2001 GRUR INT. 32, 32–35.

[60] Dieter Stauder, *Cross-Border Protection of European Patents, Part One: A Stocktaking*, 29 IIC 497, 500 (1998); Véron, *Thirty Years*, *supra* note 53, 437.

[61] Annette Kur, *International Hague Convention on Jurisdiction and Foreign Judgments: A Way Forward for I.P.*, 24 EUR. INTELL. PROP. REV. 175, 176 (2002).

[62] Jenard Report, *supra* note 18, 36.

[63] Case C-288/82, Ferdinand M.J.J. Duijnstee v. Lodewijk Goderbauer, 1983, para. 25.

raises validity the court must hand the proceedings over to the courts having exclusive jurisdiction over that issue"[64] because of the close interrelation between the issues of infringement and validity.[65] Similarly, a Belgian court noted in *Röhm Enzyme* that there "can be no infringement if the patent is invalid"; therefore, validity of the patent in issue must be considered in each infringement action.[66] Because the Belgian court suspected in this particular case that the plaintiff intended to introduce the issue of validity of foreign patents after jurisdiction had been established, the court rejected jurisdiction over the foreign patents,[67] emphasizing that the court deciding infringement should also be the court that assesses the validity of the patent in issue.[68]

Other European courts have not seen the issue of validity as dispositive of the question of where infringement proceedings should ultimately take place. The Mannheim Landgericht adopted the view that infringement proceedings could be conducted outside the country that granted the patent, but that when invalidity was raised, the court must stay the proceedings and wait for the respective foreign authority to decide the question of patent validity.[69] Dutch courts and the Düsseldorf Landgericht went even further; they emphasized their discretion in the matter and their freedom to choose either to stay or continue the infringement proceedings based on their assessment of the likelihood of success of the patent invalidity claim. When The Hague Court of Appeal decided that the chance of success of the invalidity claim raised in a foreign country was slim, it refused to suspend the infringement case.[70] The Düsseldorf Landgericht has granted stays and directed parties to resolve the validity issue in the country where the patent was granted only if the court considered the invalidity arguments to have merit.[71] For instance, in *Schwungrad* the court held that simply raising the invalidity of a foreign patent did not automatically

---

[64] Coin Controls Ltd. v. Suzo International, [1997] 3 All ER 45 (Eng.).

[65] *Id. See also* Fort Dodge Animal Health Ltd. and Others v. Akzo Nobel NV and Another, Oct. 27, 1997, [1998] FSR 222 (Eng.), reported in 1998 IIC 927. "Where questions of infringement and validity both arise it is invariably not possible to conclude there is infringement without validity being determined." *Id.*, 931. "[A]ny proceedings for infringement must in English eyes be 'concerned with' the validity of the patent." *Id.*, 932.

[66] Röhm Enzyme GmbH et al. v. DSM N.V., BASF Belgium N.V. et al., Brussels Court of First Instance, May 12, 2000, No. 2000/857/A (Belg.), reported in 32 IIC 571, 575 (2001).

[67] Röhm Enzyme GmbH et al. v. DSM N.V., *supra* note 66.

[68] *Id.*

[69] Landgericht Mannheim, 7 O 235/01, Feb. 8, 2002. *See* Osterrieth & Haft, Chapter 1, note 5. On the German approach to adjudicating foreign patents, see *infra* Section 2.1.6.2.

[70] Palmaz v. Boston Scientific BV, [1999] F.S.R. 352 (Neth.), reported in Bart J. Van den Broek, *Netherlands: Patents—Cross-Border Injunctions*, 20 Eur. Intell. Prop. Rev. N132 (1998).

[71] *Kettenbandförderer III*, Landgericht Düsseldorf, 4 O 193/87, Feb. 1, 1994. The case concerned a British patent.

trigger the exclusive jurisdiction of a foreign court.[72] However, when in another case a suit for declaration of invalidity was brought before a Belgian court, the Düsseldorf Landgericht stayed its proceedings to wait for the Belgian decision.[73]

The dissonance in the approaches of European courts to the question of deciding foreign patent validity required a unifying intervention from the CJEU,[74] and it was hoped that the *GAT* and *Roche* rulings would provide the necessary guidance. In *GAT*, the first of the two cases, two German companies contested two French patents; the case was brought by one of the companies as a declaratory action for non-infringement and invalidity.[75] The Düsseldorf Landgericht decided that it had jurisdiction to adjudicate the case.[76] On appeal, the Düsseldorf Oberlandesgericht asked the CJEU whether the exclusive jurisdiction provision of Article 22.4 applied only to suits filed for a declaration of invalidity or also to infringement suits and suits filed for a declaration of noninfringement in which the issue of patent validity was raised.[77] In *Roche* the plaintiff alleged that a Dutch defendant and eight foreign co-defendants—all from the Roche group—infringed plaintiff's patents; each of the nine defendants was alleged to have infringed the respective parallel patent in its country of incorporation.[78] The Dutch court asked the CJEU to interpret Article 6.1[79] and explain whether the provision conferred jurisdiction on a court over foreign entities infringing foreign patents abroad based on a common strategy originating from a domestic company.[80]

In response to both cases, the CJEU explained that the exclusive jurisdiction provision of Article 22.4 applies any time validity becomes an issue; even if raised as a

---

[72] *Schwungrad*, Landgericht Düsseldorf, 4 O 128/00, May 31, 2001, 2001 GRUR INT. 983; 1 ENTSCHEIDUNGEN DER INSTANZGERICHTE ZUM RECHT DES GEISTIGEN EIGENTUMS 261 (2000). The case concerned a French patent. The Landgericht relied on its own prior 1998 decision in *Kettenbandförderer III* (*supra* note 71) and the 1996 decision in *Reinigungsmittel für Kunststoffverarbeitungsgeräte. Id.*, 983.

[73] *Torsionsschwingungsdämpfer*, Landgericht Düsseldorf, 4a O 61/02, Jan. 14, 2003, 3 ENTSCHEIDUNGEN DER INSTANZGERICHTE ZUM RECHT DES GEISTIGEN EIGENTUMS 21 (2002).

[74] *E.g.*, Mario Franzosi, *Germany: Patents—Unitary Character of a European Patent*, 22 EUR. INTELL. PROP. REV. N173 (2000) ("[T]he problem of cross-border actions, torpedoes, declarations of non-infringement, etc., has gone too far. A ruling from the [CJEU] would be most desirable." *Id.*, N174.)

[75] GAT, *supra* note 57, paras. 8–10. For the background of the case, see also the decision by the Düsseldorf Oberlandesgericht in 2 U 104/01, Dec. 5, 2002, 2003 GRUR INT. 1030.

[76] GAT, *supra* note 57, para. 11.

[77] *Id.*, para. 12.

[78] Roche, *supra* note 58, para. 14.

[79] Article 6.1 states that "[a] person domiciled in a Member State may also be sued [. . .] where he is one of a number of defendants, in the courts for the place where any one of them is domiciled, provided the claims are so closely connected that it is expedient to hear and determine them together to avoid the risk of irreconcilable judgments resulting from separate proceedings."

[80] *Id.*, paras. 17, 18, 31, and 33.

defense in infringement proceedings, the validity of a patent can be decided only by a court of the country where the patent was granted. The result of the *GAT* decision was quickly written into the 2007 revision of the Lugano Convention; the relevant exclusive jurisdiction provision was amended to state explicitly that it applied "in proceedings concerned with the registration or validity of patents [. . .], *irrespective of whether the issue is raised by way of an action or as a defence*."[81] An almost identical wording has been suggested in a proposal for recasting the Brussels I Regulation that was published by the European Commission in December 2010.[82]

The CJEU in *Roche* not only reiterated the principle explained in *GAT*, but also added that a court has no jurisdiction over foreign defendants for conduct abroad that infringes foreign patents;[83] only if jurisdiction is based on defendants' domicile in the jurisdiction of the court may the court decide on infringements of foreign patents. With this decision *Roche* partly addressed the phenomenon of the cross-border relief that had been issued by some courts. *Roche* explained that Article 6.1 cannot be used as a jurisdictional hook to sue foreign entities for infringement of foreign patents along with domestic co-defendants.[84] This CJEU interpretation does not eliminate the instances in which cross-border relief may be granted but it does limit them.

Even prior to *Roche*, European courts had already narrowed the application of Article 6.1; in *Expandable Crafts Partnership v. Boston Scientific* The Hague Court of Appeal limited the application of Article 6.1 by the "spider in the web" doctrine, requiring that the defendants' center of operations had to be in the Netherlands for a Dutch court to assert jurisdiction over foreign entities.[85] In *Roche* the CJEU went further than the Dutch courts, and in agreement with an approach adopted by the

---

[81] The Lugano II Convention, *supra* note 24, Article 22.4 (emphasis added); *Explanatory Report, Fausto Pocar*, 2009 O.J. (C319) 1, 68–69.

[82] Proposal for a Regulation of the European Parliament and of the Council on jurisdiction and the recognition and enforcement of judgments in civil and commercial matters (Recast), COM(2010) 748 final, December 14, 2010, p. 32.

[83] "That issue, whether it is raised by way of an action or a plea in objection, is a matter of exclusive jurisdiction . . ." Roche, *supra* note 58, para. 40.

[84] Roche, *supra* note 58, holding of the court.

[85] Expandable Crafts Partnership v. Boston Scientific, The Hague Court of Appeal, Apr. 23, 1998 (Neth.), reported in Bart J. Van den Broek, *Netherlands: Patents—Cross-Border Injunctions*, 20 Eur. Intell. Prop. Rev. N132 (1998); Peter Meier-Beck, *Aktuelle Fragen des Patentverletzungsverfahrens*, 1999 GRUR 379. *See also* Eka Chemicals AB v. Nalco Chemicals Co., May 25, 2000 (Neth.), reported in Bart Van den Broeak, *Netherlands: Patents—Preliminary Injunction—Cross Border Relief Refused But Relief Granted in Netherlands*, 22 Eur. Intell. Prop. Rev. N111 (2000); Rößler, Chapter 1, note 5, 395 ff.

Danish High Court[86] and the Brussels Court of First Instance[87] found that even when a case concerns a group of entities acting in concert with their center of operations in the country of suit, no jurisdiction under Article 6.1 may be extended over foreign entities for infringements of foreign patents. The CJEU reasoned that no risk of irreconcilable judgments arises when the litigation of such infringements is spread among a number of respective national courts because the acts of infringement are different, and the patents at issue are also different.[88]

Although the CJEU has ruled quite clearly on the scope of the exclusive jurisdiction provision, it has not reconciled the discrepancies in the approaches of national courts to retention of jurisdiction over infringement claims once validity becomes an issue. Even after *GAT* and *Roche* it remains unclear whether national courts should dismiss an infringement case altogether or only stay the proceedings and await a decision on validity by the respective foreign authority. Although in *Roche* the CJEU mentioned a "fragmentation of the patent proceedings"[89] that follows when invalidity is raised, it did not explain what the fragmentation means or how it should occur.[90]

GAT and *Roche* have not eliminated the widely discussed and often criticized practices that are frequent in European patent litigation: the pan-European injunctions[91] and the so-called "torpedoes." Torpedoes—declaratory judgment suits filed in slow courts to prevent faster courts from deciding infringement[92]—remain possible; the alleged infringer may still file for a declaration of noninfringement in a

---

[86] Meyn Food Processing Technology BV v. Lindholst & Co. A/S, [2003] UfR 898 (Den.), reported in Nicolai Lindgreen & Louise Knudsen, *Danish High Court Rejects Pan European Injunctions in Patent Cases*, 26 Eur. Intell. Prop. Rev. 182 (2004). *Proteinderivat*, Landgericht Düsseldorf, 4 O 65/00, Mar. 22, 2001, 1 Entscheidungen der Instanzgerichte zum Recht des geistigen Eigentums146 (2000).

[87] Röhm Enzyme, *supra* note 66.

[88] Roche, *supra* note 58, paras. 31–34.

[89] *Id.*, para. 40.

[90] On this particular matter, see Klaus Grabinski, *Cross-Border Injunctions in Patent Litigations Following the ECJ Decision* in GAT v. LuK—*Life after Death?*, *in* Patents and Technological Progress in a Globalized World—Liber Amicorum Joseph Straus 565, 570–72 (Wolrad Prinz zu Waldeck und Pyrmont, Martin J. Adelman, Robert Brauneis, Josef Drexl, & Ralph Nack eds., 2009).

[91] *Cf.* Jonathan Radcliffe, *Patent and Trademark Issues in the United Kingdom*, The IP Litigator 37 (May/June 2006) ("[T]his will effectively end cross-border injunctions in patent cases." *Id.*); Paul Joseph, *The Rise and Fall of Cross-Border Jurisdiction and Remedies in IP Disputes*, 1 J. Intell. Prop. L. & Prac. 850, 857 (2006) ("[C]ross-border jurisdiction and remedies are effectively dead, at least for the all important registered rights." *Id.*); Jacob, *The Judge's Perspective*, *supra* note 55 ("The Court of Justice put an end to [the practice of enforcing patents granted in other countries] (or virtually so) with *Gat v Luk*." *Id.*).

[92] The subject of torpedoes is widely discussed in the European literature. *See, e.g.*, Vincenzo Jandoli, *The "Italian Torpedo,"* 31 IIC 783, 788 (2000); Pitz, *Torpedos*, *supra* note 59; Pierre Véron, *ECJ Restores Torpedo Power*, 35 IIC 638, 638–40 (2004).

slow jurisdiction, and since invalidity is unlikely to be raised by a right holder, the case will remain in the court first seized. Certain strategies are already being utilized to attempt to eliminate torpedoes; some national courts, for example, are taking a progressive approach that is likely to discourage litigants from resorting to this practice in the future.[93] Although these courts cannot refuse to stay infringement proceedings simply because another court is slow,[94] they can consider the launch of a torpedo to be litigation misconduct or abuse of process.[95] Some courts fend off declaration of noninfringement torpedo actions by declining to extend jurisdiction based on the place of the tortious act.[96] Of course an ideal remedy would be that no judiciary in Europe would suffer from slow proceedings.[97]

---

[93] *See, for instance*, Therex Ltd. Partnership v. Medtronic BV, Feb. 6, 2001 (Neth.), reported in Bart J. Van den Broek, *Netherlands: Patents—Belgian Torpedo—Equivalence*, 23 Eur. Intell. Prop. Rev. N121 (2001). For another example of courts' progressive approach to some of the "innovative" litigation practices, see Novamont v. Biotec (Italy), reported in Mario Franzosi, *Italy: Patents—Cross-Border Declaration of Non-Infringement—Italian Torpedo—German Torpedo*, 22 Eur. Intell. Prop. Rev. N142 (2000). The case involved a "double torpedo"; a company filed an infringement suit purposefully in the wrong court in Germany in an attempt to remove the case from the scope of the Brussels Convention and obtain an early filing date. The Italian court in a declaratory judgment action "condemned this tool as excessively clever." *Id.* Although in this case the torpedo launcher won, the court's language showed its concern over shady practices in European patent litigation.

[94] Case C-116/02, Gasser v. Misat, 2003; Véron, *ECJ*, *supra* note 92, 641–42; Mario Leitzen, *Comeback des "Torpedo"?*, 2004 GRUR Int. 1010, 1013–14. *Cf.* a pre-Gasser decision Röhm Enzyme, *supra* note 66.

[95] *Cholesterin-Test*, Landgericht Düsseldorf, 4a O 4/00, Dec. 19, 2002, 3 Entscheidungen der Instanzgerichte zum Recht des geistigen Eigentums 8 (2002); Mario Franzosi, *Torpedoes Are Here to Stay*, 33 IIC 154, 160–61 (2002). *E.g.*, a Belgian court's decision to act promptly on the issue of jurisdiction because "[i]f the court quickly rules about its jurisdiction, it is impossible for the mala fide plaintiffs to further abuse the procedure." Röhm Enzyme, *supra* note 66. The court in that case rejected jurisdiction over the foreign patents because of its suspicion that the plaintiff intended to introduce the validity issue later in the proceedings. *Id.*, 575. The court pointed out the obvious "mixed intentions" with which plaintiffs began the proceedings in Belgium (*id.*, 576) and found that plaintiffs abused the rules of jurisdiction (*id.*, 578). Johann Pitz describes how the Tribunal d'Instance in Paris declined to stay infringement proceedings endangered by an Italian torpedo (The General Hospital/Bracco, GR 99/4574, Apr. 28, 2000 (Fr.)). The court applied a "highly restrictive interpretation" to the jurisdictional rules and decided that the Italian declaratory judgment action and the French infringement action were not related. Pitz adds that the court stated that the goal of the Brussels Convention "could not consist of enabling one party to block a suit for many years." Pitz, *Torpedos*, *supra* note 59, 36. The Tribunal de Grande Instance decided similarly in Schaerer Schweiter Mettler A.G. v. Fadis SpA, 00/04083, Mar. 9, 2001, 33 IIC 225 (2002). *See also* Leitzen, *supra* note 94, 1012–14. On misuse of rights, see also *Pulverbeschichtung*, Bundesgericht, 4C.370/2002, Feb. 21, 2003 (Switz.), 2004 GRUR Int. 448.

[96] *See, e.g.*, *Verpackungsmaschine*, Tribunale di Bologna, Sept. 16, 1998 (Italy), GRUR Int. 1021; *Verpackungsmaschine II*, Corte di Cassazione, Dec. 19, 2003 (Italy), 2005 GRUR Int. 264. *See also Trägermaterial für Kartenformulare*, Bundesgerichtshof, KZR 8/10, February 1, 2011 (a decision to lodge a reference for a CJEU preliminary ruling on the interpretation of the Brussels I Regulation in declaratory judgment actions).

[97] Jandoli, *supra* note 92, 788—noting that following a reform of the Code of Civil Procedure, "several Italian courts were able to reduce the duration of proceedings"; *id.* Leitzen, *supra* note 94—pointing out the creation of specialized intellectual property chambers at Italian courts as of July 1, 2003; *id.*, 1012. Franzosi, *Torpedoes*, *supra* note 95, 161; Philippe De Jong, *The Belgian Torpedo: From Self-Propelled Armament to Jaded Sandwich*, 27 Eur. Intell. Prop. Rev. 75 (2005)—noting the "increased tempo" of the Belgian courts as one of the

Although *Roche* limited the instances in which cross-border relief could be granted, cross-border injunctions remain possible under the jurisdictional rules of the Brussels regime.[98] Injunctions can be issued as provisional measures under Article 31, which permits courts to issue such measures "even if [. . .] courts of another Member State have jurisdiction as to the substance of the matter."[99] Among these provisional measures are injunctions that Dutch courts issue in *kort geding* proceedings,[100] and indeed since the *GAT* decision The Hague District Court has confirmed that *GAT* had no effect on *kort geding* proceedings. For example, in *Bettacare Ltd. v. H3 Products B.V., Wedeka B.V.*[101] the court issued a preliminary injunction against the Dutch defendants that covered the plaintiff's German patent and thus had effects in Germany. The CJEU will have an opportunity to clarify the applicability of the rule on exclusive jurisdiction in proceedings that concern provisional measures when it responds to a reference for a preliminary ruling submitted to the CJEU by the The Hague Court of Appeal in December 2010.[102]

It is a fair conclusion that *GAT* and *Roche* did not deliver what was expected of them; experts have criticized the decisions, calls have been voiced for a revision of the Brussels I Regulation,[103] and a revision project is now being undertaken by the

sources of the torpedo's disarmament. For an overview of other mitigating approaches taken by European courts toward torpedoes, see REBEKKA HYE-KNUDSEN, MARKEN-, PATENT- UND URHEBERRECHTS-VERLETZUNGEN IM EUROPÄISCHEN INTERNATIONALEN ZIVILPROZESSRECHT 179–89 (2005).

98 Marc Döring & Francis van Velsen, *Is Cross-Border Relief in European Patent Litigation at an End?*, 1 J. INTELL. PROP. L. & PRAC. 858, 858 (2006).

99 Brussels I Regulation, *supra* note 25, Article 31. For a cross-border injunction issued as a preliminary measure, see, e.g., Colgate v. Unilever, Belgium, Sept. 14, 2001 (Belg.), reported in Fernand De Visscher, *Belgium: Patents—International Jursidiction*, 24 EUR. INTELL. PROP. REV. N30 (2002).

100 On kort geding, see Jan J. Brinkhoff, *Between Speed and Thoroughness: The Dutch "Kort Geding" Procedure in Patent Cases*, 18 EUR. INTELL. PROP. REV. 499 (1996); Jan J. Brinkhof, *The Enforcement of Patent Rights in the Netherlands*, 31 IIC 706, 710–11 (2000); Michiel Rijsdijk, *Patent Cases: 1994 to the Present*, 22 EUR. INTELL. PROP. REV. 120 (2000); XANDRA E. KRAMER, THE DUTCH KORT GEDING PROCEDURE IN AN INTERNATIONAL PERSPECTIVE: A COMPARATIVE VIEW ON PROVISIONAL MEASURES AND PRIVATE INTERNATIONAL LAW, *available at* http://papers.ssrn.com/sol3/papers.cfm?abstract_id=1122344 (last visited Sept. 2, 2011); Véron, *Thirty Years*, *supra* note 53, 438. On the practice of cross-border injunctions, see Jan J. Brinkhof, *Geht das grenzüberschreitende Verletzungsverbot im niederländischen einstweiligen Verfügungsverfahren zu weit?*, 1997 GRUR INT. 489; Pitz & Meibom, *supra* note 53.

101 Bettacare Ltd. v. H3 Products B.V., Wedeka B.V., The Hague District Court, Sept. 21, 2006, No. 266720/KG ZA 06-0694 (Neth.).

102 Reference for a preliminary ruling from The Hague Court of Appeal lodged on December 29, 2010—Solvay S.A. v. Honeywell Fluorine Products Europe B.V., Honeywell Belgium N.V., Honeywell Europe N.V., CJEU, C-616/10.

103 Marko Schauwecker, *Europäische Union/EFTA—Revidiertes Lugano-Übereinkommen kodifiziert umstrittene EuGH-Rechtsprechung zur internationalen Zuständigkeit bei grenzüberschreitenden Patentverletzungsklagen*, 2007 GRUR INT. 552; *An Industrial Property Rights Strategy for Europe, Communication from the Commission to the European Parliament, the Council and the European Economic and Social Committee*, COM(2008)

European Commission.[104] Jeremy Phillips noted that the interpretation by the CJEU in *Roche* makes it "difficult to refute the assertion that the Brussels Convention acts as a deterrent to the enforcement of patent rights against a highly organized international infringer."[105] Marta Pertegas pointed out that *GAT* "severely limits the possibility of bringing cross-border patent claims before the European courts in cases involving defendants based in the [European Union],"[106] and that both *GAT* and *Roche* "severely curtail the trend of centralising patent infringement disputes before the European courts."[107] Similarly, Marko Schauwecker wrote that the CJEU "drastically limited" the possibility of bringing an infringement suit concerning a foreign patent,[108] and Klaus Grabinski suggested that "the thorny life under the Brussels I Regulation and the Lugano Convention has become even more thorny."[109]

The fact that an alleged infringer may now easily remove any litigated patents from a centralized infringement suit by counterclaiming invalidity or raising invalidity as a defense makes centralized proceedings much less likely. Even if the result is only a stay and not a complete removal of the infringement proceedings, it clearly prolongs and complicates the enforcement effort. In the end, it appears that *GAT* and *Roche* have left only one scenario in which courts can indisputably adjudicate infringements of foreign patents: cases in which an infringement suit or a suit for declaration of noninfringement is brought against a domestic entity and the issue of validity is not raised.

---

465 final (July 16, 2008), 14. In the summer of 2008 the European Commission declared that it "will consider how cross-border enforcement of judgments can be improved in its review of the Brussels I Regulation." *Id.* The press reacted to the decision with excited headlines, as Professor Adolphsen recalls; the German press announced the decisions with the headlines *The Country's Territory Decides—No Cross-Border Judgments in Patent Proceedings* (FRANKFURTER ALLGEMEINE ZEITUNG) and *Patents Remain a National Matter* (BÖRSEN-ZEITUNG). Jens Adolphsen, *Renationalisierung von Patentstreitigkeiten in Europa*, 2007 IPRAX 15, 15.

[104] *Green Paper on the Review of Council Regulation (EC) No 44/2001 on Jurisdiction and the Recognition and Enforcement of Judgments in Civil and Commercial Matters*, COM(2009) 175 final (Apr. 21, 2009). Patent issues are addressed at pp. 6–7. Proposal for a Regulation of the European Parliament and of the Council on Jurisdiction and the Recognition and Enforcement of Judgments in Civil and Commercial Matters (Recast), COM(2010) 748 final, December 14, 2010, p. 32. *See also* Christian Heinze, *Choice of Court Agreements, Coordination of Proceedings and Provisional Measures in the Reform of the Brussels I Regulation*, Max Planck Private Law Research Paper No. 11/5, *available at* http://ssrn.com/abstract=1804111 (last visited Sept. 2, 2011).

[105] Jeremy Phillips, *Should Forum-Shopping Be a Basket Case?*, 1 J. INTELL. PROP. L. & PRAC. 683 (2006).

[106] Marta Pertegas, *EC: Patents—Cross Border Injunctions*, 28 EUR. INTELL. PROP. REV. N193, N193 (2006).

[107] *Id.*, N193.

[108] Schauwecker, *Die Entscheidung*, *supra* note 44, 188.

[109] Grabinski, *Cross-Border*, *supra* note 90, 574.

2.1.3 THE HAGUE CONVENTION

Notwithstanding the various problems that the Brussels regime created in the area of patent litigation, the regime has been viewed as a successful project that sparked an interest in creating a similar regime at a larger than regional level. Since 1994 The Hague Conference on Private International Law has held discussions about a comprehensive jurisdiction, recognition, and enforcement convention with the goal of replicating the success of the Brussels regime.[110] However, it has proved to be difficult to achieve the same level of agreement and mutual trust among countries that are significantly more diverse than the member states of the European Union. Disagreements among countries about jurisdictional rules eventually altered the scope of Conference ambitions and in 2002 led to the decision to keep the negotiations to a noncontroversial minimum—choice of court agreements.[111]

The scope of the resulting 2005 Convention on Choice of Court Agreements is extremely limited (namely, to business-to-business scenarios)[112] and is even more limited in patent matters.[113] A significant portion of patent-related litigation is excluded from the scope of the Convention; it does not apply to issues of patent validity or to infringement cases "except where infringement proceedings are brought for breach of a contract between the parties relating to such rights, or could have been brought for breach of that contract."[114] Notably, if patent invalidity is raised as a defense in a contract dispute, the court selected by the parties is expected to entertain the issue of validity; this is apparent from a provision of the Convention[115] but is also confirmed by commentary and an example included in the Explanatory Report.[116] Therefore, in a licensing dispute, for example, the court chosen by the

[110] The proposal to draft a convention on jurisdiction, recognition, and enforcement of foreign judgments in civil and commercial matters began to be discussed by the Special Commission on General Affairs and Policy of The Hague Conference in 1994. For comments on the proposal's content, see Annette Kur, *Immaterialgüterrechte in einem weltweiten Vollstreckungs- und Gerichtsstandsübereinkommen—Auf der Suche nach dem Ausweg aus der Sackgasse*, 2001 GRUR INT. 908.

[111] The First Part of the 19th Session of The Hague Conference in 2002 decided to postpone work on the draft and ordered a new draft to be prepared that would avoid conflicts among countries on rules of jurisdiction. To minimize the controversy, the informal working group proposed a draft limited to choice of court agreements.

[112] Convention on Choice of Court Agreements, June 30, 2005, Article 2(1) a).

[113] For a detailed analysis of the Convention, see Stefan Luginbuehl & Heike Wollgast, *IP Rights in The Hague Convention on Choice of Court Agreements*, *in* FESTSCHRIFT FÜR JOCHEN PAGENBERG 321 (Dietrich Beier, Laurence Brüning-Petit, & Christopher Heath eds., 2006).

[114] Convention on Choice of Court Agreements, June 30, 2005, Article 2(2) n) and o).

[115] *Id.*, Article 2(3).

[116] Explanatory Report on the preliminary draft Convention on exclusive choice of court agreements, drawn up by Trevor C. Hartley and Masato Dogauchi (Dec. 26, 2004), 13–14.

parties would rule on the issue of patent validity that might arise as an "incidental question";[117] however, according to the Report, "the ruling on validity will not itself be subject to recognition under the Convention, nor will it create an estoppel or operate as issue preclusion under the Convention."[118] It seems that such a ruling would have a formal effect that would be even less than an inter partes effect.[119]

So far, six years after it was concluded, the Convention has been signed only by the European Union and the United States, and Mexico has acceded to the Convention.[120] The Convention has therefore not yet entered into force.[121]

2.1.4 THE ALI PRINCIPLES

The failure of the general Hague Convention generated interest among intellectual property experts in the possibility of creating a private international law instrument that would solve cross-border litigation concerns in the area of intellectual property. The first initiative arising from this interest was a proposal that was presented in 2002 by Professors Rochelle C. Dreyfuss and Jane Ginsburg.[122] They built on their experience with this project later when they, together with Professor François Dessemontet, served as the reporters to the American Law Institute (ALI) project that resulted in the drafting of the ALI Principles entitled *Intellectual Property: Principles Governing Jurisdiction, Choice of Law, and Judgments in Transnational Disputes*;[123] the Principles were adopted by the ALI in May 2007.[124]

Although undertaken under the auspices of the ALI, the Principles are directed at an audience larger than just the United States. Advisors to the project included experts from Australia, Canada, England, France, Germany, Japan, and

---

117 *Id.*

118 *Id.*

119 The practical effect of such a ruling would likely transcend the case and impact the patent at issue outside the particular litigation.

120 Information by The Hague Conference on Private International Law, *available at* http://www.hcch.net/index_en.php?act=conventions.status&cid=98 (last visited Sept. 2, 2011).

121 Convention on Choice of Court Agreements, June 30, 2005, Article 31.

122 Rochelle C. Dreyfuss & Jane C. Ginsburg, *Draft Convention on Jurisdiction and Recognition of Judgments in Intellectual Property Matters*, 77 CHI.-KENT L. REV. 1065 (2001–2002). Although they offer possible provisions for patent rights enforcement, they express their preference that patent rights be excluded from the scope of the Convention.

123 Intellectual Property: Principles Governing Jurisdiction, Choice of Law, and Judgments in Transnational Disputes (ALI 2008) ("ALI Principles"). The project started in 2001. *Id.*, ix.

124 For a detailed analysis of the ALI Principles, see François Dessemontet, *The ALI Principles: Intellectual Property in Transborder Litigation*, *in* INTELLECTUAL PROPERTY IN THE GLOBAL ARENA (Jürgen Basedow, Toshiyuki Kono, & Axel Metzger eds., Mohr Siebeck 2010), 31.

South Africa,[125] and the authors declared their intent "to balance civil-law and common-law approaches"[126] in drafting the document. The Principles are not a proposal for an international convention, but rather a template offered to national authorities who may either adopt them in their entirety or adjust them to the particular circumstances of their own country.[127]

As does the Brussels regime, the Principles provide for multiple grounds of jurisdiction; the grounds are available for both infringement suits and declaratory judgment suits for noninfringement (Section 213.1). They provide for jurisdiction of the court of defendant's habitual residence (Section 201),[128] the court agreed upon by the parties (Section 202), the court in which defendant appears (Section 203), the court of the place where infringement was prepared, initiated, or furthered (Section 204.1), or the court where the infringement occurred (Section 204.2). The Principles also include a jurisdictional ground based on the relation of a nonresident defendant to a resident defendant; this provision is analogous to Article 6.1 of the Brussels I Regulation. Section 204 of the Principles states that only the court of defendant's habitual residence can adjudicate claims that arise in other countries; as under the Brussels regime, all other courts are limited as to the claims on which they may decide. Courts that base their jurisdiction on the place of conduct or the place of injury may decide only claims concerning injuries arising out of the conduct in the particular country (Section 204.1) or claims concerning injuries in the particular country (Section 204.2).[129]

The adjudication of patent validity is divided into two tracks according to whether an inter partes or erga omnes effect is sought. The only venue where an erga omnes determination of patent validity may be made is in the country of patent registration (Section 213.2). However, other courts with jurisdiction over the defendant based on the Principles may decide validity inter partes (Section 211.2 and Section 213.3). The authors of the Principles concede that even an inter partes decision is likely to have effects reaching far beyond the relationship between the parties involved in the particular litigation; however, they anticipate that the effects will be positive rather than negative because they will lead to elimination of "duplicative litigation."[130] To foster

---

[125] *See* Dessemontet, *supra* note 124, 34.

[126] ALI Principles, *supra* note 123, 3.

[127] *Id.*, 7.

[128] On the choice of "habitual residence" as opposed to domicile, see Dessemontet, *supra* note 124, 35.

[129] There is a special provision concerning jurisdiction over "[a] person who cannot be sued in a World Trade Organization" country. ALI Principles, *supra* note 123, Section 214.3.

[130] ALI Principles, *supra* note 123, 77.

such an outcome, they suggest the creation of a system of "public notification of inter se invalidity determinations."[131]

The approach to patent validity issues taken by the Principles is thus different from the approach adopted by the Brussels regime, as influenced by the *GAT* and *Roche* decisions; while under the Principles courts may decide foreign patent validity with an inter partes effect, under the Brussels regime they must completely refrain from adjudicating foreign patent validity. But this is not the only difference between the Principles and the Brussels regime; as opposed to the Brussels regime,[132] the Principles allow courts to issue protective or provisional measures only if they have jurisdiction under the Principles. Another substantial difference is the inclusion in the Principles of a system for coordinating multiple proceedings,[133] even though the introduction of such a system could clearly not be achieved by a unilateral implementation of the Principles into one country's legislation—significant cooperation among countries and their judiciaries would be essential for such a system to operate successfully.

The Principles mitigate two of the three problems that the Brussels regime has caused.[134] First, they eliminate confusion concerning exclusive jurisdiction over patent validity. If raised as an incidental question, validity will be decided inter partes; if raised by a request for a declaration of invalidity, it can be done either in the country of registration with an erga omnes effect or in another country with an inter partes effect. Second, the Principles should prevent the use of torpedoes; the options for coordination or consolidation should successfully neutralize torpedo attacks[135] and eventually lead to their elimination once their users realize that the torpedoes' destructive power is gone. As for the third phenomenon associated with the Brussels regime that has been perceived as a problem—the availability of cross-border relief—the Principles do not attempt to eliminate the problem. On the contrary, they purposefully preserve the possibility of cross-border relief because the drafters consider such relief important and desirable, not problematic, for the effective enforcement of rights.[136] Other differences from the Brussels regime exist; for example, in the area of recognition and enforcement of judgments the Principles

---

[131] *Id.*, 78.

[132] The Brussels I Regulation allows any court of a member state to issue provisional and protective measures, "even if [. . .] the courts of another Member State have jurisdiction as to the substance of the matter." Brussels I Regulation, *supra* note 25, Article 31.

[133] ALI Principles, *supra* note 123, Chapter 3.

[134] *See supra* Section 2.1.2.

[135] ALI Principles, *supra* note 123, Section 221.5. Also *id.*, 97.

[136] *Id.*, 88–90.

address the issue of recognition of punitive damages (Section 411.2), which is understandable given that the Principles were drafted in the United States, where courts are permitted to award punitive damages.

The Principles are one of the most comprehensive works in the world at the intersection of private international law and intellectual property, and their solutions reflect the experience of the Europeans under the Brussels regime. The comments and reporters' notes provide a wealth of information on the history and current state of the problems that the Principles address. However, two solutions offered by the Principles, probably the two most significant of the work, may be difficult for countries to accept. First, countries may be reluctant to accept the solution required by the Principles for adjudicating foreign patent validity; decisions on the validity of foreign patents continue to be viewed as an inappropriate reach into countries' sovereign affairs.[137] Even though countries seem to be willing to allow courts to entertain patent validity inter partes in some cases, these cases are extremely limited,[138] and countries might not be ready to go one step further and extend inter partes validity determinations to all cases, as required under the Principles. The impact that an inter partes decision on validity would have on a particular patent cannot be discounted; in practice, a technically purely inter partes decision could generate a de facto erga omnes effect. The second significant hurdle to the adoption of the Principles is the willingness, or lack thereof, of countries to coordinate and consolidate proceedings in multiple countries; such organization would require a great deal of cooperation among countries and adjustments to their procedures to create a mutually complementary system.

2.1.5 THE CLIP PRINCIPLES

Another solution to the problem of enforcement of parallel patents based on private international law has been prepared by the European Max Planck Group for Conflict of Laws in Intellectual Property (CLIP).[139] This group was established in 2004 by the Max Planck Institute for Intellectual Property and Competition Law, and since its creation the group has held more than a dozen meetings to discuss draft Principles that would address goals similar to those of the ALI Principles. The CLIP Principles have been developed to serve either as an interpretative tool and supplement to international and domestic rules, or as a set of model provisions for

---

[137] *See* CJEU decisions in *GAT* and *Roche* and the Federal Circuit decision in *Voda*.

[138] *See* the Convention on Choice of Court Agreements, June 30, 2005.

[139] European Max Planck Group for Conflict of Laws in Intellectual Property (CLIP), *available at* http://www.cl-ip.eu/ (last visited Sept. 2, 2011).

countries to adopt;[140] the authors also envisage that private parties could utilize the Principles when shaping their dispute resolution agreements.[141]

As the Brussels regime and the ALI Principles do, the CLIP Principles offer several bases of jurisdiction; these bases apply to both infringement and declaratory judgment suits (Article 2:602). The bases are the place of defendant's habitual residence (Article 2:101),[142] the court chosen by the parties (Article 2:301), the court where defendant enters an appearance (Article 2:302), the place of performance of a contract (Article 2:201), the place where infringement occurred or may occur, which includes both place of conduct and place of effect (Article 2:202), and the place where a co-defendant resides (Article 2:206).

The CLIP Principles adopt a more liberal approach to the issue of jurisdiction for determination of patent validity than the rules under the Brussels regime as interpreted by the CJEU, but the CLIP approach is stricter than the rules of the ALI Principles. According to the CLIP Principles, only the court of registration can decide disputes "having as their object" the issue of patent validity; determinations arising from such disputes have an erga omnes effect (Article 2:401(1)). However, as opposed to the ALI Principles, which apply the exclusive jurisdiction provision only to declaratory judgment actions seeking a declaration of invalidity, the CLIP Principles extend the exclusive jurisdiction rule also to counterclaims of invalidity (Article 2:401(2)). As opposed to the Brussels regime, which mandates exclusive jurisdiction of the court of patent registration whenever the issue of validity is raised, whether by way of counterclaim or defense, the CLIP Principles permit courts other than the courts in the country of registration to entertain validity when the issue is raised as a defense; the determination of validity in such instances will have only an inter partes effect (Article 2:401(2)).

The treatment of the validity issue is one area in which the CLIP Principles, like the ALI Principles, seek to mitigate problems uncovered in practice under the Brussels regime. In addition to the validity issue, the CLIP Principles also address the problem of torpedoes; in line with the ALI Principles, they coordinate multiple proceedings (Section 7) to eliminate the use of torpedoes (Article 2:701(2)(a)). The CLIP Principles are also aligned with the ALI Principles in their approach to cross-border injunctions; the CLIP draft permits injunctions to be issued for all countries for which infringement has been determined (Article 2:604(1)).

---

[140] Principles for Conflict of Laws in Intellectual Property, the European Max Planck Group for Conflict of Laws in Intellectual Property, Draft, March 25, 2011, Part 1, 8 ("CLIP Principles").

[141] *Id.*, Part 1, 8.

[142] For the definition of habitual residence, see CLIP Principles, *supra* note 140, Article 3:904.

Although similar to the ALI Principles in a number of respects, the CLIP Principles introduce additional features that do not appear in the ALI Principles. CLIP has a more elaborate provision on provisional and protective measures (Article 2:501) that lists the types of measures that may be imposed. The CLIP Principles also have a special provision concerning jurisdiction over acts committed through "ubiquitous media such as the Internet."[143] A court of a country where an infringement occurred has jurisdiction, based on the place of infringement, over a defendant who acted on the Internet, even if that court is not the court of defendant's habitual residence; the court of a place of infringement can exercise jurisdiction with respect to infringements everywhere as long as the infringements have no substantial effect in the country of defendant's habitual residence (if they do, only the court of the country of defendant's habitual residence can decide on infringements in foreign countries) and either 1) substantial infringement activities occurred in the country of infringement, or 2) substantial harm was caused in that country in relation to the entire harm caused by the infringements.[144] Another special provision deals with injunctions on the Internet, extending them to all countries "where the signals can be received," unless the activity at issue is "strictly limited" to countries whose laws were not applied by the court imposing the injunction (Article 2:604(2)).

2.1.6 OBSTACLES TO IMPLEMENTATION OF PRIVATE INTERNATIONAL LAW SOLUTIONS

There are two major obstacles to implementation of the ALI and CLIP Principles:[145] First, both Principles expect a high degree of cooperation among courts of various countries, cooperation that cannot be achieved by changes to the law of only one country. Such a high degree of cooperation would require an orchestrated effort by countries and their judiciaries to achieve the necessary compatibility of procedures, and success would necessitate the building of a strong mutual trust and reliable and flexible channels of communication among countries.[146] Consequently, the Principles are not the appropriate vehicle for achieving these goals and an instrument that binds countries—an international convention—would be necessary to establish a functioning system with such a degree of cooperation.

---

143 CLIP Principles, *supra* note 140, Article 2:203(2).

144 *Id.*, Article 2:203(2)(a) and (b).

145 For additional proposals from Japan and Korea, see *supra* note 10.

146 Although mutual trust and information exchange might not appear to be significant hurdles for some courts (such as courts in Europe, or courts in Europe and the United States), the mutual trust and information exchange must also exist among other courts in the world if the system is to function effectively.

The second obstacle to adoption of the Principles is the issue of deciding foreign patent validity. Both the ALI and the CLIP Principles require countries to overcome their view of a patent grant as an act of a sovereign state that cannot be scrutinized by the courts of a foreign country; however, for now courts remain reluctant to decide the validity of foreign patents in all but a few cases.[147] The following sections review how courts in the United States and Germany address the problem of adjudicating foreign patents, and point out that although courts in both countries have entertained cases involving foreign patents, such instances have been rare and have shown that courts are willing to adjudicate cases involving foreign patents only if they do not have to decide the validity of the foreign patents.

2.1.6.1 Foreign Patents in U.S. Courts

In the United States, some courts have asserted jurisdiction over foreign patents, while others have declined to do so. The current position of the U.S. Court of Appeals for the Federal Circuit, as outlined in its decision in *Voda v. Cordis*,[148] is that supplemental jurisdiction cannot be used to bring foreign patents before U.S. courts; the decision also suggests that the court is not in favor of extending jurisdiction over foreign patents even if other grounds of jurisdiction are claimed.

U.S. courts have considered two important issues when deciding whether to extend their jurisdiction in cases involving foreign patents. First, if jurisdiction over foreign patents is based on supplemental jurisdiction, courts must evaluate whether claims concerning foreign patents are related closely enough to claims concerning parallel U.S. patents to comply with the condition of supplemental jurisdiction, according to which courts can extend jurisdiction over related claims only if the claims are related to such a degree that they can be considered parts of the same case or controversy.[149] Second, regardless of the jurisdictional basis, courts must consider whether the act of state doctrine prevents them from adjudicating claims involving foreign patents.[150]

---

[147] For instance, in Japan a court extended jurisdiction over a case in which the validity of a U.S. patent was at issue. Coral Co. Ltd. v. Marin Bio Co. Ltd. ("Coral Powder Case"), 1151 HANREI TAIMUZU 109 (Tokyo Dist. Ct., Oct. 26, 2003) (Japan). *See also* Toshiyuki Kono, *Intellectual Property Rights, Conflict of Laws and International Jurisdiction: Applicability of ALI Principles in Japan?*, 30 BROOK. J. INT'L L. 865 (2005). "[T]he Court stated that the Japanese court has jurisdiction since the defendant has its principal place of business in Japan, which justifies the exercise of jurisdiction of Japanese courts over any kind of claim against the defendant." *Id.*, 871.

[148] Jan K. Voda, M.D. v. Cordis Corporation, 476 F.3d 887 (Fed. Cir. 2007).

[149] 28 U.S.C. §1367.

[150] Even if supplemental jurisdiction is found, courts may use "other compelling reasons" to decline jurisdiction. 28 U.S.C. §1367(c)(4).

When discussing the jurisdictional requirement of claim relatedness, proponents of foreign patent adjudication cite the 1967 decision by the U.S. Court of Appeals for the Seventh Circuit in *Ortman v. Stanray Corp.*,[151] in which the court held that ancillary jurisdiction over parallel foreign patents existed if there was a strong enough relationship between the claims related to U.S. patent law and those related to foreign patent laws. The relationship existed in this case because "the actions of defendant of which complaint [was] made [were] the result of defendant doing similar acts both in and out of the United States."[152] Ultimately, neither the district court nor the Circuit Court had to rule on the infringement of the foreign patents in the case; the parties agreed to limit their dispute to contract issues, which eliminated the need to decide the infringement claims.[153]

The U.S. Court of Appeals for the Federal Circuit considered the issue of relatedness in *Voda*, but because it relied on other factors to decline jurisdiction over the foreign patents, the court offered its opinion on the issue only in dicta. The court first looked for a "common nucleus of operative fact,"[154] and pointed to its earlier decision in *Stein Associates v. Heat and Control, Inc.*,[155] where it affirmed a lower court's decision to decline to issue a preliminary injunction concerning parallel patents granted in the United Kingdom; the court concluded that the issues in claims involving patents that were granted in different countries were not the same.[156] Similarly, in deciding *Mars Inc. v. Kabushiki-Kaisha Nippon Conlux*[157] the court found no sufficient relationship between a claim of infringement of a U.S. patent and a Japanese patent. In *Voda* the court went on to discuss the second part of the relatedness requirement for supplemental jurisdiction—the question of whether it would "ordinarily [be] expected to try [the claims] in one judicial proceedings."[158] The court suggested only that this requirement might not be met "if the norm is that patent claims are adjudicated by the courts within the jurisdiction where the patents are created."[159]

---

[151] Ortman v. Stanray Corp., 371 F.2d 154 (7th Cir. 1967).

[152] *Id.*, 158.

[153] Ortman v. Stanray Corp., not Reported in F.Supp., 1969 WL 9596, *2 (N.D.Ill. 1969). "[T]he contract action was in the alternative to the four patent counts in that if the court found that the assignment was not terminable or was not effectively terminated, plaintiff's relief would be in damages for breach of contract or for benefits thereunder and not for patent infringement."

[154] United Mine Workers of America v. Gibbs, 383 U.S. 715, 725 (1966).

[155] Stein Associates v. Heat and Control, Inc., 748 F.2d 653 (Fed. Cir. 1984).

[156] *Id.*, 658.

[157] Mars Inc. v. Kabushiki-Kaisha Nippon Conlux, 24 F.3d 1368 (Fed. Cir. 1994).

[158] United Mine Workers of America v. Gibbs, 383 U.S. 715, 725 (1966).

[159] Jan K. Voda, M.D. v. Cordis Corporation, 476 F.3d 887, 897 (Fed. Cir. 2007).

The court's rejection of jurisdiction over any foreign patent infringement in *Voda* related only to the supplemental jurisdiction of federal courts[160] and theoretically did not foreclose jurisdiction on other grounds; jurisdiction over foreign patents could be found, for example, under diversity jurisdiction in federal courts, or in state courts.[161] Practically, however, one other doctrine can block those options—the act of state doctrine. The court in *Voda* relied heavily on the argument that foreign patent claims cannot be entertained by courts in the United States because of the act of state doctrine.

Not all courts agree that the act of state doctrine applies to foreign patents. The U.S. Court of Appeals for the Third Circuit stated that the doctrine is misplaced in patent cases when it decided *Mannington Mills v. Congoleum Corp.*,[162] a case concerning a claim of fraud in obtaining foreign patents. The court rejected the notion that a grant of patents should fall within the act of state doctrine and stressed that "[t]he grant of patents for floor coverings is not the type of sovereign activity that would be of substantial concern to the executive branch in its conduct of international affairs."[163]

However, in *Voda* the U.S. Court of Appeals for the Federal Circuit expressed a different view. On the one hand, the court recognized the strong "harmonization trend"[164] among the patent systems of various countries, but on the other hand, the court insisted that "the U.S. judiciary should not unilaterally decide either for [the U.S.] government or for other foreign sovereigns that our courts will become the adjudicating body for any foreign patent."[165] Judge Newman disagreed; in her dissent she argued inter alia that a grant of a patent by a foreign authority does not fall within the scope of the act of state doctrine. Judge Newman contended that "patent validity and infringement are legal and commercial issues, not acts of state."[166]

It remains to be seen whether *Voda* will completely extinguish foreign patent litigation before U.S. federal and state courts; since *Voda*, only three district court decisions have been issued that have concerned federal jurisdiction over foreign patents.

---

[160] *Id.*, 905.

[161] Eric Chan, *Asserting Foreign Patent Claims in U.S. Federal Courts: What's Left After* Voda v. Cordis?, 18 ALB. L.J. SCI. & TECH. 1, 45–46 (2007); see also the concurring opinion by Judge Fairchild in Ortman v. Stanray Corp., 371 F.2d 154, 159 (7th Cir. 1967).

[162] Mannington Mills v. Congoleum Corp., 595 F.2d 1287 (3rd Cir. 1979).

[163] *Id.*, 1294. "Although enforcement of a decree in the present litigation may possibly present problems of international relations [. . .], the granting of the patents per se, in substance ministerial activity, is not the kind of governmental action contemplated by the act of state doctrine or its correlative, foreign compulsion." *Id.*

[164] Jan K. Voda, M.D. v. Cordis Corporation, 476 F.3d 887, 900 (Fed. Cir. 2007).

[165] *Id.*, 900.

[166] *Id.*, 915.

In the first, a U.S. district court asserted diversity jurisdiction over infringements of foreign patents;[167] however, the case settled two months after the decision on jurisdiction was issued and was not adjudicated on the merits. In the second decision a different U.S. district court rejected claims of foreign patent infringements as frivolous.[168]

The third post-*Voda* decision concerning foreign patents is *Fairchild Semiconductor Corp. v. Third Dimension (3D) Semiconductor, Inc.*,[169] in which the plaintiff asked for a declaration of noninfringement of U.S. and Chinese patents covered by a licensing agreement. The parties to the case, which were both U.S. companies,[170] agreed on the jurisdiction of the U.S. District Court for the District of Maine, but the defendant moved to have the claim concerning the Chinese patent dismissed. The court refused to dismiss the claim pertaining to the Chinese patent, and using the reasoning of the U.S. Court of Appeals for the Federal Circuit in *Voda* pointed out that the act of state doctrine was not implicated in the case because the validity of the Chinese patent was not contested.[171]

Although *Fairchild* eventually settled,[172] and although no appellate decision is available on the issue of jurisdiction over foreign patents in the case, the district court decision seems to confirm that in the United States, as in Europe under the Brussels regime, the only instance in which courts may decide a case involving a foreign patent is when there is a dispute involving a domestic infringer in which the issue of the validity of a foreign patent is uncontested. *Voda* thus brought about in the United States the same result that *GAT* and *Roche* instituted in Europe.[173]

Finally, the decision in *Voda* may have influenced the outcome in a case where a reverse consideration of the problem was necessary. If a recent decision by the U.S. District Court for the District of Columbia is an indication of the future approach

---

[167] Baker-Bauman v. Walker, Not Reported in F.Supp.2d, 2007 WL 1026436 (S.D.Ohio 2007).

[168] Igbinadolor v. TiVo, Inc., Slip Copy, 2008 WL 4925023 (N.D.Ga.2008), 2 ("After full review, the Court concludes that Plaintiff's Complaint includes no special allegations that would overcome the Federal Circuit Court of Appeals' serious admonition to district courts to decline to exercise jurisdiction over foreign patent infringement claims.")

[169] Fairchild Semiconductor Corp. v. Third Dimension (3D) Semiconductor, Inc., D.Me., 2:08-cv-00158-DBH.

[170] *Id.*, the original complaint, docket document number 1, filed on May 17, 2008, and the first amended complaint, docket document number 184, filed on January 22, 2009.

[171] *Id.*, Decision and Order on Motion to Dismiss, Dec. 10, 2008.

[172] The case was settled in June 2009. *Id.*, Stipulation of Dismissal, June 9, 2009.

[173] When considering various factors mentioned by the Federal Circuit Court in *Voda*, the Maine District Court in *Fairchild* contemplated potential enforcement problems but pointed out that it "will not be asking any other court to enforce" royalties if awarded in the case. Fairchild Semiconductor Corp. v. Third Dimension (3D) Semiconductor, Inc., D.Me., 2:08-cv-00158-DBH, Decision and Order on Motion to Dismiss, Dec. 10, 2008, 22.

of U.S. courts, it will be difficult for holders of U.S. patents to bring suits concerning those patents outside the United States. In *Juniper Networks, Inc. v. Abdullah Ali Bahattab*[174] the defendant, a resident of Saudi Arabia, filed suit in Dubai claiming infringement of his U.S. patent by the plaintiff. Before the court in Dubai decided the case, the plaintiff filed a declaratory judgment suit in the U.S. District Court for the District of Columbia, where the court relied on *Voda* to "decline[. . .] to defer the consideration of the issues related to the [U.S.] patent to a foreign jurisdiction."[175]

2.1.6.2 Foreign Patents in German Courts

German courts approach patent validity from a different viewpoint than their U.S. counterparts. In Germany, German patent validity may be contested only before the German Patent and Trademark Office and the German Federal Patent Court;[176] contrary to the practice in the United States, the option to file a declaratory judgment suit for patent invalidity in a regular German court does not exist. The decisions of the Patent Office may be appealed only to the German Federal Patent Court, the Bundespatentgericht, a body that was created solely to deal with these appeals and patent validity issues; it does not decide any infringement actions.[177]

Although trial courts do not decide declaratory judgment actions for invalidity, issues of patent validity do arise in proceedings before them, usually in the context of infringement proceedings. If the validity of a patent is raised in an infringement action, a court will consider whether the invalidity claim appears to have merit; if the court decides that there is a likelihood that the claim will be successful, it will stay the infringement proceedings[178] and wait for a decision on validity by the Patent Office or the German Federal Patent Court. However, if the court concludes that the invalidity claim is without merit and unlikely to succeed, it will proceed with the infringement action.[179]

---

[174] Juniper Networks, Inc. v. Abdullah Ali Bahattab, Slip Copy 2009 WL 6781382 (D.D.C. 2009).

[175] *Id.*, *6.

[176] Deutsches Patent- und Markenamt, *available at* http://www.dpma.de/ (last visited Sept. 2, 2011).

[177] Bundespatentgericht, *available at* http://www.bundespatentgericht.de/ (last visited Sept. 2, 2011). The court was established in 1961. On the court, see, e.g., KRASSER, Chapter 1, note 15, 68 and 450–58. On the background of this dualism, see Peter Mes, *Reflections on the German Patent Litigation System*, *available at* http://www.springerlink.com/content/t71311177w294105/fulltext.pdf (last visited Sept. 2, 2011), 405–07.

[178] Zivilprozessordnung, §148. According to the provision, the court may stay the proceedings if its decision depends "fully or partially on whether a legal relationship exists or not." *Id.*

[179] According to one commentator, "German infringement courts quite rarely stay the infringement case under [§148 of the Code of Civil Procedure]." Mes, *supra* note 177.

Given the structure of the German system it would be misleading to claim that any regular German court decides that a patent is valid or invalid. Rather, courts presume patents to be valid if they find good reasons to rely on the presumption, in which case they continue with infringement proceedings. If a court finds in favor of the presumption of validity[180] and continues the proceedings, that action might be interpreted as meaning that the court has rendered an interim decision on patent validity inter partes. However, any decision rendered is subject to a later ruling on patent validity by the Patent Office or the Federal Patent Court.[181]

Two aspects of the German practice are notable: first, the system removes from trial courts the ultimate decision on patent validity, so judges are accustomed to respecting the patent authority and to deferring patent validity decisions to this authority; second, judges are accustomed to exercising discretion in deciding the strength of the presumption of patent validity and proceeding with infringement suits whenever they find it warranted. Given the context of the Brussels regime, however, this approach will change in cases involving patents granted in the Brussels regime countries (and possibly even in cases involving patents granted in other countries)[182] if the CJEU decision in *GAT* is interpreted to mandate a stay of infringement proceedings every time an issue of foreign patent validity is raised.[183]

The earliest notion held by German courts was that they could not decide cases involving foreign patents. The Reichsgericht initially rejected the jurisdiction of German courts over foreign patents, but courts in Düsseldorf, the capital of German patent litigation, eventually espoused a different view. The Reichsgericht reiterated the impossibility of deciding foreign patent infringements in 1934 when it referred to its decision from 1890[184] and emphasized the need to avoid intrusion into the sovereignty of foreign countries.[185] However, it held a much different opinion about

---

180 "Since patents have a limited lifespan and the law does not attribute to opposition and revocation proceedings the power to suspend the prohibitive rights conferred by a patent, the courts very rarely resort to suspension. To protect the patent proprietor, the appellate courts regularly insist on a clear and high probability that the patent in suit will be declared invalid." Thomas Kühnen, *What Becomes of Judgments on Infringement When the Patents in Suit Are Revoked: The Legal Situation in Germany*, 14th European Patent Judges' Symposium, European Patent Office, O.J. 1/2009, Spec. ed., 56.

181 On the status of the infringement judgment after the patent is invalidated, see Kühnen, *What Becomes, supra* note 180, 57–63.

182 For an explanation of the potentially different treatment of foreign patents granted in a Brussels regime country and in a country outside the regime, see *supra* Section 2.1.1.

183 *See* Mes, *supra* note 177, 408–10 on recent criticism of the dualism in German proceedings.

184 Reichsgericht, June 18, 1890, 1890 Juristische Wochenschrift 280; *see also Kunststofflacke*, Oberlandesgericht Düsseldorf, 2 U 93/65, Mar. 25, 1966, 1968 GRUR Int. 100, 100.

185 Reichsgericht, I 243/33, June 6, 1934, 1934 GRUR 657; summarized in Matthias Zigann, Entscheidungen inländischer Gerichte über ausländische gewerbliche Schutzrechte und Urheberrechte, VVF Verlag, 2002, 53.

"claims arising from domestic contracts involving foreign patents,"[186] which, according to one of its 1931 decisions "[could] be brought before German courts."[187] Similarly, in 1936 the Hamm Oberlandesgericht[188] confirmed that jurisdiction was possible in a case concerning licensing obligations that involved foreign patents.[189]

Gradually, the idea of German court jurisdiction over infringements of foreign patents became accepted. In 1958 the Düsseldorf Landgericht suggested that if the Bundesgerichtshof accepted universal jurisdiction in trademark matters in cases where a suit concerned a German defendant,[190] the same approach should be adopted in patent matters.[191] Additionally, the court stated that it should make no difference whether the case involved only German entities or whether it involved foreign entities against German entities.[192] In 1966 the Düsseldorf Oberlandesgericht asserted jurisdiction in a case of infringement of a foreign patent; the case involved two German parties contesting the infringement of a Swiss patent.[193] The court recognized the earlier decisions by the Reichsgericht but pointed to the contemporary scholarship that rejected the earlier Reichsgericht approach and advocated jurisdiction over foreign patents; it emphasized that the decision would be effective only in Germany and would therefore not offend the sovereignty of any foreign country. Shortly thereafter the Düsseldorf Landgericht cited the decision when it confirmed its jurisdiction over the infringement of a foreign patent;[194] the court repeated that in general, German courts could exercise jurisdiction over foreign patents as long as they had jurisdiction over the defendant.[195]

At the end of the 1960s German jurisprudence and German legal literature became aligned in rejecting the initial approach of the Reichsgericht and in agreeing that cases involving foreign patents could be litigated before German courts;[196] however,

---

[186] Reichsgericht, I 131/39, June 14, 1940, 1940 GRUR 437, 438.

[187] *Id.*

[188] Oberlandesgericht Hamm, 1936 GRUR 744; referred to in Landgericht Düsseldorf, Mar. 18, 1958, 1958 GRUR INT. 430, 430.

[189] In 1940 the Reichsgericht decided that German courts had jurisdiction over a claim concerning the inventorship of an English patent; however, the case was decided during World War II. Reichsgericht, I 131/39, June 14, 1940, 1940 GRUR 437.

[190] *Flava–Erdgold*, Bundesgerichtshof, I ZR 9/54, Oct. 2, 1956, 1957 GRUR 215, 218.

[191] Landgericht Düsseldorf, Mar. 18, 1958, 1958 GRUR INT. 430, 430.

[192] *Id.*, 431.

[193] *Kunststofflacke*, *supra* note 184; *see also* Tetzner, *Die Verfolgung*, *supra* note 19, 669.

[194] *Frauenthermometer*, Landgericht Düsseldorf, 4 O 127/63, Oct. 27, 1966, 1968 GRUR INT. 101.

[195] *Id.*

[196] Rudolf Nirk, *Grundfragen des deutschen Internationalen Privat- und Zivilprozeßrechts im Patent- und Lizenzrecht*, 60 MITTEILUNGEN DER DEUTSCHEN PATENTANWÄLTE 328, 331 (1969); Tetzner, *Die Verfolgung*, *supra* note 19, 669.

the ultimate decision on patent validity has always been understood in Germany to be reserved for the patent authority of the country granting the patent.[197] As noted earlier, until the CJEU decision in *GAT* there was a split between the Mannheim Landgericht and the Düsseldorf Landgericht on what courts were to do once an issue of patent validity was raised in a case that fell within the scope of the Brussels regime. After *GAT* courts have had no discretion in the matter, and as soon as invalidity is raised they must stay their proceedings or dismiss the case and refer the parties to the courts of the country that granted the patent.[198] Ironically, *GAT* means that holders of patents issued in Brussels regime countries may find themselves in a worse position than holders of patents issued in other countries; in cases involving patents from non–Brussels regime countries, German courts may exercise discretion in deciding the presumption of patent validity and decide to continue proceedings over infringements of such patents if they find the strength of the presumption to be adequate.[199]

2.2 Institutional Solutions to the Problem of Enforcement of Parallel Patents

Institutional solutions to the problem of enforcement of parallel patents are similar to private international law solutions in that they also rely on concentrating litigation before only one court. However, as opposed to private international law solutions, the institutional solutions that have been proposed eliminate the two significant problems that any private international law solution generates, namely, the problem that arises when one national court has to decide the validity of patents issued in other countries, and the problem of coordination among courts of multiple countries when parallel patents are litigated before them simultaneously. The institutional solutions eliminate these two problems by concentrating the litigation—either at the appellate instance or at both the first and appellate instances—in a multinational court.

The idea of a multinational court is particularly appealing to countries that share strong economic ties, high cross-border trade, and the resulting and potentially significant volume of cross-border patent litigation. As mentioned above in Chapter 1, Section 1.2, it was proposed in 1919 that a single patent court be created for the

---

[197] Nirk, *Grundfragen*, *supra* note 196, 331.

[198] On the ambiguity of Article 22.4 and the CJEU decision in *GAT*, see *supra* Section 2.1.2.

[199] *See supra* Section 2.1.1 for a discussion of the problem of exclusive jurisdiction over patent validity under Article 22.4 of the Brussels I Regulation.

British Empire;[200] however, the proposal never materialized. In Europe the idea of a multinational patent court has also been discussed and also not implemented; the failure of the idea is related to the particular institutional situation in Europe, which is worthy of mention.

In Europe, proposals have been developed inside two somewhat competing institutions, the Commission of the European Union (Commission) and the European Patent Organization. To understand the differences between the proposals discussed within these institutions and the obstacles to their adoption, it is important to remember the relationship between the two bodies. First, the European Union and the European Patent Organization have overlapping membership, and second, the Commission and the European Patent Organization have an overlapping agenda. All European Union member states are members of the European Patent Organization, but the Organization has additional members that are not in the European Union.[201] Although it is not the European Union that is a member of the European Patent Organization but rather the individual member states of the European Union, the Commission has had ambitions to influence and coordinate the actions of European Union member states within the European Patent Organization. These ambitions have been met with opposition among European Union member states, which have not always appreciated the Commission's tendencies to extend the influence of the European Union over affairs that member states have considered matters of their own policy; the dynamics present are in many cases similar to the tensions in other areas of law and policy in the United States between the federal government and the individual states. Notwithstanding any Commission ambitions, the European Patent Organization appears to present a more suitable vehicle than the European Union for patent cooperation; it has, through decades of operation, strengthened cooperation among national patent offices, and the European Patent Office has developed into an institution that is highly specialized and well respected in the field.[202]

---

[200] Theobald, Chapter 1, note 31, 30.

[201] As of July 2011, the European Union has twenty-seven member states; the European Patent Organization has thirty-eight members and two "extension states." The non-European Union members of the European Patent Organization are Albania, Croatia, the Former Yugoslav Republic of Macedonia, Iceland, Liechtenstein, Monaco, Norway, San Marino, Serbia, Switzerland, and Turkey. The extension states are Bosnia and Herzegovina and Montenegro. EPO Member States, *available at* http://www.epo.org/about-us/epo/member-states.html (last visited Sept. 2, 2011).

[202] The EPC framework is less likely to fall victim to bargains made in exchange for favors in areas outside patents; the European Union, given its general scope, frequently experiences negotiations that are conducted across fields, a practice that is sometimes to the detriment of highly technical areas. For a critique of Commission work in the area of patent litigation, see, e.g., Jochen Pagenberg, *Another Year of Debates on Patent Jurisdiction in Europe and No End in Sight?*, 38 IIC 805, 820–25 (2007).

The tension that exists between the European Patent Organization and the Commission in patent policy probably explains why proposals at the European Union level have not been adopted or implemented even though the European Union has been successful in other intellectual property areas, such as trademarks.[203] The first European Union patent initiative was the Convention for the European Patent for the Common Market (also known as the Luxembourg Convention), which was signed in 1975; it was later followed by the 1989 Agreement Relating to Community Patents and the 1989 Litigation Protocol. None of these instruments ever came into force. In 1997 the Commission reintroduced the idea for a European Union patent in a Green Paper,[204] but as Professor Joseph Straus remarked, it was "a shy attempt to revitalize" European Union activity in the patent area.[205] Eventually, the Commission announced that it would begin preparing a draft Regulation on a European Union—then "Community"—patent in 1999; the announcement included an indication that the draft would also address enforcement of such a patent. In 2000 a proposal for a Council Regulation on the Community Patent was prepared by the Commission;[206] it included a vision for a two-instance Community Patent Court, a vision that was influenced by a proposal developed earlier by the European Patent Organization for an optional European Patent Litigation Agreement (EPLA).[207]

The EPLA itself had its origins in the 1999 Intergovernmental Conference of European Patent Organization members, which initiated the work on the proposal for an "integrated judicial system."[208] The EPLA envisaged the establishment of a European Patent Court, which would consist of a Central Division and a number of

---

[203] Council Regulation (EC) No. 40/94 of 20 December 1993 on the Community trade mark, in effect since 1994; Council Regulation (EC) No 207/2009 of 26 February 2009 on the Community trademark (codified version).

[204] *Green Paper on the Community Patent and the Patent System in Europe*, COM(97) 314 final (June 24, 1997).

[205] Straus, *supra* note 30, 419.

[206] *Proposal for a Council Regulation on the Community Patent*, COM(2000) 412 final (Aug. 1, 2000).

[207] Stefan Luginbuehl, *A Stone's Throw Away from a European Patent Court: The European Patent Litigation Agreement*, 25 EUR. INTELL. PROP. REV. 256, 258 (2003) ("The proposal is clearly influenced by the outcome of the negotiations for an Optional European Patent Litigation Agreement." *Id.*)

[208] 1999 OJ EPO 546, 548. In anticipation of the outcome of the work, the 2000 amendment to the EPC inserted a provision specifically addressing the possibility of concluding agreements on such a judicial system. Article 149a(a) and (b) of the EPC state that "[n]othing in [the EPC] shall be construed as limiting the right of some or all of the Contracting States to conclude special agreements on any matters concerning European patent applications or European patents which under this Convention are subject to and governed by national law, such as, in particular (a) an agreement establishing a European patent court common to the Contracting States party to it; (b) an agreement establishing an entity common to the Contracting States party to it to deliver, at the request of national courts or quasi-judicial authorities, opinions on issues of European or harmonised national patent law." The amendment came into force on Dec. 13, 2007.

regional divisions. The Central Division would make declaratory judgments on patent validity with erga omnes effect; patent invalidity raised in infringement proceedings before a regional division would be decided only inter partes.

The EPLA proposal was enthusiastically welcomed by judges, patent attorneys, and industry;[209] however, the EPLA initially was not appreciated by the Commission, which, as Jochen Pagenberg recalls, "had regarded EPLA as detrimental to European integration."[210] In his detailed 2007 description of the developments, Pagenberg, who had been an advisor to the EPLA Working Party, explained that although it seemed that the Commission's position had changed in 2006 when it recognized the preferences of patent system users for the EPLA,[211] the Commission shortly thereafter reiterated its former position opposing the EPLA and instead promoted a solution at the European Union level.[212]

In 2009, after three years of discussions on the European Union patent project and a possible litigation framework,[213] the Commission finally decided to approach the issue in a comprehensive manner (albeit without the involvement of the European Patent Office), and the Council of the European Union gave its approval to the framework of the project in December 2009. What was sought by the European Union was "a package of measures for an Enhanced Patent System in Europe," which would have consisted of the European and EU Patents Court (EEUPC) and the European Union patent.[214] The EEUPC would have consisted of a Court of Appeal and a Court of First Instance with a central division and regional and local divisions.[215] The EEUPC was designed to have exclusive jurisdiction in matters of infringement and validity of European patents and the expected newly created

---

[209] Pagenberg, *Another Year*, *supra* note 202, 806–10; Assessment of the Impact, Chapter 1, note 20, 9; Jacob, *The Judge's Perspective*, *supra* note 55. "We are, uniformly or almost uniformly of the view that the way forward is EPLA and not via some sort of EU Court." *Id.*

[210] Pagenberg, *Another Year*, *supra* note 202, 807.

[211] *Id.*

[212] For the reasons that the European Commission changed its position, see Pagenberg, *Another Year*, *supra* note 202, 809; Fröhlinger, Chapter 1, note 173, 36–37.

[213] *Proposal for a Council Decision Conferring Jurisdiction on the Court of Justice in Disputes Relating to the Community Patent*, COM(2003) 827 final (Dec. 13, 2003); *Proposal for a Council Decision Establishing the Community Patent Court and Concerning Appeals Before the Court of First Instance*, COM(2003) 828 final (Dec. 13, 2003); *Draft Agreement on the European Union Patent Court and Draft Statute, Council of the European Union*, 14970/08 (Nov. 4, 2008).

[214] *Conclusions on an Enhanced Patent System in Europe, Council of the European Union* (Dec. 4, 2009), *available at* http://www.consilium.europa.eu/uedocs/cms_data/docs/pressdata/en/intm/111744.pdf (last visited Sept. 2, 2011), para. 4.

[215] *Id.*, para. 11.

European Union patents.[216] However, the proposal for the European patent litigation framework suffered a setback in March 2011 when the CJEU opined that the proposed instrument was incompatible with the law of the European Union.[217] Any future proposals for a European Union unified litigation framework will have to address the CJEU opinion.

Apart from the CJEU objections, the obvious limitation of the proposed European Union solution is its focus not only on a specific region but also on particular patents—European patents and future European Union patents. For European Union patents the existence of a unified court system is indispensible; only such a system can secure the necessary uniformity of jurisprudence concerning European Union patents. For European patents—the patents under the European Patent Convention (EPC)—the court system could finally bring the desired legal certainty and predictability[218] because it would eliminate differences that exist in decisions concerning national patents arising from the same European patent.[219] However, the system would not be available to litigants who pursue infringements of national patents that do not arise out of a European patent, and would not solve the problems encountered by those whose enforcement efforts reach outside of Europe.

2.3 Obstacles to the Enforcement of Parallel Patents

It would be revolutionary to find a workable solution to the problem of enforcement of parallel patents and to end what Justice Laddie referred to as "the tyranny of the necessity of multiple litigation."[220] The costs of multiple litigation and the logistics of enforcing patents for the same invention in multiple countries are overwhelming. There are no estimates of how many cases of enforcement of parallel patents are brought in the world; Professor Dietmar Harhoff suggested in 2009 that "between 146 and 311 infringement cases [were] being duplicated annually in the

---

[216] *Id.*, para. 10.

[217] The Draft Agreement on the Creation of a European and Community Patent Court Is Not Compatible with European Union Law, Court of Justice of the European Union, Press Release No. 17/11, March 8, 2011.

[218] On complaints about legal uncertainty and unpredictability associated with the enforcement of parallel national patents arising from a European patent, see *supra* the introductory section of Chapter 2.

[219] See an analysis of the reasons for differences in interpretation of European patents in Dieter Brändle, *Kann und darf Auslegung und Ermittlung des Schutzbereichs eines europäischen Patents in verschiedenen Ländern zu unterschiedlichen Ergebnissen führen*, 1998 GRUR 854. The current proposal for a European Union patent builds on the existing European patent under the EPC. *See* Proposal for a Regulation of the European Parliament and of the Council Implementing Enhanced Cooperation in the Area of Creation of Unitary Patent Protection, COM(2011) 215/3, 6 and 16.

[220] De Ranitz, *Mr. Justice Laddie*, Chapter 1, note 37, 535.

[European Union] Member States."[221] He estimated that by 2013 the numbers will increase to 202–431 parallel cases litigated each year.[222] However, what would be more important to know, and something that seems impossible to show empirically, is how many cases are *not* brought because patent holders simply cannot afford to litigate on two or more fronts. Proponents of the solutions to parallel patent enforcement hope that the proposed solutions would make litigating infringements of multiple parallel patents less costly and rectify the problem of inconsistent judgments concerning parallel patents for the same inventions.[223]

Solutions to the problem that have been offered by private international law have both positive and negative implications. What makes these solutions appealing is that they can be introduced gradually; they do not necessarily require a dramatic multinational upheaval of the status quo. Although the introduction of such solutions through an international convention would be preferable, the solutions can also be adopted through changes in national laws, country by country. Another positive feature of these solutions is that they do not require the creation of new institutions but rely only on existing national court structures. This reliance on national courts can also be problematic, however, because the various national courts would need to agree on a high level of cooperation for the solutions to be truly effective. The proposal that courts be entrusted to decide the validity of foreign patents is sometimes viewed with distrust; Justice Jacob criticized it quite harshly when he said that "[i]t is all part of the keep things tidy approach which ignores, because it has no or little experience of, the practical implications."[224]

Judges and other practitioners lean toward an institutional solution to the problem of enforcement of parallel patents, which would purportedly eliminate both of the negatives of the private international law solutions—the problems of coordination and of decisions about the validity of foreign patents. However, any creation of a multinational court is significantly complicated and has proved to be difficult even for the purposes of adjudicating such highly harmonized patents as the European patent and the proposed European Union patent.[225] As suggested in the discussion

---

221 Harhoff, Economic Cost-Benefit, *supra* note 5, 5 (emphasis omitted).

222 *Id.*

223 Cost Estimates for European Patent Litigation (under EPLA) *in* Assessment of the Impact, Chapter 1, note 20, 10–12. "The rough cost estimates also indicate that it will be cheaper to litigate before the European Patent Court than before national courts in three European states which is today's average parallel litigation." *Id.*, 11 (emphasis omitted). "[T]he costs of parallel litigation before two national courts (with the exclusion of Great Britain courts) in a medium-scale patent case are higher than the expected litigation costs before the European Patent Court." *Id.*, 10 (emphasis omitted).

224 Jacob, *The Judge's Perspective*, *supra* note 55.

225 *See supra* Section 2.2 for the patent litigation system proposed in Europe.

of a world patent in Chapter 1, Section 1.2, any multinational court will inevitably work toward and support the unification of patents litigated before it; it is apparent that a multinational court would ultimately serve as a backdoor mechanism for the unification of patent law and patent jurisprudence, even in cases of patents that do not originate from a unitary regime.[226] If a court is created under the European Union proposal to adjudicate both European Union patents and European patents, we may expect the court to bring not only uniformity to the interpretation of European Union patent law, but also harmonization of national courts' interpretations of their own national patent laws and national courts' interpretations of the EPC; the national courts' interpretations of the EPC have been subject to the differing jurisprudence of individual countries. The question at that point will be whether European Patent Organization members are ready to surrender their national particularities and agree on a single interpretation of the EPC.

The story of cross-border enforcement thus maintains its underlying theme—the unwillingness of countries to accept substantive patent law harmonization, thereby preventing them from reaching agreement on a world (or a uniform regional) patent and preventing a workable solution for the enforcement of parallel patents. It is not only institutional solutions that carry a "danger" of gradual harmonization, according to harmonization critics; any solution based on private international law will also lead to the alignment of national patent laws. In the process of examining the patent laws of other countries, national courts will learn more about foreign patent law interpretations, which will lead to a judicial cross-pollination of ideas. This is the phenomenon that Christopher Heath labeled a "cross-border exchange of judicial minds," which, he admits, "could provide an excellent forum for harmonisation."[227] In a less appealing scenario, gradual harmonization will result from an erroneous application of foreign law.[228] In any event, as noted earlier, increased harmonization is not a result that many countries are willing to accept.

If a European Union patent system is created, a single patent litigation structure will be indispensable to the system. A patent litigation project that would allow for centralization of proceedings concerning multiple parallel patents has had strong

---

[226] The proposed European Union patent would operate as a unitary regime but the existing European patent does not.

[227] Christopher Heath, *Methods of Industrial Property Harmonisation—The Example of Europe*, *in* Intellectual Property Harmonisation Within ASEAN and APEC 39, 55 (Christopher Antons, Michael Blakeney, & Christopher Heath, eds., 2004).

[228] *See, e.g.*, Brief for the United States as Amicus Curiae in Support of the Appellant, Jan K. Voda, M.D. v. Cordis Corporation, No. 05-1238 (Fed. Cir. June 15, 2005), 11. "[H]owever diligently the court may apply itself to the task [of adjudicating foreign patents], the risk of error is far greater than it would be if the infringement claim were heard in the courts of the foreign country whose patent law is being applied." *Id.*

support from the patent bar,[229] and although the current European Union proposal is not without critics or implementation difficulties, the fact that the proposal builds on the existing European patents under the EPC might help reduce the tensions between the European Patent Organization and Commission that have impeded progress in the area of multiple-country patent litigation until now.[230] And, as Professor Joseph Straus has stressed, the project "is overdue both politically and economically."[231] Once organized and operational, the new European court system could be an excellent laboratory for testing an institutional solution to the problem of enforcement of parallel patents; perhaps like the Brussels regime it might inspire intellectual property experts to seek similar solutions above the regional level.

Until a solution to the enforcement problem is found, holders of parallel patents will continue to face difficult times when pursuing enforcement in multiple countries. Jan Brinkhof, a renowned patent law expert and former Presiding Judge of the Intellectual Property Chamber of The Hague Court of Appeal,[232] described the persisting situation as "rather depressing" and concluded that under the current circumstances, "cross-border enforcement is all but impossible."[233]

---

[229] As Justice Jacob noted, "the need for a strong and fast Central Patents Court for Europe sticks out a mile." Robin Jacob, Patents and Pharmaceuticals—A Paper Given on 29th November at the Presentation of the Directorate-General of Competition's Preliminary Report of the Pharma-Sector Inquiry, 2008, *available at* http://ec.europa.eu/competition/sectors/pharmaceuticals/inquiry/jacob.pdf (last visited Sept. 2, 2011), 10.

[230] Proposal for a Regulation of the European Parliament and of the Council Implementing Enhanced Cooperation in the Area of Creation of Unitary Patent Protection, COM(2011) 215/3, 6 and 16. See also a positive reaction by the President of the EPO on the current proposal in *European Commission Presents Its Draft Regulations on Unitary Patent Protection*, EPO, Apr. 13, 2011, *available at* http://www.epo.org/news-issues/news/2011/20110413a.html (last visited Sept. 2, 2011).

[231] Straus, *supra* note 30, 420 (2000). *See also* Jacob, *The Judge's Perspective*, *supra* note 55.

[232] Jan Brinkhof at http://www.brinkhof.com/en/Lawyers/Jan_Brinkhof (last visited Sept. 2, 2011).

[233] Jan Brinkhof, *Wish List in the Area of Patent Law*, 35 IIC 407, 414 (2004).

3 Protecting an Invention outside the Protecting Country

THE COSTS OF obtaining patents in multiple countries and the additional costs of any enforcement actions place limits on the number of patents that inventors can secure and the number of countries in which they can enforce their patents. If patent holders face exploitation of their inventions in countries where they hold no patents or where they cannot afford to litigate, they can turn to a protecting country in which they hold patents and attempt to use that country's patent laws to fight the exploitation of their inventions in other countries. Additionally, patent holders may have other reasons why they might attempt to "stretch" the patent law of one protecting country. Relying on the patent law of some particular protecting country will allow a patent holder to place infringement litigation into that country and take advantage of the country's procedural and substantive rules. This chapter analyzes the various doctrines that have been developed and applied to extend national patent protection to the exploitation of inventions beyond the borders of protecting countries.

There is nothing to stop a third party from exploiting an invention outside a protecting country; inventions not protected may be freely utilized, and inventors enjoy no exclusive rights in countries where they have no protection. The only possibility inventors have to benefit directly[1] from the exploitation of their inventions outside protecting countries is to apply quickly for patents in other countries. As long as the term during which international priority is afforded to their applications[2] has not expired, they may apply for patents in any of the countries in the world that are parties to the Paris Convention.[3] However, expiration of the international priority period is not the only hurdle to patenting in other countries; high costs and varying standards of patentability are also barriers to applying for and obtaining patents in multiple countries.[4]

For inventors, free exploitation outside the protecting countries is at minimum an economic loss; the disclosure of their inventions is not limited to the protecting countries, but is global, and yet the benefits promised in exchange for the disclosure are limited to the protecting countries. Additionally, it may be impossible to segregate the exploitation of inventions outside the protecting countries from the effects of such exploitation on the markets of the protecting countries; the exploitation can contribute to subsequent acts of infringement inside the protecting countries. For instance, a manufacturer of a patented vehicle air conditioning unit may be acting entirely outside the protecting country but its units may eventually be installed by others in vehicles imported into a protecting country.[5] Inventors will attempt to mitigate losses they have incurred that were the result of a lack of patent protection in certain countries; for instance, some patentees may introduce upgrades or accessory products that they will patent in those countries to capture some of the income lost because of the lack of patent protection for the original invention. Inventors may also try to rely on protection under other intellectual property doctrines, such as trademark or copyright law, to remedy the losses. However, such mitigating approaches will not fully replace the losses suffered because of the original lack of patent protection.

The use of the patent law of a protecting country to cover acts that occur in a non-protecting country has long been employed by patentees; observations of the phenomenon were made many decades ago. For instance, in 1931 a patent expert

[1] There may be indirect benefits to inventors stemming from widespread use of their inventions; for instance, the inventions may become standards in an industry and help the inventors to introduce their related inventions to the markets in countries where they had no protection.

[2] Paris Convention, Chapter 1, note 63, Article 4.

[3] There were 173 contracting parties to the Paris Convention as of July 2011. Information by the WTO, *available at* http://www.wipo.int/export/sites/www/treaties/en/documents/pdf/paris.pdf and http://www.wipo.int/treaties/en/statistics/StatsResults.jsp?treaty_id=2&lang=en (last visited Sept. 2, 2011).

[4] *See* Chapter 1, note 2 and Chapter 2, note 5 and the accompanying text for discussions of the costs of patenting and enforcing patent rights.

[5] *See infra* note 210.

suggested that this avenue was an understandable and required strategy for small and medium-sized enterprises. The expert, a German patent attorney, pointed out that because such enterprises lacked the resources to patent their inventions outside Germany, they needed to rely on German law to protect them worldwide.[6]

This chapter analyzes the doctrines used to prevent the exploitation of inventions outside protecting countries. Section 3.1 covers the first mid-nineteenth-century cases that involved inventions embedded in foreign ships that entered ports of protecting countries. Section 3.2 discusses the cases in which the transit of goods through territories of protecting countries provided an opportunity for inventors to block the utilization of their inventions in other countries; the section also reviews border measures developed to block the importation of infringing products. Sections 3.3 and 3.4 analyze offers to sell and the issue of preventing patent infringements through the supply of components of a patented invention for assembly abroad. Acts of indirect infringement performed abroad may be also infringing, as discussed in Section 3.5. The standard used to localize an infringing act, if defined flexibly enough, may also place an act committed abroad within the scope of the patent law of a protecting country, and such possibilities are discussed in Section 3.6, which also addresses infringements committed on the Internet. Section 3.7 summarizes the various doctrines and explores the limitations of their territorial reach.

The chapter examines the doctrines from a comparative perspective by drawing from legislation and jurisprudence in the United States and Germany. Because any analysis of German law must include the European Union framework applicable in Germany, references are made to European Union law and case law of the Court of Justice of the European Union (CJEU). By reviewing the situation in both the United States and Germany this chapter provides a unique comparative and comprehensive picture of the issues as they arise in both jurisdictions; although various concepts analyzed in this chapter have been discussed in the literature of both countries,[7] the doctrines and their application in the U.S. and German legal regimes have rarely been compared side by side,[8] and never in a comprehensive manner. The analysis shows that U.S. law does not exceed the reach of German patent law,

---

[6] Siegfried Meier in 1931 MITTEILUNGEN VOM VERBAND DEUTSCHER PATENTANWÄLTE 95.

[7] In the United States, see, for instance, Dan L. Burk, *Patents in Cyberspace: Territoriality and Infringement on Global Computer Networks*, 68 TUL. L. REV. 1 (1993); Curtis A. Bradley, *Territorial Intellectual Property in an Age of Globalism*, 37 VA. J. INT'L L. 505 (1997); Chisum, Chapter 1, note 173; Holbrook, *Territoriality*, Chapter 1, note 5; Timothy R. Holbrook, *Extraterritoriality in U.S. Patent Law*, 49 WM. & MARY L. REV. 2119 (2008). In Germany, see, for instance, DIETER STAUDER, PATENTVERLETZUNG IM GRENZÜBERSCHREITENDEN WIRTSCHAFTSVERKEHR (1975); Stauder, *Cross-Border*, Chapter 2, note 60, 497–504.

[8] Dieter Stauder, *Patent Infringement in Export Trade—The Vulnerable Combination Patent*, 3 IIC 491 (1972); Jacob A. Schroeder, *So Long as You Live Under My Roof, You'll Live By . . . Whose Rules?: Ending the Extraterritorial*

and suggests that the problems of cross-border enforcement, which are further studied in detail in Chapter 4, are not unique to U.S. law, but are problems that are shared by other legal systems as well.

It is important to note that the goal of this chapter is not to address all legal and practical problems associated with the doctrines and their applications, since most of the doctrines deserve their own independent studies. Rather, the goal is to provide an overview of all the various ways in which patent laws of one country have been applied to cover acts committed outside that country and compare the situations in the United States and Germany. The two countries, which are the primary patent litigation jurisdictions in the world,[9] have a great number of materials for the study of the phenomenon;[10] they are not the jurisdictions of choice only because they provide advantageous legal mechanisms, but also because they are among the primary countries in the world for the exploitation of inventions.

3.1 Inventions in the Means of Transportation

What might be the oldest reported cases that evidence attempts to reach inventions beyond the borders of a protecting country are those involving devices embedded in ships. Ideally, inventors of those devices should have obtained patent protection in the countries where the ships were manufactured or from which they were operated or both; patent protection in those countries would have allowed the inventors to stop the manufacture or operation of the ships. Because they did not secure patents in those countries, the inventors turned to the patent protection that they had in countries to which the ships sailed, and by claiming infringement of their patents in these countries of destination, the inventors at least tried to prevent the temporary presence of the ships in the territory of these protecting countries. The cases brought by patent holders in these instances did not test the territorial boundaries of patent laws; rather, they tested the limits of the temporariness of the allegedly infringing act.

Countries eventually agreed on a unified approach to the problem of inventions embedded in a means of transportation when the 1925 Revision Conference on the

---

Application of Patent Law, 18 TEX. INTELL. PROP. L.J. 55, 77–81 (2009); Lucas S. Osborn, *Deconstructing an "Offer to Sell" in the Patent Infringement Context*, draft paper, on file with the author.

[9] For statistics on and a discussion of the German patent litigation system, see Mes, Chapter 2, note 177.

[10] In the United States, 2,847 patent cases were filed in federal district courts in 2010. Lex Machina, Chapter 4, note 6, as of June 6, 2011. According to estimates, about 1,200 patent cases are filed in Germany every year. Mes, Chapter 2, note 177, 402.

Paris Convention added Article 5*ter* dealing specifically with the issue of inventions in means of transportation; since that time attacks on such inventions appear only sporadically to test the limits of the provision. The two cases that paved the way to the approach that was adopted in 1925 were an English case from 1851 and a U.S. case from 1855; because there is an interesting connection between the cases it is useful to examine both of them.

The issue of a patented device in the construction of a foreign ship was first addressed in an English court in 1851.[11] Vice-Chancellor Turner had a case before him in which the assignees of a patent concerning a propeller[12] requested an injunction to prevent the defendant's steam vessel from entering English waters, which the vessel regularly did on its route between Amsterdam and London. It was the first and apparently the only instance in which the assignees, who were serial plaintiffs,[13] targeted these particular foreign defendants. The defendants did not dispute the fact that ships in English waters were subject to English laws; they argued instead that they knew nothing about the plaintiff's English patent and that the plaintiffs held no corresponding patent in Holland where the vessel was built.

Strong policy arguments were made by both sides. The plaintiffs suggested that no exception should be made for foreigners and urged the court to rule against the Dutch defendants because permitting the defendant's behavior would mean that in any similar situation "any foreigner [could] infringe an English patent."[14] In an affidavit introduced by the defendants, the master of the ship emphasized the importance of steamship transportation at that time and noted that ships using the propeller were the prevailing means of transportation between Holland and England and facilitated trade that "in his judgment and belief, [was] of great advantage to both the said countries."[15]

The Vice-Chancellor granted the injunction. He noted that he could not deny an injunction merely because the defendants were foreigners; "foreigners," in his words, "are in all cases subject to the laws of the country in which they may happen to be."[16] As for the argument relating to the impediment of trade between the two countries,

[11] Caldwell v. Van Vlissengen, 1851 (Eng.), reported by Francis Fisher, Esq., 16 Jurist o.s. 115 (1853).

[12] The patent at issue was "granted to James Lowe, in the year 1838, for a mode of propelling vessels by means of one or more curved blades set or affixed on a revolving shaft below the water line of the vessel, and running from stem to stern of the vessel." Caldwell, *supra* note 11, 116.

[13] It is notable that the plaintiffs litigated several cases in which they successfully withstood attacks on the validity of the patent by reaching settlement with defendants before the issue of validity was decided.

[14] Caldwell, *supra* note 11, 117.

[15] The affidavit by Tzebbe Swart, quoted in Caldwell, *supra* note 11, 117.

[16] Caldwell, *supra* note 11, 118. In support of his conclusion he quoted several authorities, including Justice Story and Ulrich Huber, cited the applicable English statute, and also referred to natural justice. *Id.*, 119.

he reasoned that an equal treatment of English and Dutch ships would actually level the playing field, as all ships would be required to obtain licenses to use the invention patented in England if they wanted to service English waters.

At the conclusion of his decision, Vice-Chancellor Turner suggested that it was upon the legislature to change the law if policy considerations dictated a different result.[17] Thereafter, his words were rapidly translated into action by Parliament and also confirmed by later developments in the United States. As Turner envisioned, his decision was legislatively overruled; the Solicitor General, who was personally involved in the case, authored the relevant amendment to the Patent Act that inserted a provision protecting foreign vessels against the claims of holders of English patents.[18] When the similar case of *John Brown v. Duchesne*[19] was brought later before the Circuit Court of the United States, Massachusetts District, and ultimately before the U.S. Supreme Court, American justices inquired about the outcome of the English case, and their decisions were influenced by the developments in England.

Although the facts and governing law in *Duchesne* were similar to those faced by Vice-Chancellor Turner, the outcome in *Duchesne* was completely different from the one in the English case because the U.S. decisions followed the legislative overruling of the English case in the English Patent Act. The patent involved in *Duchesne* covered a device used in a French vessel that was alleged to have infringed a U.S. patent when the vessel entered the port of Boston. Judge Curtis of the Massachusetts District, having recognized the prescriptive and adjudicatory power of countries to regulate ships that enter their ports,[20] interpreted the U.S. patent statute as not "designed to touch the subject of the structure or equipment of foreign vessels." He also suggested that at minimum it was "extremely questionable" whether patentees should be able to obtain damages or compensation in situations similar to the one presented in *Duchesne*; in his opinion the use of an invention covered by a U.S. patent in U.S. waters by a foreign ship would be "almost an unappreciable part of the use of a thing patented."[21]

The U.S. Supreme Court agreed with Judge Curtis;[22] having emphasized the territorial scope of patent laws, the Court noted that "[t]he chief and almost only advantage which the defendant derived from the use of the [invention] was on the

---

[17] Caldwell, *supra* note 11, 120.

[18] H. Geoffrey Lynfield, *Patent Infringement on British and American Ships*, 37 J. PAT. OFF. SOC'Y 389, 390 (1955).

[19] John Brown v. Duchesne, 4 Am. L. Reg. 152 (C.C. Mass. 1855); Brown v. Duchesne, 60 U.S. 183 (1856).

[20] John Brown v. Duchesne, 4 Am. L. Reg. 152, 155 (C.C. Mass. 1855).

[21] *Id.*, 157.

[22] Brown v. Duchesne, 60 U.S. 183 (1856).

high seas and in other places out of the jurisdiction of the United States."[23] The Court saw no damage to the plaintiff and no advantage to the defendant stemming from the use of the invention in this case; even if there was some damage or advantage, the Court deemed it to be "so minute that it [was] incapable of any appreciable value."[24] The Court held that "the rights of property and exclusive use granted to a patentee [did] not extend to a foreign vessel lawfully entering one of [the U.S.] ports."[25]

Following the decisions in *Caldwell* and *Duchesne* on the issue of inventions of components used in the building of ships, countries began to protect ships temporarily entering their ports from patent infringement claims. In the United States the problem was solved by the statutory interpretation in *Duchesne*; a specific statutory provision on the issue was adopted only much later in 1952.[26] Other countries, including Germany, followed the lead of Great Britain and adopted statutory provisions protecting foreign ships in their waters even earlier than the United States.[27]

At the international level the exception was embraced in 1925 through the insertion of Article 5*ter* to the Paris Convention;[28] this article provides protection to those who use inventions on board the vessels of countries of the Paris Union as long as the vessels "enter the waters of the country" only "temporarily or accidentally" and the invention is "used there exclusively for the needs of the vessel."[29] Article 5*ter* also resolved the question of whether the same exception should apply for means of transportation that use air or ground instead of water; the 1925 Revision Conference included both air and ground transportation.[30] Article 5*ter* paragraph 2 states that inventions may be used in countries of the Union if they are used "in the construction or operation of aircraft or land vehicles" and also under the condition that they enter only "temporarily or accidently."[31]

---

[23] *Id.*, 196.

[24] *Id.*, 196.

[25] *Id.*, 198.

[26] 35 U.S.C. §272.

[27] Lynfield reported that by 1907 six other countries had adopted such a provision, including the Austro-Hungarian Empire and Germany. Lynfield, *supra* note 18, 394. *See* §5 of the German Patent Act of Apr. 7, 1891; reprinted in JULIUS KÜSTER, PATENT-, MUSTER- UND MARKEN-SCHUTZ IN DER MOTOREN- UND FAHRZEUG-INDUSTRIE 51 (1908).

[28] BODENHAUSEN, Chapter 1, note 68, 82.

[29] Paris Convention, Chapter 1, note 63, Article 5*ter*(1).

[30] By this time, in fact, the 1919 Convention Relating to the Regulation of Aerial Navigation already protected foreign aircraft from seizures in protecting countries. *Cf.* Joseph H. Beale, who in 1923 remarked that it was "perhaps too soon to assert dogmatically" whether air transportation was to be viewed analogously. Joseph H. Beale, *The Jurisdiction of a Sovereign State*, 36 HARV. L. REV. 241, 262 (1922–1923).

[31] Paris Convention, Chapter 1, note 63, Article 5*ter*(2). On details of the negotiations of Article 5*ter*, see Lynfield, *supra* note 18, 397–98. *See also* Convention on International Civil Aviation, Dec. 7, 1944 (Chicago Convention), Article 27; the United States adhered to the Convention in 1946, and Germany in 1956. As of September 2011,

Since the 1925 Revision of the Paris Convention, cases have been brought that have further refined the notion of "temporariness" used in Article 5*ter*. For instance, in 1974 the U.S. District Court for the Eastern District of New York interpreted the term in *Cali v. Japan Air Lines*,[32] in which the defendants, who were various international air carriers, were accused of infringing a U.S. patent concerning JT-4 jet engines. The plaintiff argued that there was nothing "temporary or accidental" in "the maintenance of a regular and systematic international aircraft service to the U.S."[33] The court noted that the exception provided by Article 5*ter* of the Paris Convention and the corresponding provision of Section 272 of the U.S. Patent Act was a substantial "subtraction from the grant" to the patent holder in *Cali*, and although it found that the magnitude of operations of the foreign carriers was comparable to those of U.S. carriers, the court adopted a broad interpretation of the term "temporarily" and found no infringement of the patent.[34] Recently, the U.S. Court of Appeals for the Federal Circuit formulated its own definition of the term as used in Section 272; in *National Steel Car, Ltd. v. Canadian Pacific Ry., Ltd.* it stated that "'temporarily' [. . .] is entering for a period of time of finite duration with the sole purpose of engaging in international commerce."[35]

3.2 Inventions in Transit and Border Measures

Even after inventions in the means of transportation that only temporarily entered protecting countries became protected from attacks by patent holders, the activities of transportation or transit of goods through protecting countries continued to offer opportunities for inventors to block transportation channels and fully or partially

---

there were 190 contracting parties to the Convention. *See* http://www.icao.int/icao/en/leb/chicago.pdf (last visited Sept. 2, 2011). For issues of patent protection in outer space and other "extraterritorial areas," see, e.g., Dieter Stauder, *Patent Protection in Extraterritorial Areas (Continental Shelf, High Seas, Air Space, and Outer Space)*, 7 IIC 470 (1976); Friedrich-Karl Beier & Dieter Stauder, *Weltraumstationen und das Recht des geistigen Eigentums*, 1985 GRUR INT. 6; Karl-Heinz Böckstiegel, Paul Michael Krämer, & Isabel Polley, *Kann der Betrieb von Satelliten im Weltraum patentrechtlich geschützt werden?*, 1999 GRUR 1.

[32] Cali v. Japan Air Lines, 380 F. Supp. 1120 (E.D.N.Y. 1974).

[33] *Id.*, 1124.

[34] A similar refinement of "temporariness" was provided in the United Kingdom in Stena Rederi AB and Stena Line AB v. Irish Ferries Ltd., [2003] EWCA Civ 66; [2003] R.P.C. 36 (Eng.). Although the vessel at issue, a catamaran, which included in its construction an invention patented in the United Kingdom, sailed between Ireland and the United Kingdom three or four times a day, the court held that unless the vessel's presence in U.K. waters was permanent, no injunctive relief could be granted.

[35] National Steel Car, Ltd. v. Canadian Pacific Ry., Ltd., 357 F.3d 1319, 1331 (Fed. Cir. 2004). On the opportunity to take advantage of the exception, see J. Jonas Anderson, *Hiding Behind Nationality: The Temporary Presence Exception and Patent Infringement Avoidance*, 15 MICH. TELECOMM. & TECH. L. REV. 1, 40–44 (2008).

prevent utilization of their inventions abroad. Countries have hesitated to permit such actions targeting goods in transit—there are important reasons to ensure that goods be allowed to be transported safely through the territory of a protecting country on their way from one country to another.

An inventor who holds a patent in a country through which the goods are transported must find a "hook"—a reason for the country to be willing to entertain an action targeting the goods. A danger that the goods might "leak" from transit into the market of the protecting country is such a reason. Countries have distinguished between pure transit, where the goods should be protected from such attacks, and other activities that go beyond pure transit, may result in "leakage," and should be subject to attacks; as two German commentators explained, the difference is between pure transit that is "the simple uninterrupted transport through or over the territory"[36] and "other forms of transit [that] may include activities such as storage in a customs free zone, repackaging, etc."[37]

Given the different geographical locations of the United States and Germany, it is not surprising that the issue of transit has been discussed frequently in Germany but has not been developed in U.S. case law. German jurisprudence provides numerous cases on patent infringing goods in transit, and recent German cases reflect developments in the European Union that may have far-reaching consequences for those who transport goods patented in member states of the European Union through the territories of those member states.

The issue of transit was a subject of discussion in Germany from the time of the enactment of the first Patent Act of the German Empire in 1877,[38] as recalled by the Reichsgericht in an 1899 decision.[39] The 1877 and 1891 Patent Acts granted exclusive rights to manufacture, sell, offer to sell, and use the patented invention,[40] and the question from early on was one of demarcation between pure transit and an activity that was more accurately labeled a sale or offer to sell. The oldest transit cases

---

[36] Alexander von Mühlendahl & Dieter Stauder, *Territorial Intellectual Property Rights in a Global Economy—Transit and Other "Free Zones," in* PATENTS AND TECHNOLOGICAL PROGESS IN A GLOBALIZED WORLD—LIBER AMICORUM JOSEPH STRAUS 653, 659 (Wolrad Prinz zu Waldeck und Pyrmont, Martin J. Adelman, Robert Brauneis, Josef Drexl, & Ralph Nack eds., 2009).

[37] Mühlendahl, Stauder, *supra* note 36, 659.

[38] For the pre-1877 history of patent law in the German territory, see, e.g., KLOSTERMANN, Chapter 1, note 60, 103 ff.; Margrit Seckelman, *Industrial Engineering and the Struggle for the Protection of Patents in Germany, 1856–1877*, 5 QUADERNS D'HISTÒRIA DE L'ENGINYERIA 234 (2002–2003); KRASSER, Chapter 1, note 15, 58–64. For an overview of German patent law since 1877, see *id.*, 64–69.

[39] Reichsgericht, I 324/99, Dec. 2, 1899, RGZ 45, 147. The court noted that the decision in that particular case did not require it to take a position on the controversy surrounding the issue of transit. *Id.*, 148.

[40] §4 of the Patent Act of 1877; §4 of the Patent Act of 1891. The terms used being "herstellen, in Verkehr bringen, feilhalten, gebrauchen."

before the German Supreme Court—at that time called the Reichsgericht—bore two characteristic features: first, they were criminal cases, since criminal prosecution for patent infringement was possible under the Patent Act, and if one knowingly infringed patent rights, he could be criminally prosecuted;[41] and second, they involved transit through the port of Hamburg, which was not only an extremely important transportation hub but also a customs-free zone.

In the early cases defendants relied on the status of the customs-free zone to provide protection for their dealings with products that included patented inventions. For instance, in 1884 the Reichsgericht considered a case in which goods were shipped from a manufacturer in Holland to the defendants' storage in the port of Hamburg, where the defendants repackaged the goods and offered them for sale to their customers abroad.[42] Both the Hamburg Landgericht and the Reichsgericht interpreted the conduct as acts of infringement (sale, offer to sell) committed by the defendants in Germany. The Reichsgericht reached the same result in a similar criminal case in 1890; in that decision the court emphasized that although the goods at issue were not subject to German customs because of the customs-free zone in the port of Hamburg, the presence in the zone did not exclude the goods from application of German laws, including the Patent Act.[43]

A case that seemed more difficult was decided by the Reichsgericht in 1899;[44] the defendants arranged for goods to be sent from Milan to their corporate headquarters in Hamburg from which they shipped the goods to customers in Sydney. The goods remained in the customs-free zone in Hamburg and were not removed from their original packaging. Although the lower court classified the activity as transit and found no infringement, the Reichsgericht disagreed and held that the defendants acted not as carriers but as buyers and sellers of the infringing product, and that therefore their acts were not acts of transit but of import and export involving the sale of goods.

In later cases German courts continued to distinguish between "transit in a strict sense" and "transit in a broader sense," holding that only the former is a noninfringing activity.[45] For instance, in 1981 in *Rollwagen*[46] the Karlsruhe Oberlandesgericht

---

[41] §34 of the Patent Act of 1877; §36 of the Patent Act of 1891.

[42] *Schmierbüchsen*, Reichsgericht, 626/84, Apr. 3, 1884, RGZ 104, 349.

[43] *Antipyrin*, Reichsgericht, 1865/90, Oct. 25, 1890, RGZ 76, 205. In this case the defendant bought the patented product in Basel and had it shipped to the Hamburg customs-free zone, where he stored it and only from there sold it to clients abroad.

[44] Reichsgericht, I 324/99, Dec. 2, 1899, RGZ 45, 147.

[45] *Taeschner-Pertusin*, Bundesgerichtshof, Jan. 15, 1957, 1957 GRUR 195 (a trademark case). The Bundesgerichtshof speaks in the case about a "Durchfuhr im engeren Sinne" and a "Durchfuhr im weiteren Sinne." *Id.*

[46] *Rollwagen*, Oberlandesgericht Karlsruhe, 6 U 173/80, Dec. 23, 1981, 1982 GRUR Int. 752, 1982 GRUR 295.

refused to hold that the defendant's shipment of goods to Kuwait constituted a transit, even when the shipment was made from Switzerland free on board[47] to the German port of Bremerhaven and from Bremerhaven to Kuwait on board a ship under the Dutch flag. The court noted that the product was in fact offered for sale and sold in Germany and that the defendant personally attached its own label to the product when it was loaded on the ship in the customs-free zone of the port of Bremerhaven. The court restated the rule that although customs-free zones are excluded from certain customs regulations, they fall within the territorial scope of German patent law;[48] the court then reiterated the position of the Bundesgerichtshof that "[t]he criterion that distinguishes a mere transit permitted by patent laws and importation for the purposes of export that infringes a patent is whether the product that falls within the scope of a German patent is an item of sales business that exhibits sufficient connection with [Germany]."[49]

The rule, then, is that shipment free on board does not protect an infringer if the infringer in fact takes control over the goods in Germany.[50] In *Rollwagen* the Karlsruhe Oberlandesgericht attached significance to the fact that although the goods were shipped free on board, they were in defendant's control in the German port when the defendant personally attached his own label to the goods. Similarly, in *Trimethoprim*[51] the Hamburg Hanseatisches Oberlandesgericht ruled that if goods are shipped from abroad and while in Germany they become available to the defendant, the situation does not qualify as pure transit; there is infringement, and it does not make a difference "whether the goods are supposed to remain in [Germany] or be exported abroad."[52]

As the cases above illustrate, German jurisprudence on the issue of transit is consistent; however, there was a brief period of uncertainty in 2004–2007 caused by the CJEU's interpretation in two trademark cases of the notion of transit under European Union law,[53] specifically, the European Union Customs Regulation.[54] Although the TRIPs Agreement does not require countries to adopt customs

---

[47] *See infra* note 231 and the accompanying text on the term "free on board."

[48] *Rollwagen*, *supra* note 46.

[49] *Id.*, 299–300.

[50] *See also infra* Section 3.6 for a discussion of the effects of a free on board shipment.

[51] *Trimethoprim*, Hanseatisches Oberlandesgericht Hamburg, 3 U 1/90, Oct. 25, 1990, 1990 GRUR INT. 301.

[52] *Id.*, 301 and 302. *See also Imidazol*, Oberlandesgericht Hamburg, 3 U 12/85, Apr. 25, 1985, 1985 GRUR 923.

[53] Case C-383/98, Polo/Lauren v. Dwidua, 2000; Case C-60/02, Re Montres Rolex SA, 2004.

[54] Council Regulation (EC) No 1383/2003 of 22 July 2003 concerning customs actions against goods suspected of infringing certain intellectual property rights and the measures to be taken against goods found to have infringed such rights, 2003 O.J. (L 196) 7 ("2003 Customs Regulation"); Council Regulation (EC) No 3295/94 of 22 December 1994 laying down measures to prohibit the release for free circulation, export, re-export,

measures to target patent infringing goods in transit,[55] the Regulation does; its original 1994 version did not cover patents, but the amended 2003 version does cover patents.[56] Inclusion of patents in the regulation was not without controversy; for example, during the legislative process Spain warned that extending the scope of the regulation to cover process patents would create difficulties in practice.[57]

The two trademark decisions by the CJEU[58] seemed to suggest that the Regulation would require that many transit situations be classified as importations,[59] and the Hamburg Landgericht adopted the reasoning of these CJEU trademark cases in a 2004 patent case.[60] The Landgericht explained that the CJEU case law in the trademark area required the court to interpret the concept of importation in line with the Customs Regulation, which enables customs officials to seize goods that infringe a patent of a member state[61] when they are transported from a third country to another third country.[62] This 2004 decision by the Hamburg Landgericht contradicted

or entry for a suspensive procedure of counterfeit and pirated goods, 1994 O.J. (L 341) 8 ("1994 Customs Regulation").

[55] "[T]here shall be no obligation to apply [customs procedures] to [. . .] goods in transit." Article 51, fn. 13, TRIPs. "Members may enable such an application [for the suspension by the customs authorities] to be made in respect of goods which involve other infringements of intellectual property rights." (Meaning other than trademarks and copyright.) Article 51, TRIPs. The Paris Convention includes provisions on seizure of goods upon importation but they concern only marks and trade names. Paris Convention, Chapter 1, note 63, Article 9.

[56] 2003 Customs Regulation, *supra* note 54, Article 2(1)(c)(i).

[57] General Affairs Council Meeting, 5455/99 (Jan. 25, 1999), XI.

[58] *See supra* note 53.

[59] In *Polo/Lauren* T-shirts were in transit from Indonesia to Poland when they were temporarily detained by Austrian customs pursuant to a request by the trademark holder. Polo/Lauren, *supra* note 53, paras. 16 and 17. Responding to the observation submitted by the government of Germany, the CJEU rejected the interpretation that the 1994 Customs Regulation did not apply to goods that were merely in transit from one nonmember country to another. *Id.*, paras. 24 and 25. In *Rolex* watches were transported from Italy to Poland, meaning, at that time, from a member state to a nonmember country. The CJEU confirmed that the 1994 Customs Regulation applied "to situations in which goods in transit between two countries not belonging to the European Community are temporarily detained in a Member State by the customs authorities of that State." Rolex, *supra* note 53, para. 64.

[60] Landgericht Hamburg, 315 O 305/04, Apr. 2, 2004.

[61] 2003 Customs Regulation, *supra* note 54, Article 2(1)(c).

[62] *Id.*, Article 1. It is worth noting that under the particular facts of the case the Hamburg Landgericht might have found infringement through importation even without making any changes to the interpretation of the term "transit." The products were transported through Germany on their way from a Chinese manufacturer to Russian customers. In addition to a somewhat suspicious routing, there was some evidence that at least some of the infringing products were intended for the German market; the court did not believe that German labels on the products that included information likely to be understandable only to a German customer ("TüV," "GS," and "Grüne Punkt") were intended solely to provide the products a "western touch," highly desirable on the Russian market.

previous German court decisions on the issue of transit, and joined the CJEU trademark decisions as a target of criticism by various commentators.[63]

The CJEU further clarified its position concerning goods in transit in a 2006 trademark case, *Montex Holdings Ltd. v. Diesel SpA*,[64] which concerned the transit of jeans through Germany en route from Poland to Ireland. The court described the transit as an "uninterrupted transit from the Polish customs office to the customs office in Dublin" with goods "protected against any removal in the course of transit by a customs seal affixed on the means of transport by the Polish authorities."[65] The transit was thus from a then-non-member country to a member state, and although the trademark at issue was protected in Germany where the jeans were detained, the trademark was not protected in Ireland—the destination member state of the goods. The CJEU confirmed that pure transit does not infringe trademarks;[66] however, it added that pure transit must not involve offers for sale or a sale "effected while the goods are placed under the external transit procedure or the customs warehousing procedure and [the placement] necessarily entails their being put on the market"[67] in the European Union, or "goods [being] subject to the act of a third party while they are placed under the external transit procedure which necessarily entails their being put on the market in the Member State of transit."[68]

Since *Diesel*, the Bundesgerichtshof reconfirmed its approach to transit in the trademark case *Durchfuhr von Originalware*,[69] which concerned a U.S. defendant

---

[63] Iouri Kobiako, *Durchfuhr als Patentverletzungshandlung?—Zugleich Anmerkung zum Urteil des LG Hamburg vom 2. Apr. 2004*, 2004 GRUR Int. 832, 834, 836, and fn. 29. Commentators rejected the proposition that a particular solution for a procedural issue pursued in the Customs Regulation should justify a new interpretation of a substantive right. Kobiako also suggested that the CJEU jurisprudence concerning trademarks might not be relevant in cases involving patents; while in cases involving trademarks the Regulation concerns goods bearing without authorization a registered trademark, in cases involving patents the Regulation speaks of goods that infringe a national patent. Kobiako concludes that a finding of patent infringement must first be made by a court before the Regulation may apply.

[64] Case C-281/05, Montex Holdings Ltd. v. Diesel SpA, 2006.

[65] *Id.*, para. 11.

[66] *Id.*, para. 21. "In the field of trade marks, placing non-Community goods bearing a mark under a suspensive customs procedure such as that of external transit is not, per se, interference with the right of the proprietor of the mark to control the initial marketing in the Community [. . .]." *Id.*

[67] *Id.*, para. 22. "The external Community transit (T1) procedure, applies mainly to the movement of non-Community goods." Transit Manual, TAXUD/A3/0007/2010, July 1, 2010, *available at* http://ec.europa.eu/taxation_customs/resources/documents/customs/procedural_aspects/transit/common_community/transit_manual_consolidation_en.pdf (last visited Sept. 2, 2011), 37–38.

[68] *Id.*, para. 23. The CJEU added that "[i]t is [. . .] irrelevant whether goods whose destination is a Member State come from an associated State or a third country, or whether those goods have been manufactured in the country of origin lawfully or in infringement of the existing trade mark rights of the proprietor in that country." *Id.*, the ruling, para. 2.

[69] *Durchfuhr von Originalware*, Bundesgerichtshof, I ZR 66/04, Mar. 21, 2007, 2007 GRUR 875.

that bought plaintiffs' products in Russia. The plaintiffs intended for the products to be sold in Russia, but the defendant wanted to import them into the United States. The defendant transited the products through Europe; they were flown from Russia, unloaded in Germany at the Frankfurt-Hahn airport, and from there they were supposed to be transported by ground to the port of Bremen and shipped to Miami. German Customs seized the products at the Frankfurt-Hahn airport under suspicion of trademark infringement. In holding that there was no infringement, the court pointed out that trademark laws, legislative history, and the jurisprudence of the CJEU all require that something in addition to pure transit must exist in order to warrant a finding of infringement.[70] In this case there was no indication that the defendant intended to sell any of the products in Germany; a possibility that the products could end up on the German market was insufficient.

Regardless of the CJEU's decision in *Diesel* and the position of German courts on the issue of transit, courts of other European Union member states are split in their interpretations of the Customs Regulation and the impact of the Regulation on substantive patent laws; the matter is thus subject to a significant and continuing debate[71] that has extended beyond European Union borders. Following a seizure by Dutch customs officials of 500 kilograms of generic medicines traveling through the Netherlands in a shipment from India to Brazil, Brazil filed an intervention with the World Trade Organization (WTO) General Council in March 2009.[72] In the intervention Brazil claims that the action by Dutch customs was a breach of Article V of the General Agreement on Tariffs and Trade (GATT), which codifies the principle of "freedom of transit."[73] In May 2010 Brazil and India filed requests with the WTO to institute official consultations with the European Union and the Netherlands to resolve the problem of seizures of goods in transit.[74] For now, the consultations have

---

[70] *Id.*, 875.

[71] Frederick M. Abbott, *Seizure of Generic Pharmaceuticals in Transit Based on Allegations of Patent Infringement: A Threat to International Trade, Development and Public Welfare*, 1 World Intell. Prop. Org. J. 43, 43 (2009). Frederick M. Abbott explains that although customs authorities in other member states have also seized goods that allegedly infringed patents, "[t]he customs authorities of the Netherlands have been the most aggressive." *Id.*, 47.

[72] *Intervention by Brazil, available at* http://www.keionline.org/blogs/2009/02/03/intervention-by-brazil-at-wto-general-council-on-seizure-of-500-kilos-of-generic-medicines-by-dutch-customs-aut (last visited Sept. 2, 2011).

[73] Article V, General Agreement on Tariffs and Trade, Oct. 30, 1947, *available at* http://www.wto.org/english/docs_e/legal_e/gatt47_01_e.htm (last visited Sept. 2, 2011).

[74] Information by the WTO concerning the request by Brazil, *available at* http://www.wto.org/english/tratop_e/dispu_e/cases_e/ds409_e.htm (last visited Sept. 2, 2011), and Information by the WTO concerning the request by India, *available at* http://www.wto.org/english/tratop_e/dispu_e/cases_e/ds408_e.htm (last visited Sept. 2, 2011).

been halted in anticipation of a CJEU decision that should clarify the contentious provisions of the Customs Regulation; the CJEU should issue the decision in response to a request for a preliminary ruling that was submitted by the English Court of Appeal in *Koninklijke Philips Electronics NV v. Lucheng Meijing Industrial Co. Ltd.*[75]

Although German customs do not prevent the mere transit of goods that embed an invention protected in Germany, they continue to employ measures to prevent the importation of goods; both the 2003 European Union Customs Regulation and German patent law provide for seizures of patent-infringing goods by customs. In Germany, goods are seized based on a request filed by a patent holder. Under the German Patent Act, the alleged infringer has two weeks to object to the seizure.[76] Once the patent holder is notified of the objection, the holder must produce a court order that mandates an impounding or defines the limitations of disposition rights.[77] Under the 2003 Customs Regulation, the patent holder has ten working days from receipt of notification of suspension of release or of detention of goods to initiate proceedings concerning infringement of goods, which in Germany will be held before a court.[78]

According to statistics by the European Commission, out of over 118 million articles seized at European Union borders in 2009 because of alleged intellectual property rights infringements, 4.99 percent were targeted because the articles were claimed to infringe a patent.[79] According to German customs statistics, of all goods subject to actions by German customs in 2009 because of intellectual property rights violations 8.93 percent (measured by value of goods) concerned products claimed to infringe patents; that percentage represented a value of €32.5 million.[80]

---

[75] *See* the Request for Preliminary Ruling in *Nokia Corp. v. HM Commissioners of Revenue & Customs*, Nov. 9, 2009, *available at* http://www.eplawpatentblog.com/2010/January/Court%20of%20Appeal%20Order%20Nokia.pdf (last visited Sept. 2, 2011), and the Opinion of Advocate General Cruz Villalón in *Koninklijke Philips Electronics NV v. Lucheng Meijing Industrial Co. Ltd.*, CJEU, C-446/09.

[76] Patentgesetz, §142a(3).

[77] Patentgesetz, §142a(4).

[78] 2003 Customs Regulation, *supra* note 54, Articles 9–13. The period may be extended by ten working days, and the period is only three working days for perishable goods. *Id.*, Article 13. *See id.*, Article 11, for the possibility of a simplified procedure.

[79] Report on EU Customs Enforcement of Intellectual Property Rights—Results at the EU Border—2009, 2 and 17, *available at* http://ec.europa.eu/taxation_customs/resources/documents/customs/customs_controls/counterfeit_piracy/statistics/statistics_2009.pdf (last visited Sept. 2, 2011).

[80] Gewerblicher Rechtsschutz, Statistik für das Jahr 2009, 9 and 11, *available at* http://www.zoll.de/DE/Fachthemen/Verbote-Beschraenkungen/Gewerblicher-Rechtsschutz/Marken-und-Produktpiraterie/Statistik/statistik_node.html (last visited Sept. 2, 2011). Most of the actions concerned products claimed to infringe trademarks (76.3 percent of value of goods). *Id.*, 11. The total value of all goods subjected to actions by German customs in 2009 because of alleged intellectual property rights violations was €363.7 million, or about

The United States has powerful customs proceedings to fight the importation of goods that infringe intellectual property rights, including patents. Section 337 investigations before the International Trade Commission (ITC) enable holders of U.S. patents to obtain exclusion orders to prevent importation of infringing goods.[81] Each year two to three dozen cases are brought before the ITC;[82] as of April 2011, of the total of eighty-one outstanding Section 337 exclusion orders, forty-three concerned patents.[83] The effect of the exclusion orders is strictly limited to U.S. territory, as they "exclude from entry for consumption into the United States, entry for consumption from a foreign trade zone, or withdrawal from a warehouse for consumption, for the remaining term of the patent, except under license of the patent owner."[84]

Orders are issued either as "limited exclusion orders" or "general exclusion orders." "General exclusion orders" concern a particular product and any downstream product, wherever the product may originate. "Limited exclusion orders" cover only a particular product by parties specified in the order. Until the 2008 decision by the U.S. Court of Appeals for the Federal Circuit in *Kyocera Wireless Corp. v. ITC*,[85] "limited orders" were used to cover not only the infringing products per se, but also downstream products by entities not named as respondents in the particular ITC investigation; however, since *Kyocera* the ITC may no longer issue limited orders covering downstream products.[86]

ITC proceedings provide a number of advantages when compared to infringement proceedings before a court. Among the advantages that have been appreciated by patentees are the speed of the proceedings, which tends to be faster than proceedings

---

$525 million. *Id.*, 9. The value of goods targeted by U.S. customs for such violations in fiscal year 2008 was $188.1 million, or about €130.3 million. Intellectual Property Rights—Fiscal Year 2010 Seizure Statistics, 2, *available at* http://www.ice.gov/doclib/news/releases/2011/110316washington.pdf (last visited Sept. 2, 2011).

[81] 19 U.S.C. §1337. On Section 337 investigations, see, e.g., Colleen Chien, *Patently Protectionist? An Empirical Analysis of Patent Cases at the International Trade Commission*, 50 Wm. & Mary L. Rev. 63 (2008). On the issue of standing and the "domestic industry" requirement see the ITC decision in *Certain Multimedia Display and Navigation Devices and System Components Thereof and Products Containing Same*, Inv. No. 337-TA-694, July 22, 2011.

[82] In 2010 there were fifty-six cases instituted, in 2009 there were thirty-one. *See* ITC statistics *available at* http://www.usitc.gov/intellectual_property/documents/cy_337_institutions.pdf (last visited Sept. 2, 2011).

[83] See list of outstanding Section 337 exclusion orders *available at* http://www.usitc.gov/intellectual_property/ (last visited Sept. 2, 2011). The number includes orders concerning design patents.

[84] *E.g.*, limited exclusion order in the matter of Certain Coupler Devices for Power Supply Facilities, Components Thereof, and Products Containing the Same, 337-TA-590, Dec. 20, 2007, 2–3; general exclusion order in the matter of Certain Plastic Food Containers, 337-TA-514, May 23, 2005, 2.

[85] Kyocera Wireless Corp. v. ITC, 543 F.3d 1340 (Fed. Cir. 2008).

[86] For the impact of *Kyocera* on ITC proceedings, see Bas de Blank & Bing Cheng, *Where Is the ITC Going After Kyocera?*, 25 Santa Clara Computer & High Tech. L.J. 701 (2009).

before a district court,[87] availability of the "general exclusion orders" that may cover downstream products,[88] jurisdictional rules that can extend further than the rules applicable to civil litigation in district courts,[89] the fewer defenses that ITC proceedings allow, as compared to district court proceedings,[90] and the absence of a four-part equity test for obtaining an exclusion order.[91] ITC proceedings are often sought by patentees as a complement to the filing of a suit in a U.S. district court;[92] the patentees seek rapid relief, and although no damages can be awarded in ITC proceedings, exclusion orders may be valuable both as a prospective remedy and a powerful negotiating tool.

The advantages of ITC proceedings are why they have recently become popular for fighting infringements by domestic infringers, although Section 337 investigations were designed to fight infringing importations by foreign competitors. As Colleen Chien noted in her study on ITC investigations, the "venue [. . .] has outgrown its original purpose: the ITC is no longer reserved for the specific threat of foreign piracy."[93] Her survey of recent cases shows that only 14 percent of investigations were initiated solely against foreign respondents;[94] in 72 percent of cases, investigations concerned both foreign and domestic respondents.[95] The remaining investigations targeted only domestic respondents.[96]

Although border measures are by definition directed against infringements that emanate from outside the protecting country, they do not generally create cross-border enforcement difficulties; the measures, like the ones in Germany and the United States, rely on domestic enforcement—enforcement by the countries' respective national customs authorities—and no need for cross-border enforcement arises.

---

[87] De Blank & Cheng, *supra* note 86, 704.

[88] *Id.*, 705.

[89] *Id.*, 707.

[90] Chien, *supra* note 81, 79; de Blank & Cheng, *supra* note 86, 707–08.

[91] Chien, *supra* note 81, 78–79.

[92] *E.g.*, Apple filed against Taiwanese High Tech Computer Corp. and its two subsidiaries (one in the United States and one in the British Virgin Islands) in both a federal district court and the ITC. Apple Inc. et al. v. High Tech Computer Corp. et al., D.Del., 1:10-cv-00166-RK, complaint filed on Mar. 2, 2010. The ITC complaint was filed on the same day.

[93] Chien, *supra* note 81, 71. Chien observed that "perhaps one of [the] most surprising findings is that Section 337 cases have been brought against purely foreign defendants in only a small minority of recent cases (14 percent)." *Id.*, 87.

[94] Chien, *supra* note 81, 87. Compare to 5 percent of district court cases brought solely against foreign defendants in 2004; *see* Chapter 4, Section 4.1.

[95] Chien, *supra* note 81, 87. Compare to 10 percent of district court cases brought against both foreign and domestic defendants in 2004; *see* Chapter 4, Section 4.1.

[96] Chien, *supra* note 81, 87.

Undeniably, the actions have an impact on foreign companies or activities outside the protecting country because the resulting exclusion orders and the threat of seizures of goods at the border affect the activities of foreign manufacturers, who lose particular markets for their goods.

3.3 Offers to Sell

When courts hold that what a defendant claims to be a transit is in fact not a pure transit, the determination may result in a finding of infringement through importation; however, importation was not originally understood as an act of direct infringement—importation as an exclusive right was not included in patent acts in Germany until 1981[97] and in the United States until 1994.[98] Before importation was added as an additional exclusive right, courts often found that infringement in transportation situations was committed through an infringing offer to sell in the protecting country.[99]

If an offer is made in a protecting country to sell a patented invention outside the protecting country, right holders may be able to claim that the offer itself infringes their patent in the protecting country; by doing so they can fight foreign utilization of their patented inventions outside the protecting country. However, such a strategy works against intended or actual sales outside the protecting country only if courts view offers to sell as stand-alone tortious acts of direct infringement and do not require that the sale that is being offered occur in the same country as the offer itself. This section reviews the doctrine of an infringing "offer to sell" and its application in assisting patent holders in fighting the utilization of their inventions outside protecting countries.

Jurisprudence concerning the issue of offers to sell developed during different periods in Germany and the United States and brought remarkably different results. In Germany "offer to sell" was first included in the Patent Act of 1877,[100] and after

[97] The German patent acts always included the act of "in Verkehr bringen," which is not only "selling"; it may also be understood as importation. According to Rudolf Kraßer, "[t]he importation as such is Inverkehrbringen only for the (foreign) exporter, not for the [German] importer." He admits that the jurisprudence and literature have not been consistent in differentiating between importation and "Inverkehrbringen." KRASSER, Chapter 1, note 15, 786.

[98] The 1994 Uruguay Round Agreements Act; TRIPs, Chapter 1, note 19, Article 28(1); 35 U.S.C. §154(a)(1).

[99] The infringing sale can also be found in these scenarios if the method of localization permits them to be captured. *See infra* Section 3.6. on the issue of localization of a sale.

[100] §4 of the Patent Act of 1877. The Act used the term "feilhalten," as opposed to the term "anbieten" that was used later. The term "feilhalten," somewhat more limited than "anbieten," was eventually interpreted so broadly

1891 "offer to sell" was expanded to prohibit offers in situations where products that were not themselves patented were made through patented processes. Based on the 1891 Act, holders of patents to processes held the same rights to products made through the patented processes as they did to the processes themselves, including the right to offer for sale.[101]

In the United States "offer to sell" was inserted into the U.S. Patent Act in 1994 as part of the implementation of U.S. obligations under the TRIPs Agreement, which in Article 28 includes "offering to sell" among the rights conferred upon a patent holder. "Offer to sell" was also added to Section 271(g) of the U.S. Patent Act,[102] which since 1988 has protected products in the United States that were made abroad by processes patented in the United States.[103] Prior to the 1994 amendment, offers to sell appeared in U.S. patent-related case law as forms of indirect infringement.[104] Whether an offer to sell is considered to be an act of direct or indirect infringement is significant because an "offer to sell", if considered only an act of *indirect* infringement, cannot apply to offers to sell where the sale is to occur abroad; only if an "offer to sell" is an act of direct infringement in the protecting country may an offer that concerns a sale abroad be actionable in the protecting country.

Before it can be determined whether offers made in a protecting country for sales that should or will occur abroad are infringing, it must be clarified what behavior constitutes an offer that will qualify as a patent-infringing act. The choice might fall anywhere on a continuum, with an advertisement on one end and a formal offer as defined by contract law on the other.[105] The closer the definition is to an

that it overlapped with "anbieten." On the history of the terminology, see Gerhard Schricker, *Anbieten als Verletzungstatbestand im Patent- und Urheberrecht*, 2004 GRUR INT. 786, 787–88.

[101] §4 of the Patent Act of 1891.

[102] *See infra* note 131.

[103] *See also* 35 U.S.C. §154(a)(1). The sections have been in the U.S. Patent Act since the 1988 Process Patent Amendments Act but did not mention "offer to sell" until the 1994 Uruguay Round Agreements Act. As Professor Chisum noted, although "[t]he focus of the legislation is upon foreign activity [(using a process abroad that is patented in the protecting country)], technically, the Process Act has no extraterritorial effect." Chisum, Chapter 1, note 173, 607. *See also* Ajinomoto Co., Inc. v. Archer-Daniels-Midland Co., 228 F.3d 1338, 1348 (Fed. Cir. 2000) (It "applies to unauthorized actions within the U.S.; it is irrelevant that the product was authorized to be produced outside the U.S."). The German provision also protects products made by patented processes not only in Germany but also abroad. *See, e.g., Diazepam*, Landgericht Düsseldorf, 4 O 99/68, Sept. 18, 1969, 1970 GRUR 550 ("Offer to sell and use of [an] ingredient in the [protecting country] is a patent infringement even when it [was] produced [by the patented process] abroad." *Id.*, 551.). On the relevant provision of the Paris Convention, see BODENHAUSEN, Chapter 1, note 68, 85.

[104] *See infra* Section 3.5.

[105] For a discussion of the various definitions of an offer to sell see Lucas S. Osborn, *Deconstructing an "Offer to Sell" in the Patent Infringement Context,* draft paper, on file with the author, 14 ff.

advertisement, the better for any patent holder, including a patent holder who attacks an offer that concerns a sale abroad.

German courts decided early on that an offer to sell for purposes of the Patent Act should *not* be defined in terms of contract law; instead, the courts have used economic criteria to assess whether particular conduct constitutes an offer to sell.[106] Therefore, negotiations of an individual contract were not the only activity that was deemed to constitute an infringing offer to sell;[107] showing marketing materials to potential buyers was also viewed as an infringing offer to sell.[108] For instance, the Düsseldorf Landgericht noted that acts of a Chinese company that exhibited infringing products at the CeBIT international fair in Hannover would be considered infringing offers to sell.[109] Although German courts recognize an exception for advertising at "general exhibitions" ("allgemein Leistungsschau"), which are exhibitions designed to "provide the expert circles and the public an overview of the state of the field, but do [. . .] not have a character of a sale exhibition or a fair,"[110] courts have construed this term narrowly. In the case of CeBit, the Düsseldorf Landgericht declined to extend the exception to CeBIT because CeBIT, as "the largest computer and electronics fair in the world[,] provides for establishment of contacts and making business,"[111] and therefore, exhibiting an infringing product at such an event is an infringing offer to sell.

In the United States after the 1994 Act introduced the "offer to sell," and as the first cases on the issue appeared in courts, commentators began to debate the proper definition of an "offer to sell." Some commentators advocated a definition of infringing conduct in strict contract law terms, reasoning that economic considerations dictated a limited approach. Others argued for a broader construction of the term that would "extend[. . .] beyond contractual offers"[112] because such an interpretation

---

[106] *E.g.*, *Kupplung für optische Geräte*, Bundesgerichtshof, X ZR 179/02, Sept. 16, 2003; *Thermocycler*, Oberlandesgericht Düsseldorf, 2 U 58/05, Dec. 21, 2006, 2007 GRUR-RR 259 ("The term 'offer' used in §9 [of the Patent Act] must be understood in the economic sense and does not coincide with the legal term of a contract offer." *Id.*, 261.). *See also* Schricker, *supra* note 101, 787.

[107] *Kreuzbodenventilsäcke*, Bundesgerichtshof, I ZR 109/58, Mar. 29, 1960, 1960 GRUR 423.

[108] *E.g.*, *Kupplung für optische Geräte*, *supra* note 106; Reichsgericht, I 137/33, Jan. 13, 1934, RGZ 29, 173; *Zeitlagenmultiplexverfahren*, Landgericht Düsseldorf, 4a O 124/05, Feb. 13, 2007.

[109] *Zeitlagenmultiplexverfahren*, *supra* note 108.

[110] *Zeitlagenmultiplexverfahren*, *supra* note 108; *Heißläuferdetektor*, Bundesgerichtshof, X ZR 52/67, Dec. 18, 1969, 1970 GRUR 358. "An exhibition and presentation at a 'Leistungsschau' is only then an 'industrial use' within the meaning of §6(1) of the Patent Act when the exhibitor pursues a mercantile purpose." *Id.*, 360.

[111] *Zeitlagenmultiplexverfahren*, *supra* note 108.

[112] Edwin D. Garlepp, *An Analysis of the Patentee's New Exclusive Right to "Offer to Sell,"* 81 J. Pat. & Trademark Off. Soc'y 315, 319 (1999).

would serve better the needs of patent holders[113] and reflect "[t]he history of the GATT implementing legislation,"[114] which led to Congress's intent "to significantly strengthen patent law."[115]

The U.S. Court of Appeals for the Federal Circuit first addressed the offer to sell problem in 1998 in *3D Systems, Inc. v. Aarotech Laboratories, Inc.*[116] in the context of a discussion of personal jurisdiction. For the purposes of personal jurisdiction, the court adopted an approach broader than that of contract law and found that "price quotation letters [could] be regarded as 'offer[s] to sell.'"[117] Some thirteen months later the court had its first opportunity to consider the term in a decision on the merits in *Rotec Indus., Inc. v. Mitsubishi Corp.*[118] The court derived guidance from a then-recent Supreme Court decision on the "on sale" bar to patentability;[119] because the Supreme Court construed a "commercial offer for sale" in contract law terms[120] the Circuit Court concluded that the definition of an "offer to sell" for infringement purposes should be guided by "the norms of traditional contractual analysis."[121] Since in *Rotec* the defendant's communication with the potential purchaser did not comply with the definition of an offer in contract law the court found no "offer to sell" within the meaning of the Patent Act.[122]

The current definition of "offer to sell" used by the U.S. Court of Appeals for the Federal Circuit thus differs dramatically from the definition used in German courts; as a result a much wider range of acts fall within the scope of an infringing "offer to sell" in Germany than in the United States.[123] The rigid approach taken by the

---

[113] Garlepp, *supra* note 112, 319.

[114] Robert Ryan Morishita, *Patent Infringement After GATT: What Is an Offer to Sell?*, 1997 UTAH L. REV. 905, 912.

[115] Morishita, *supra* note 114. For a review of the relevant legislative history, see *id.*, 912–13.

[116] 3D Systems, Inc. v. Aarotech Laboratories, Inc., 160 F.3d 1373 (Fed. Cir. 1998).

[117] *Id.*, 1379. The court explicitly declined to "import the authority construing the 'on sale' bar."

[118] Rotec Indus., Inc. v. Mitsubishi Corp., 215 F.3d 1246 (Fed. Cir. 2000).

[119] Pfaff v. Wells Electronics, Inc., 525 U.S. 55 (1998). "On sale bar" is a term that describes a bar to patentability presented by a sale in the United States "more than one year prior to the date of the application for patent in the United States." 35 U.S.C. §102(b).

[120] Pfaff v. Wells Electronics, Inc., 525 U.S. 55, 67 (1998). The Supreme Court looked at an acceptance of the purchase order (clearly a contract law concept) to conclude that "the sale was commercial rather than experimental in character." *Id.*

[121] Rotec Indus., Inc. v. Mitsubishi Corp., 215 F.3d 1246, 1254–55 (Fed. Cir. 2000). *See also* Transocean Offshore Deepwater Drilling, Inc. v. Maersk Contractors USA, Inc., 617 F.3d 1296, 1308 (Fed. Cir. 2010).

[122] The court used the definition of an offer in the Restatement (Second) of Contracts, §24 (1979): "An offer is the manifestation of willingness to enter into a bargain, so made as to justify another person in understanding that his assent to that bargain is invited and will conclude it." Rotec Indus., Inc. v. Mitsubishi Corp., 215 F.3d 1246, 1257 (Fed. Cir. 2000).

[123] The court in *Rotec* commented on the situation in the United Kingdom where "the common law of contract does not limit the meaning of 'offer for sale' in the context of patent infringement." Rotec Indus., Inc. v. Mitsubishi Corp., 215 F.3d 1246, 1253 (Fed. Cir. 2000).

U.S. Court of Appeals for the Federal Circuit to the interpretation of an "offer" contrasts with the liberal approach that U.S. courts have adopted in their interpretation of a "sale"; the definition of a sale becomes important when the place of an infringing sale needs to be determined, as discussed below in Section 3.6. Although the interpretation by the U.S. Court of Appeals for the Federal Circuit of an infringing "offer" is quite limited and is likely to have an adverse impact on patent holders' abilities to reach those who utilize their inventions anywhere, what is even more important for evaluating the usability of the "offer to sell" provision for fighting conduct outside a protecting country is whether patent holders may use an "offer to sell" to capture an offer that concerns a sale outside the protecting country. In other words, would an offer made in the United States be infringing if it concerned a sale of goods that should occur in China?

In Germany courts have held that an offer to sell is infringing regardless of where the eventual sale is intended to occur or where it actually occurs. For an offer to sell that is made in Germany to be infringing, goods at issue need not be present in Germany at the time of the offer or at any later time, or even be intended to ever enter Germany.[124] Therefore, even offers to sell made at trade fairs in Germany with the intent for the sale to take place outside Germany were found sufficient acts of infringement.[125] An offer made in Germany to sell goods abroad resulted in a finding of an infringing offer to sell in Germany even when the goods were marked clearly as "for sale outside Germany."[126]

It is remarkable that the elements controlling whether there is an infringing offer to sell are the opposite in the United States and Germany; in the United States the controlling element is the location of the sale, while in Germany it is the location of the offer itself. Under the current interpretation that the U.S. Court of Appeals for the Federal Circuit pronounced in *Transocean Offshore Deepwater Drilling, Inc. v. Maersk Contractors USA, Inc.*,[127] "the location of the contemplated sale controls

---

[124] Reichsgericht, I 137/33, Jan. 13, 1934, RGZ 29, 173; *Kreuzbodenventilsäcke*, *supra* note 107.

[125] *Messeangebot ins Ausland I*, Landgericht München I, 21 O 6421/01, June 23, 2004, 5 ENTSCHEIDUNGEN DER INSTANZGERICHTE ZUM RECHT DES GEISTIGEN EIGENTUMS 13 (2004); appeal denied in *Messeangebot ins Ausland I*, Oberlandesgericht München, 6 W 2048/04, Sept. 16, 2004. The appeals court rejected the opinion of Jochen Pagenberg that the offer to sell, even though an independent tort, should be interpreted in a restrictive manner. *Id. See* Jochen Pagenberg, *Ausstellen und Anbieten auf internationalen Messen—eine Verletzung inländischer gewerblicher Schutzrechte?*, 1983 GRUR INT. 560.

[126] *Messeangebot ins Ausland I*, *supra* note 125. *See also Infrarot-Messgerät*, Landgericht Düsseldorf, 4b O 388/03, Feb. 5, 2004, 4 ENTSCHEIDUNGEN DER INSTANZGERICHTE ZUM RECHT DES GEISTIGEN EIGENTUMS 90 (2003). In this case the device was exported from Germany, rebuilt in the United States and labeled as "assembled in USA with parts from Germany." The court referred to *Kreuzbodenventilsäcke* when it decided that there was also an infringing offer to sell. *Id.*

[127] Transocean Offshore Deepwater Drilling, Inc. v. Maersk Contractors USA, Inc., 617 F.3d 1296 (Fed. Cir. 2010).

whether there is an offer to sell within the United States,"[128] which means that an offer made anywhere in the world for a sale in the United States will be infringing under U.S. patent law, but an offer made in the United States for a sale outside the United States will not constitute a patent infringing act.[129]

Prior to the 2010 decision in *Transocean Offshore*, the interpretation of the U.S. statutory language was unclear, and no relevant legislative history existed that would shed light on the problem.[130] When the "offer to sell" concept was introduced into the Patent Act in 1994[131] Congress omitted any explanation as to what the subsequent phrase "within the United States" modified.[132] Three options appeared possible: the offer to sell itself must be made in the United States but the place of sale does not matter,[133] the offer to sell can be made anywhere but the sale must occur or be intended to occur in the United States,[134] or both the offer to sell must occur and the sale must occur or be intended to occur in the United States.[135] Commentators disagreed on the correct interpretation of the ambiguous language of the Act;[136] one commentator suggested that "a reading that requires only that an offer be within the United States to infringe §271(a) may be an impermissible expansion of the territorial scope of U.S. patent laws."[137]

---

[128] *Id.*, 1309.

[129] Although the holding in the case refers only to the specific scenario in which two U.S. companies negotiate abroad a contract for performance in the United States (Transocean Offshore Deepwater Drilling, Inc. v. Maersk Contractors USA, Inc., 617 F.3d 1296, 1310 (Fed. Cir. 2010)), dicta suggest that the rule will apply even if non-U.S. companies are involved: "The focus should not be on the location of the offer, but rather the location of the future sale that would occur pursuant to the offer." *Id.*, 1309.

[130] Even if it considered offers to sell, pre-1994 case law would not be of assistance because it had only considered offers to sell in the context of indirect infringement. *See infra* Section 3.5 for a discussion of the territorial scope of provisions on indirect infringement.

[131] "Offer to sell" was added in 35 U.S.C. §271 in paragraphs (a), (c), (e), and (g).

[132] In paragraphs (a) and (g) the words "within the United States" remained from the previous versions of the law; however, in (c) and (e) the words "within the United States" were added by the 1994 Act. It has been debated what, if anything, the insertion of "within the United States" should mean; however, a review of the 1994 Act reveals that the legislator probably wished only to make the wording in all four paragraphs consistent and used the wording from paragraph (a) for this purpose. Professor Chisum noted that "[t]here appear[ed] to be no policy reason for restricting Section 271(c) in this fashion. The change may have been a grammatical indiscretion." Chisum, Chapter 1, note 173, 615.

[133] Garlepp, *supra* note 112, 325.

[134] Holbrook, *Territoriality*, Chapter 1, note 5, 728.

[135] Garlepp, *supra* note 112, 325.

[136] "With legislative history silent, an interpretation based solely on the mechanics of the English language may indicate Congressional intent to adopt the broader reading." Garlepp, *supra* note 112, 325. "Given the lack of guidance in the legislative history and the ambiguous statutory language, the presumption should not be conclusive as to the extraterritorial reach of 'offers to sell,' and the appropriate scope merits further discussion." Holbrook, *Territoriality*, Chapter 1, note 5, 731. *See also* Chisum, Chapter 1, note 173, 615.

[137] Garlepp, *supra* note 112, 326.

In 2000 *Rotec* offered an opportunity to clarify whether the sale needed to occur or be intended to occur in the United States, but the majority in that case avoided the issue; only Judge Newman in her concurring opinion addressed the issue, opining that only if the intended sale would infringe a U.S. patent could the offer to sell be infringing.[138] She reasoned that the statutory requirement that the offered "sale will occur before the expiration of the term of the patent"[139] meant that the patent must be valid under U.S. law at the time of the intended sale, and therefore the sale must have been envisaged in the United States because it was only in the United States where a U.S. patent could be valid.[140]

In *Transocean Offshore*[141] the U.S. Court of Appeals for the Federal Circuit explained that because the place of the intended sale is controlling, an offer made in Norway for delivery and use in the United States will infringe a U.S. patent.[142] This interpretation finally provides needed guidance to district courts, which split in their decisions on the issue prior to *Transocean Offshore*; some courts held that the sale need not occur or be intended to occur in the United States, while other courts insisted that the sale must occur or be intended to occur in the United States.[143] For instance, in *Wesley Jessen Corp. v. Bausch & Lomb, Inc.*[144] the U.S. District Court for the District of Delaware noted that "[t]he geographic location and physical destination of the subject matter of the 'offer' appear to be immaterial to the analysis, so long as the 'offer' was made in the United States."[145] The court decided that "the 'sale' contemplated by the 'offer to sell' need not take place in the United States or be intended to take place in the United States for there to be infringement because of the 'offer to sell.'"[146] Other courts disagreed; for instance, in *Semiconductor Energy Laboratory Co., Ltd. v. Chi Mei Optoelectronics Corp.*[147] the U.S. District Court for

[138] Rotec Indus., Inc. v. Mitsubishi Corp., 215 F.3d 1246, 1258–60 (Fed. Cir. 2000).

[139] 35 U.S.C. §271(i).

[140] 35 U.S.C. §271(i) does not actually specify that the patent must be a U.S. patent, an omission that has generated debate over whether the Act could have contemplated a foreign patent as well. Holbrook, *Territoriality*, Chapter 1, note 5, 748 ff.

[141] Transocean Offshore Deepwater Drilling, Inc. v. Maersk Contractors USA, Inc., 617 F.3d 1296 (Fed. Cir. 2010).

[142] "In order for an offer to sell to constitute infringement, the offer must be to sell a patented invention within the United States." *Id.*, 1309.

[143] For a helpful recent overview of various district court decisions, see, e.g., Transocean Offshore Deepwater Drilling, Inc. v. Stena Drilling Ltd., 659 F.Supp.2d 790 (S.D.Tex. 2009).

[144] Wesley Jessen Corp. v. Bausch & Lomb, Inc., 256 F.Supp.2d 228 (D. Del. 2003).

[145] *Id.*, 233.

[146] *Id.*, 234.

[147] Semiconductor Energy Laboratory Co., Ltd. v. Chi Mei Optoelectronics Corp., 531 F.Supp.2d 1084 (N.D.Cal. 2007).

the Northern District of California emphasized "the strong presumption against extraterritorial application," and decided that "an 'offer of sale' may constitute direct infringement only if the sale is intended to take place within the United States."[148]

The requirement that a sale must occur or be intended to occur in the United States for the offer to sell to be infringing significantly limits the usefulness of the prohibition against an "offer to sell" in any fight in the United States against foreign utilization of patented inventions. By contrast, the broad interpretation that German courts attach to offers to sell and the fact that the sale need not occur in Germany or be intended to occur in Germany enables holders of German patents to reach those who engage in acts leading to foreign utilization of their inventions. In the United States the utility of the offer to sell in fighting foreign exploitations of the invention will depend on where the act of selling is localized; this problem is discussed below in Section 3.6.

3.4 Inventions Assembled Abroad from Components from a Protecting Country

Another means of stopping or curtailing the utilization of an invention abroad is to prevent exportation from a protecting country of components that are to be used in assembling the patented product abroad. If patent holders can prevent the exportation of components from the protecting country, they will likely have a significant impact on possible utilization of the assembled product abroad. Often cases involving these facts include situations in which manufacturers or suppliers of components in a protecting country realize that they would infringe a patent if they manufactured or supplied the product fully assembled; therefore, they try to circumvent the patent protection by avoiding the final assembly and manufacturing, and supplying only disassembled components of the final product.

In Germany and the United States the mechanisms to fight the supplying of parts developed in different manners but arrived at a similar, though not identical, result. German courts were successful very early at prohibiting conduct involving component supply by applying the existing doctrines of direct infringement through manufacture and offer to sell. As the following paragraphs show, a finding of intent on the part of an alleged infringer was the key to these cases. In the United States the landmark decision of *Deepsouth Packing Co. v. Laitram Corp.*[149] revealed that U.S. case

[148] *Id.*, 1111.

[149] Deepsouth Packing Co. v. Laitram Corp., 406 U.S. 518 (1972).

law would not extend the then-current doctrines to cover scenarios involving components supplied abroad; the realization that such a loophole existed in U.S. law led to legislative intervention that introduced new forms of direct infringement specifically tailored to address component situations.

In Germany direct infringements through manufacture or offer to sell have been found when there was knowledge on the part of the infringer about the subsequent use of the components. For instance, in 1888 the Reichsgericht held that infringement would be found whenever a defendant intended for noninfringing components to be assembled outside Germany into a product that would have infringed a German patent if it were assembled in Germany.[150] It is interesting that in these scenarios the intent of the alleged infringer matters, because normally no intent is required for a finding of direct patent infringement.

The intent of an infringer may be apparent either from acts performed by the infringer (such as an offer to sell accompanied by information about how to assemble the components abroad) or from the nature of the components. The fact that the components at issue are not "neutral"[151] but "are exclusively suitable to be assembled into the product"[152] suggests that when dealing with the components the alleged infringer must have been aware of their singular use. These "specific components"[153] in the German patent law correspond to what the U.S. Patent Act calls "material part[s] of the invention," which are defined as parts "especially made or especially adapted for use in an infringement of [the] patent."[154] The U.S. Patent Act further explains that "staple article[s] or commodit[ies] of commerce suitable for substantial noninfringing use" are not "material parts" of an invention.[155] As long as the "specific components" are at issue, German courts find direct infringement; for "neutral components" they require that specific knowledge of the intended use of the components be proven.[156]

---

[150] Reichsgericht, I 86/88, May 5, 1888, RGZ 22, 165; Reimer, *Patentverletzung*, Chapter 1, note 6, 88.

[151] The Reichsgericht in an 1897 decision characterized "neutral components" as parts that were of general purpose, could be generally replaced, and therefore did not "embody any special value." Reichsgericht, I 98/97, Sept. 18, 1897, RGZ 22, 78.

[152] *Diffusor*, Landgericht Düsseldorf, 6 Entscheidungen der Instanzgerichte zum Recht des geistigen Eigentums 130 (2005); *Isolierglasscheiben II*, Landgericht Düsseldorf, 4aO 220/07, Aug. 5, 2008.

[153] "Die erfindungsfunktionell individualisierte Teile."

[154] 35 U.S.C. §271(c), §271(f)(2).

[155] 35 U.S.C. §271(c), §271(f)(2). In 1871 the Connecticut District Court in *Wallace v. Holmes* considered a person to be indirectly liable for patent infringement; what was dispositive of the case was "the certain knowledge" by the defendant that the unpatented components were "to be used, as they [could] only be used," in the assembled product. Wallace v. Holmes, 29 F. Cas. 74, 80 (D. Conn. 1871).

[156] In *Verbolzung* the Düsseldorf Oberlandesgericht found no direct infringement because no manufacture or use was proven that would indicate that the components were specifically prepared to be used in

An 1897 case illustrates the approach taken by German courts with regard to the manufacture of components intended for foreign assembly; the Reichsgericht in the case held that the defendant infringed when it manufactured components in Germany and shipped them to Denmark and Switzerland for assembly.[157] The court reasoned that "manufacturing of a patent encompasses the entire activity necessary for a production of the product from its very beginning";[158] the court rejected as against the meaning of the statutory text and purpose of the law the argument that the term "manufacturing" would encompass only "the activities immediately leading up to the completion"[159] of the product. The court suggested that it was indefensible to define the place of manufacture as only the place of assembly abroad; such a narrow definition would permit the manufacture of components in Germany in preparation for assembly of the final product abroad where the invention was not protected.[160]

The same conclusion was reached in other German cases concerning the manufacture of components. For instance, in 1935 the Reichsgericht found infringement where the defendant manufactured two parts of a patented invention that were individually noninfringing; the defendant exported the parts abroad where customers could easily assemble them and use the invention in the form in which it was patented in Germany.[161] In a 2004 case the Düsseldorf Landgericht held that it was an infringement in the form of manufacture when the defendant manufactured a product in Germany that the defendant then sold to a customer abroad in a noninfringing form but with the understanding that the defendant would provide instructions and a component to convert the product abroad into a product corresponding to the device patented in Germany.[162] Although one commentator recently expressed doubts "whether the broad interpretation of the term 'making' favored by German courts in the past [could] still be applied,"[163] for now the law in Germany

infringing products. The defendant supplied one component abroad but did not do so with the intent that the component be combined with another component (which happened to be supplied by the plaintiff—the exclusive license holder) into the final product that corresponded to the German patented invention. *Verbolzung*, Oberlandesgericht Düsseldorf, 2 U 133/61, Jan. 11, 1963, 1964 GRUR 203.

[157] Reichsgericht, I 98/97, Sept. 18, 1897, RGZ 22, 78.

[158] *Id.*, 79.

[159] *Id.*, 79.

[160] *Id.*, 80.

[161] *Stabeisenbiegevorrichtung*, Reichsgericht, Aug. 30, 1935, 1936 GRUR 236; *see also* Stauder, *Patent Infringement*, *supra* note 8, 495–96. *See also Dia-Rämchen V*, Bundesgerichtshof, X ZR 4/65, July 14, 1970, 1971 GRUR 78, 80 (in a purely domestic context but summarizing the relevant jurisprudence).

[162] *Infrarot-Messgerät*, *supra* note 126.

[163] Rainer Moufang, *The Extraterritorial Reach of Patent Law*, *in* PATENTS AND TECHNOLOGICAL PROGRESS IN A GLOBALIZED WORLD—LIBER AMICORUM JOSEPH STRAUS 601, 607 (Wolrad Prinz zu Waldeck und

remains that manufacture of components in Germany for assembly abroad is patent infringing.[164]

In addition to the manufacture of components, offers to sell components for assembly abroad have also been considered acts of direct infringement actionable under the German Patent Act; again, the defendant's knowledge of the intended use of the components was dispositive of the issue. For instance, in *Kreuzbodenventilsäcke*[165] the Bundesgerichtshof found infringement where the manufacturer offered to deliver noninfringing components abroad with the promise that it would send its own technicians to set up the product abroad so that it would correspond to the invention patented in Germany. The court agreed with plaintiff's contention that the defendant engaged in an infringing offer to sell when it offered to supply the noninfringing components and explained that "an offer to sell is infringing when it is obvious that the recipient of the offer is supposed to receive the product in its patent infringing form."[166]

When the United States extended the protection of the patent law to "specific parts"—"material parts of inventions"—in 1952, it limited the protection to acts of sale; "making" was left out of the provision. However, and more importantly, the provision was drafted to codify existing case law on contributory infringement,[167] which meant that it would cover only acts of indirect infringement related to an act of direct infringement committed in the United States;[168] it was not drafted to apply to instances in which the related assembly occurred outside the United States.[169] For this reason the provision was of no assistance in the landmark case of *Deepsouth*, which was decided by the U.S. Supreme Court in 1972 and which prompted a legislative response.

In *Deepsouth*, Laitram held patents on a shrimp deveining machine that Deepsouth allegedly infringed; Deepsouth argued that it should be permitted to manufacture components of the machine in the United States and sell them to

---

Pyrmont, Martin J. Adelman, Robert Brauneis, Josef Drexl, & Ralph Nack eds., 2009). "Even in situations where the facts indicate that the alleged infringer actively induces or even controls the ultimate step in the process of manufacture carried out abroad, it cannot be neglected that it is outside the territory of production where this ultimate step takes place, *i.e.* where the patented product is made." *Id.*, 607–08.

[164] Rudolf Busse, Patentgesetz 222 (1999).

[165] *Kreuzbodenventilsäcke*, *supra* note 107.

[166] *Id.*

[167] For a further discussion of acts of indirect infringement under the U.S. Patent Act, see *infra* Section 3.5.

[168] Wallace v. Holmes, 29 F. Cas. 74 (D. Conn. 1871).

[169] *See infra* Section 3.5 for a discussion of provision 35 U.S.C. §271(c).

customers abroad for assembly of the machines outside the United States.[170] The U.S. Supreme Court rejected the holding of the U.S. Court of Appeals for the Fifth Circuit that the "substantial manufacture of the constituent parts of [a] machine" constituted an act of direct infringement[171]—a holding by the Circuit Court that had matched the German approach. In rejecting the argument that direct infringement had occurred, the Supreme Court reiterated its earlier position that "a combination patent protects only against the operable assembly of the whole and not the manufacture of its parts."[172] The Court was divided in its decision—four Justices filed a dissenting opinion—and, not surprisingly, a legislative response overruled the decision in 1984.

The 1984 amendment to the U.S. Patent Act introduced two new forms of direct patent infringement;[173] one focuses on "material parts" of inventions, and the second covers "non-material parts" of inventions, or what German courts call "neutral parts." Section 271(f)(2) states that a direct infringement occurs when a component that is a material part of the invention is supplied or caused to be supplied "in or from the United States" with knowledge that it is a material part of an invention and with the intent that the component be combined into a final assembled product outside the United States.[174] Section 271(f)(1) covers "non-material parts" and considers as a direct infringer one who "supplies or causes to be supplied in or from the United States all or a substantial portion of the components [. . .] in such manner as to actively induce the combination of such components outside the United States."[175]

Notwithstanding the differing approaches of their legislative solutions, the German and U.S. results are largely overlapping. German law, however, has broader scope because it covers acts that could be described as being in preparation for "supplying or causing to supply"—it covers the manufacture of components and offers to sell when the acts are accompanied by knowledge that components will be assembled, but an act of actual supplying abroad is not required for a finding of infringement. By contrast, Section 271 of the U.S. Patent Act does not prohibit the manufacture of components in the United States or offers made in the United States

[170] Deepsouth Packing Co. v. Laitram Corp., 406 U.S. 518, 523 (1972). As the Supreme Court noted in a footnote, "Deepsouth [was] entirely straightforward in indicating that its course of conduct [was] motivated by a desire to avoid patent infringement." *Id.*

[171] Laitram Corp. v. Deepsouth Packing Co., 443 F.2d 936, 939 (5th Cir. 1971).

[172] Deepsouth Packing Co. v. Laitram Corp., 406 U.S. 518, 528 (1972).

[173] 35 U.S.C. §271(f)(2) does not incorporate contributory infringement; it is a new category of direct infringement. Waymark Corp. v. Porta Sys. Corp., 245 F.3d 1364, 1460 (Fed. Cir. 2001).

[174] 35 U.S.C. §271(f)(2). The provision was added in 1984.

[175] 35 U.S.C. §271(f)(1). The provision was added in 1984. *See infra* Section 3.5 for a discussion of the requirement of intent under the U.S. Patent Act.

to sell components abroad;[176] it is questionable whether "supplying or causing to supply" components under the U.S. Patent Act could cover all acts involved in "making, offering to sell, selling, using or importing" components that may be actionable under the German Patent Act.

3.5 Acts Abroad Contributing to Infringements in the Protecting Country

The previous sections discussed scenarios in which acts in the protecting country led to further utilization of an invention abroad. The opposite scenario involves an act abroad (offer to sell, sale, or export of an invention or its components) that is directed at the protecting country and leads to further acts in the protecting country (importation, use, further offer of sale, sale) that infringe a patent. Although in such situations it should be possible to target direct infringers in the protecting country (importers, distributors, end users), patent holders may sometimes attempt to attack abroad "at the source"; such a tactic may be motivated by patent holders' hopes that attacking at the source will significantly reduce future infringements that are or may be unrelated to the current channels of distribution. Additionally, patent holders may pursue actors abroad because it is impractical to target direct infringers in the protecting country; direct infringers might lack sufficient assets or be difficult to identify, as is typically the case with end users.[177] Alternatively, there could be tactical reasons to attempt to pull a party acting abroad into the litigation in the particular protecting country; it might be more difficult to attack "the source" abroad, in the country where the acts were committed, or it might be inconvenient for the patent holder or even impossible if he lacks a parallel patent in the other country.

Sometimes defining the location of the acts will help to fight such acts abroad; if the acts can be localized in multiple locations, including in the protecting country, the conditions of direct infringement may be satisfied in the protecting country.[178] But even if the acts can only be localized abroad, the doctrine of indirect infringement[179] may still allow courts to adjudicate these acts—as long as the doctrine extends to the acts of indirect infringement committed abroad. While it is established law that indirect infringement requires related acts of direct infringement in

[176] 35 U.S.C. §271(c) and (f).

[177] Sometimes there may be public relations reasons for not targeting end users.

[178] *See infra* Section 3.6 for a discussion of localization of infringing acts.

[179] "Mittelbare Patentverletzung" in German.

the protecting country,[180] the answers may vary to the question of where the acts of indirect infringement must occur—whether the acts of indirect infringement must also be committed in the protecting country, or whether they can occur abroad as long as the related acts of direct infringement can be localized in the protecting country.

Prior to the adoption of legislation on indirect patent infringement, doctrines had existed in both Germany and the United States that covered some of the acts that were committed abroad; before the 1952 amendment to the U.S. Patent Act, which added two forms of indirect infringement, the tort law concept of aiding and abetting was applied to circumscribe the behavior of those "who did not commit an act of direct infringement but rather enabled others to do so."[181] In Germany the general doctrines of participating in and aiding and abetting a tortious activity[182] covered acts committed abroad, and the doctrines continue to be used today, even after a specific provision on indirect infringement was included in the German Patent Act.

The provisions on indirect infringement added to the U.S. Patent Act in 1952 divided indirect infringements into inducement under Section 271(b) and contributory infringement under Section 271(c).[183] The legislative treatment of inducement tracked cases in which "efforts to induce infringement" were treated "as evidence supporting the requisite affirmative intent for a case of [indirect] infringement."[184] The fact that the provision does not explicitly include the requirement of "knowing" created uncertainty about the requirement of intent; the U.S. Supreme Court clarified the requirement of intent in *Global-Tech Appliances, Inc. v. SEB, S.A.* by ruling that Section 271(b) "requires knowledge that the induced acts constitute patent

[180] For the requirement of direct infringement for a finding of inducement in the United States, see Joy Techs., Inc. v. Flakt, Inc., 6 F.3d 770, 774 (Fed. Cir. 1993); Read Corp. v. Powerscreen of America, Inc., 44 Fed. Appx. 502 (Fed. Cir. 2002); Ricoh Company, Ltd. v. Quanta Computer, Inc., 550 F.3d 1325, 1341–43 (Fed. Cir. 2009). For the requirement of direct infringement for a finding of contributory infringement in the United States, see Aro Manufacturing Co. v. Convertible Top Replacement Co., 365 U.S. 366 (1961). For the requirement of a finding of intent of direct infringement for indirect infringement in Germany, see *Funkuhr II*, Bundesgerichtshof, X ZR 53/04, Jan. 30, 2007; *Flügelradzähler*, Bundesgerichtshof, X ZR 48/03, May 4, 2004, BGHZ 159, 76, 2004 GRUR 758. *But cf. Deckenheizung*, Bundesgerichtshof, X ZR 153/03, June 13, 2006, 2006 GRUR 839, 841.

[181] Chisum, Chapter 1, note 173, 614–15. *See, e.g.*, Wallace v. Holmes, 29 F. Cas. 74 (D. Conn. 1871).

[182] Civil Code, §830.

[183] "Before 1952, both the conduct now covered by 35 U.S.C. §271(b) (inducement of infringement) and the conduct now addressed by 35 U.S.C. §271(c) (sale of a component of a patented invention) were viewed as falling within the overarching concept of 'contributory infringement.'" Global-Tech Appliances, Inc. v. SEB, S.A., 131 S.Ct. 2060, 2066 (2011).

[184] Mark Lemley, *Inducing Patent Infringement*, 39 U.C. Davis L. Rev. 225, 227 (2005). On the interpretation of the terms "inducement," "active," and the issue of the required intent in 271(b) see *id.*, 228–41.

infringement,"[185] and this requirement may be satisfied by an infringer's willful blindness.[186]

The treatment of contributory infringement under Section 271(c) of the U.S. Patent Act followed cases that involved components of patented inventions where the nature of the components alone evidenced intent of subsequent direct infringement. A contributory infringer is one who "offers to sell or sells within the United States or imports into the United States a component" of a patented invention knowing that the component is "a material part of the invention."[187]

An act of inducement may be committed outside the U.S. territory,[188] and given the broad language of Section 271(b), the possibility exists that a wide variety of acts abroad may be viewed as inducement of patent infringement.[189] The provision on contributory infringement in Section 271(c), however, applies only to acts of offers to sell or sales "within the United States" and importation "into the United States."[190] Language that was intended to territorially limit the scope of the contributory infringement provision was added to the Act in 1994, and it prevents use of the provision against acts committed abroad. Before 1994 courts had found that conduct outside the United States could lead to contributory liability under the provision; since 1994 the provision has been limited solely to conduct in the United States. Of course, the recent interpretation by the U.S. Court of Appeals for the Federal Circuit in *Transocean Offshore*[191] of "offer to sell" in the context of Section 271(a) opens the door to the possibility that the "offer to sell" under Section 271(c) could also encompass offers made outside the United States for sale of components in the United States.[192]

---

[185] Global-Tech Appliances, Inc. v. SEB, S.A., 131 S.Ct. 2060, 2068 (2011).

[186] *Id.*

[187] A "material part of the invention" is a part "made or especially adapted for use in an infringement of [the] patent"; a component that is either "a staple article" or "a commodity of commerce suitable for substantial noninfringing use" is excluded from the protection under this provision. *See supra* Section 3.4.

[188] Holbrook, *Territoriality*, Chapter 1, note 5, 717; *see also* Honeywell Intern. Inc. v. Acer America Corp., 655 F.Supp.2d 650 (E.D.Tex. 2009) ("[U]nder the current state of the law, the scope of section 271(b) can extend to extra-territorial activities." *Id.*, 660); Wing Shing Products (BVI), Ltd. v. Simatelex Manufactory Co., Ltd., 479 F.Supp.2d 388, 410 (S.D.N.Y. 2007).

[189] *See, e.g.*, the decision allowing discovery against a Taiwanese defendant concerning the defendant's activities outside the United States in Honeywell Intern. Inc. v. Acer America Corp., 655 F.Supp.2d 650 (E.D.Tex. 2009).

[190] 35 U.S.C. §271(c).

[191] Transocean Offshore Deepwater Drilling, Inc. v. Maersk Contractors USA, Inc., 617 F.3d 1296 (Fed. Cir. 2010).

[192] *See supra* Section 3.3 for a discussion of the territorial extent of the "offer to sell."

As discussed earlier in Section 3.3, the current interpretation in the United States of an infringing "offer to sell" in Section 271(a) rendered the "offer to sell" de facto an act of indirect infringement. Although it may appear from the statutory text that an offer to sell should be an act of direct infringement, as are the other acts enumerated in Section 271(a), by making the place of the intended sale the decisive element of the analysis[193] the U.S. Court of Appeals for the Federal Circuit placed the act of offer to sell in the category of indirect infringement, which requires a related act of direct infringement (the act of sale) in the United States. This is not the first time that a court has interpreted an act of infringement as an act of indirect infringement notwithstanding the fact that Congress placed the act among the acts of direct infringements. In *Subafilms, Ltd. v. MGM-Pathe Communications Co.*[194] the U.S. Court of Appeals for the Ninth Circuit explained that the legislative addition of the acts of "authorization" to the exclusive rights under the U.S. Copyright Act did not result in the creation of new grounds for finding direct infringement but only ratified the existing grounds of indirect liability.[195] Under the U.S. Court of Appeals for the Federal Circuit's interpretation of "offer to sell" it also appears that the addition of the act of "offer to sell" to the Patent Act only reiterated a form of indirect infringement that in most cases could probably be covered by the inducement provision of Section 271(b).[196]

The provision on indirect infringement that was inserted into the German Patent Act in 1980[197] is also limited to acts committed "within the territory of the application of the Act," i.e., in Germany.[198] Under Article 10, a contributory infringer is one who offers to sell or supplies a component "related to an essential element of the invention" "for use of the invention in Germany."[199] For an indirect infringement to

[193] *See supra* note 129.

[194] Subafilms, Ltd. v. MGM-Pathe Communications Co., 24 F.3d 1088 (1994).

[195] *Id.*, 1093.

[196] Inducement could not have been found in *Transocean Offshore* because there the alleged infringer did not induce infringement; instead, the alleged infringer reserved "the option to alter the rig to avoid infringement." Transocean Offshore Deepwater Drilling, Inc. v. Maersk Contractors USA, Inc., 617 F.3d 1296, 1308 (Fed. Cir. 2010).

[197] The provision was modeled after Article 30 of the 1975 Community Patent Convention. Convention for the European Patent for the Common Market, 1976 O.J. (L 17) 1. Cyrill P. Rigamonti, *Theorie und Praxis der mittelbaren Patentverletzung*, 2009 Mitteilungen der deutschen Patentanwälte 57, 58.

[198] The condition of the so-called "double connection" requires that 1) the offer or the supply be directed at Germany, and 2) the expected use following the offer or the supply (the acts of direct infringement) also occur in Germany. *See, e.g., Luftdruck-Kontrollvorrichtung*, Landgericht Mannheim, 7 O 412/03, June 25, 2004, 5 Entscheidungen der Instanzgerichte zum Recht des geistigen Eigentums 179, 181 (2004).

[199] Article 8(4) of the Patent Act of Dec. 16, 1980; Article 10(1) of the current Patent Act. For a history of the concept of "mittelbare Patentverletzung"—or "indirect patent infringement"—in Germany, see Jan Busche, *Mittelbare Patentverletzung—zu den dogmatischen Grundlagen eines Rechtsinstituts*, 2009 GRUR 236, 237–38.

be found under this provision, the indirect infringer must have known—or it had to be obvious to the indirect infringer from the circumstances—that the components "are suitable and intended to be employed in the use of the invention."[200] Components "commonly available on the market" are generally excluded from the provision on indirect infringement, with one exception: an indirect infringement will occur when someone offers to sell or supplies "components commonly available on the market" that pertain to a patented process when the infringer induces the purchaser or the entity supplied to either use the components to run the patented process, or offer the components for use in the patented process.[201]

Although acts of indirect infringement committed outside of Germany are excluded from Article 10, this exclusion does not preclude patent holders from using the provision against someone involved in utilizing their inventions abroad. In *Funkuhr II*[202] the Bundesgerichtshof explained that a German company may be liable under the provision when it supplies a component from Germany abroad; the court reiterated that "[a]n indirect patent infringement can [. . .] be committed by supplying means that relate to an essential element of the invention abroad if they are to contribute to the manufacture there of a product according to the invention which is intended for supply to Germany."[203] The court noted that while normally an act of supplying abroad would not trigger the application of the provision on contributory infringement, the provision does apply in cases where the ultimate goal is the use of the invention in Germany.[204]

While Article 10 may affect the utilization of an invention abroad only when the foreign utilization is associated with an act of indirect infringement in Germany,

---

On the concept of "essential components," see, e.g., THOMAS KÜHNEN & EVA GESCHKE, DIE DURCHSETZUNG VON PATENTEN IN DER PRAXIS 84–86 (2008); Michael Nieder, *Die mittelbare Patentverletzung—eine Bestandsaufnahme*, 2006 GRUR 977, 977–78.

[200] "Pursuant to Sec. 10 of the Patent Act the effect of the patent is that, without the patent holder's consent, any third party is prohibited from offering or supplying within the territory of the application of the Patent Act any means related to an essential element of the invention to persons [other than the persons entitled to use the patented invention in Germany], provided that the third party knows or it is obvious in the light of the circumstances that these means are capable of being applied and intended to be applied for the use of the inventions." *Funkuhr II*, *supra* note 180.

[201] Articles 9(2) and 10(2).

[202] *Funkuhr II*, *supra* note 180.

[203] *Id.* "[I]f the delivery is made in order for use to be made of the invention in Germany, this is precisely the threat to the rightholder's domestic patent rights that [Article] 10 of the Act is intended to prevent." *Id.* The issue in this case was whether a German supplier had standing to sue the patent holder for sending unjustified cease and desist letters to a distributor when the patent was allegedly infringed by a foreign company that made the product at issue abroad from an essential component delivered by the German supplier. The product was then supplied to Germany and the patent holder sent the letter to the distributor.

[204] *Funkuhr II*, *supra* note 180.

a much wider net is cast for activities abroad through the doctrines of participating and aiding and abetting;[205] these doctrines have allowed German courts to reach persons involved in the utilization of inventions abroad. In *Funkuhr*[206] a Dutch company, aware of the German patent covering a certain device in Germany, supplied devices to another Dutch company, which, as the supplier knew, supplied them into Germany. The court found infringement by the first Dutch company because that company "knew of the patent and knew of the country of destination and therefore willingly and willfully helped to cause the domestic distribution."[207] Similarly, the Düsseldorf Landgericht decided in *Sitz-Stützelement*[208] that an Austrian manufacturer infringed when it supplied a device patented in Germany into the United Kingdom where the device was installed into cars that were thereafter distributed in several countries, including Germany. The court emphasized that the Austrian manufacturer was liable because it knew of the patent and of the country of destination. In *Herkranzgefäß-Dilatationskatheter*[209] the Düsseldorf Landgericht found an Israeli manufacturer liable when the manufacturer supplied catheters to a dealer in the United States who then supplied them to various countries, including Germany, and offered them on the Internet to German customers. What was again dispositive in the decision was that the Israeli company knew of the German patent and of the U.S. supplier's intent to offer and distribute the device in Germany. The Mannheim Landgericht dealt with a similar case, *Kondensator für Klimaanlage*,[210] in the context of personal jurisdiction. The court decided that an Austrian defendant could have infringed a patent when supplying devices to car manufacturers in Italy (Alfa Romeo), and France and Spain (Citroen); some of the cars with the devices installed were shipped to Germany.[211]

---

[205] Civil Code, §830.

[206] *Funkuhr*, Bundesgerichtshof, X ZR 36/01, Feb. 26, 2002, 2002 GRUR 599.

[207] Erhard Keller, *Patentverletzungen durch Handlungen im patentfreien Ausland*, *in* FESTSCHRIFT FÜR EIKE ULLMANN 449, 454 (Hans-Juergen Ahrens, Joachim Bornkamm, & Hans Peter Kunz-Hallstein eds., 2006).

[208] *Sitz-Stützelement*, Landgericht Düsseldorf, 4a O 395/02, Nov. 18, 2003; *see also* Keller, *supra* note 207, 457.

[209] *Herkranzgefäß-Dilatationskatheter*, Landgericht Düsseldorf, 4a O 311/02, Oct. 28, 2003, 3 ENTSCHEIDUNGEN DER INSTANZGERICHTE ZUM RECHT DES GEISTIGEN EIGENTUMS 174 (2002); *see also* Keller, *supra* note 207, 456–57.

[210] *Kondensatore für Klimaanlage*, Landgericht Mannheim, 7 O 506/04, Aug. 26, 2005, 6 ENTSCHEIDUNGEN DER INSTANZGERICHTE ZUM RECHT DES GEISTIGEN EIGENTUMS 9 (2005). The court pointed to a Swiss Bundesgericht decision in *Testkassetten* in which the Swiss court confirmed that "one who participates in an infringement [in the protecting country may be] held civilly liable when the participant acts solely abroad but from there caused or supported patent infringement in [the protecting country]. [. . .] The required connection [to the protecting country] is created by the knowing and willful support of [the result in the protecting country]." *Id.*, 12.

[211] *See also Kombi-Sicherheitsnetz*, Landgericht Düsseldorf, 4a O 56/09, July 13, 2010.

The German law thus reaches the kind of infringements that Nicholas Oros aptly termed "infringement twice removed";[212] these infringements appear to be reachable also under U.S. law. For example, in the United States in *Crystal Semiconductor Corp. v. TriTech Microelectronics Intern., Inc.*,[213] a foreign manufacturer was found indirectly liable when the manufacturer dealt solely with another company that supplied infringing products into the United States; the foreign defendant manufacturer TriTech sold chips to OPTi, which then sold them into the United States. The U.S. Court of Appeals for the Federal Circuit found that "TriTech's acts in connection with selling its chip to OPTi [. . .] constitute[d] active inducement under 35 U.S.C. §271(b)."[214]

The patent laws of Germany and the United States overlap in scope with respect to acts committed abroad that contribute to an infringement in Germany or the United States as the protecting country. The acts prohibited by the U.S. Patent Act as acts of inducement are covered as acts of indirect infringement under the German Civil Code provision for participating in or aiding and abetting a direct infringement. Additionally, under the recent interpretation by the U.S. Court of Appeals for the Federal Circuit,[215] "offers to sell" are treated as acts of indirect infringement because offers made outside the United States for sale of a patented product (or a product made by a patented process) in the United States will be actionable under the "offer to sell" provisions of the U.S. Patent Act.[216]

3.6 Acts in Multiple Locations

One of the ways in which acts committed outside the protecting country may be drawn into the scope of the patent law of the protecting country is when a finding is made that the same act has been committed in multiple locations, one of which is in the protecting country.[217] Localization of an act in a certain place may be important

---

[212] Nicholas Oros, *Infringement Twice Removed: Inducement of Patent Infringement for Overseas Manufacture of Infringing Products Imported by Another*, 10 COMPUTER L. REV. & TECH J. 163 (2006).

[213] Crystal Semiconductor Corp. v. TriTech Microelectronics Intern., Inc., 246 F.3d 1336 (Fed. Cir. 2001).

[214] *Id.*, 1351.

[215] Transocean Offshore Deepwater Drilling, Inc. v. Maersk Contractors USA, Inc., 617 F.3d 1296 (Fed. Cir. 2010).

[216] *See supra* Section 3.3 for a discussion of the infringing "offer to sell."

[217] Generally on ambiguity of the place of an infringing act, see Edward Geller, *International Intellectual Property, Conflicts of Laws and Internet Remedies*, 22 EUR. INTELL. PROP. REV. 125, 126 ff. (2000). An appropriate characterization of the acts may also be a problem, although perhaps less so in patent infringement cases than in other cases. *Id.*, 126.

for establishing personal jurisdiction over the infringer; in cases where an infringer's domicile is outside the protecting country it is often necessary to base personal jurisdiction on tortious acts occurring in the protecting country.[218] Furthermore, even if courts have personal jurisdiction over an alleged infringer based on other grounds, such as the domicile of the alleged infringer, if the courts of a country do not consider patent infringement to be a transitory cause of action, and they therefore refuse to adjudicate infringements under foreign patent laws, those courts will not adjudicate infringements at all unless the localization of the act places the act within the scope of the country's patent law. Therefore, the proper localization of an act is of crucial importance when patent holders hold patents in only one country or a limited number of countries and they must deal with an infringement that originates in a country where their invention is not protected. In such cases the localization in the protecting country will determine whether an infringement can be found at all, and therefore whether any remedies are available.

Although regular choice of law provisions for torts should provide sufficient guidance for localization of acts of patent infringement,[219] the limited territorial scope of patent law requires that acts be examined in the context of the potential applicability of the patent law of the particular country.[220] For instance, choice of law provisions in the 2007 Rome II Regulation,[221] which apply in the countries that are members of the European Union, including Germany,[222] point in cases of torts in general to the "law of the country in which the damage occurs."[223] However, the special provision on infringement of intellectual property rights in Article 8.1 of the Regulation, which is designed to comply with "the universally acknowledged principle of the *lex loci protectionis*,"[224] calls for application in such infringement cases of

---

[218] *E.g.*, Restatement (Second) of Conflict of Laws, §36, §37, §49, and §50; Brussels I Regulation, Chapter 2, note 25, Article 5(3). *See also* ALI Principles, Chapter 2, note 123, Section 204.

[219] In the United States almost half of U.S. states apply the law of the state with the "most significant relationship" under Restatement (Second) of Conflict of Laws §145 (1971); ten states apply the traditional *lex loci delicti* rule. *See* Symeon C. Symeonides, *Choice of Law in the American Courts in 2008: Twenty-Second Annual Survey*, 57 Am. J. Comp. L. 269, 279 (2009).

[220] For a discussion of this phenomenon see Alexander Peukert, *Territoriality and Extraterritoriality in Intellectual Property Law*, in Beyond Territoriality: Transnational Legal Authority in the Age of Globalization (Gunther Handl & Joachim Zekoll eds., 2011).

[221] Regulation (EC) No 864/2007 of the European Parliament and of the Council of 11 July 2007 on the law applicable to noncontractual obligations (Rome II), 2007 O.J. (L 199) 40 ("Rome II Regulation").

[222] Prior to the effective date of the Rome II Regulation (Jan. 11, 2009) the German choice of law provisions concerning noncontractual obligations were in Articles 27–37 of the Introductory Act to the Civil Code (Einführungsgesetzes zum Bürgerlichen Gesetzbuche).

[223] Rome II Regulation, *supra* note 221, Article 4(1).

[224] *Id.*, Recital 26.

the "law of the country for which protection is claimed." To ascertain whether protection may be claimed for Germany, a determination is required as to whether the acts at issue may be viewed as acts that infringe a patent under German patent law; the territorial scope of the German Patent Act, as interpreted by German courts, will determine how far the Act extends as applicable law.[225]

The importance of localization may be demonstrated by an example using a sale. In the United States, if a "sale" occurs "within the United States"[226] it is infringing, and therefore it is essential to know what facts are sufficient for courts to deem certain acts to fall within the scope of the term "sale." A sale may be defined in either legal or physical terms; as the U.S. Court of Appeals for the Federal Circuit has noted, legal terms concentrate only on "the single point at which some legally operative act took place, such as the place where the sales transaction would be deemed to have occurred as a matter of commercial law."[227] Physical terms, however, offer courts the opportunity to view various facts as determinative of the location of the sale; for instance, "the location of the seller and the buyer"[228] or "the points along the shipment route."[229] U.S. and German courts both look beyond purely legal terms and consider physical terms when localizing a sale.[230]

Some sellers try to protect themselves from the reach of the patent law of a particular country by selling goods from abroad and shipping them to customers in the protecting country "free on board."[231] A shipment "free on board" means that the title to the goods is transferred when the seller delivers the goods to a carrier; therefore, sellers have argued that it should be at this point that the act of sale occurs, because this is where sellers no longer have responsibility for the goods. U.S. courts, however, do not view the issue of the shift in liability for goods as dispositive of the issue of the place of sale for the purposes of the U.S. Patent Act. In *MEMC Electronic Materials, Inc. v. Mitsubishi Materials Silicon Corp.*[232] the U.S. Court of Appeals for

---

[225] This is different from torts in general, which concern rights that have no explicit territorial limits and for which the forum's choice of law provisions set the territorial reach.

[226] 35 U.S.C. §271(a), (b) and (g).

[227] North American Philips Corp. v. American Vending Sales, Inc., 35 F.3d 1576, 1579 (Fed. Cir. 1994).

[228] *Id. See also* Litecubes, LLC v. Northern Light Products, Inc., 523 F.3d 1353, 1369 (Fed. Cir. 2008); cert. denied on Nov. 10, 2008.

[229] *Id.*

[230] As noted *supra* in Section 3.3, while both U.S. and German courts have adopted a liberal approach to the interpretation of a "sale" (by looking beyond pure contract law terms), U.S. courts have adopted a rigid approach to the interpretation of an "offer to sell" by requiring that acts fall into the contract law definition of an offer for the acts to constitute an infringing offer to sell under the U.S. Patent Act.

[231] For a definition of the term "free on board," see Incoterms 2000 by the International Chamber of Commerce, *available at* http://www.iccwbo.org/incoterms/preambles/pdf/FOB.pdf (last visited Sept. 2, 2011).

[232] MEMC Electronic Materials, Inc. v. Mitsubishi Materials Silicon Corp., 420 F.3d 1369 (Fed. Cir. 2005).

the Federal Circuit stated that a sale is not necessarily precluded from occurring in the forum "simply because an article is delivered 'free on board' outside of the forum";[233] according to the court, other factors, such as places of contracting and performance may be more important when a sale needs to be localized.[234]

Localization may also be difficult in cases involving use, particularly if the infringing use concerns patented inventions that consist of various parts—either steps in cases of process patents, or components in cases of system patents. The localization is complicated when individual components of the system are used or steps in the process are performed in different countries; the U.S. case *NTP v. Research in Motion*[235] exemplified these problems. The case concerned a technology that enables receipt of e-mails on mobile devices through a wireless network; the extraterritorial component was a relay located in Canada through which the e-mails were routed.[236] The defendant argued that U.S. patent law could not be applied because it does not extend extraterritorially and thus cannot cover acts committed in Canada.[237] The U.S. Court of Appeals for the Federal Circuit relied on an earlier decision of the U.S. Court of Claims in *Decca Ltd. v. United States*[238] to conclude that the use of a *system* may be infringing under U.S. patent law even if a component of the system is located abroad; however, it suggested that a different analysis must be performed for *method* claims that make up the processes covered by a patent.[239] The court localized the use of the system as "the place where control of the system is exercised and beneficial use of the system obtained,"[240] which was the United States. However, the use of the process could not be localized in the United States; the court explained that for a process to be infringed through use, each of the steps of the process has to be performed, and therefore a process cannot be infringed in the United States through use unless all of the steps are performed in the United States.[241]

---

[233] *Id.*, 1377.

[234] *See supra* Section 3.2 for examples of German cases. *See also* Chapter 4, Section 4.2.1, for a discussion of the case *Litecubes, LLC v. Northern Light Products, Inc.*, 523 F.3d 1353 (Fed. Cir. 2008).

[235] NTP v. Research in Motion, 418 F.3d 1282 (Fed. Cir. 2005), cert. denied.

[236] *Id.*, 1289–90.

[237] *Id.*, 1313.

[238] Decca Ltd. v. United States, 210 Ct.Cl. 546 (Ct. Cl. 1976).

[239] "The term 'process' means process, art, or method, and includes a new use of a known process, machine, manufacture, composition of matter, or material." 35 U.S.C. §100(b).

[240] NTP v. Research in Motion, 418 F.3d 1282, 1317 (Fed. Cir. 2005), cert. denied.

[241] *Id.*, 1317–18. In Cardiac Pacemakers the U.S. Court of Appeals for the Federal Circuit held that process patents cannot be infringed through acts under 35 U.S.C. §271(f). Cardiac Pacemakers, Inc. v. St. Jude Medical, Inc., 576 F.3d 1348, 1365 (Fed. Cir. 2009). On the so-called "divided infringement claims," see Mark A. Lemley, David O'Brien, Ryan M. Kent, Ashok Ramani, & Robert Van Nest, *Divided Infringement Claims*, 33 AIPLA Q.J. 255 (2005); Melissa Feeney Wasserman, *Divided Infringement: Expanding the Extraterritorial Scope of*

The question of whether a process patent can be infringed in one country when some of the steps of the process are performed in different countries was also addressed by German courts. In 2007 the Bundesgerichtshof decided a case of infringement of a "method to control the elevation of the temperature of electrically heated parts"[242] in *Rohrschweissverfahren*;[243] in that case the initial steps of the process were performed in Switzerland and the subsequent steps were performed in Germany.[244] The court held that the patent was infringed in Germany through the final steps of the process.[245] A fact situation that raised a mirror-image question appeared in 2009 before the Düsseldorf Oberlandesgericht; in *Prepaid-Karten II* the initial steps of a process were performed in Germany and the subsequent steps in other countries.[246] The court held that the "method of processing telephone cards" at issue was infringed in Germany "notwithstanding the undeniable cross-border aspect."[247] The court emphasized that in accordance with the principle of territoriality, acts that occur entirely abroad cannot infringe a German patent; however, the result will be different if at least a portion of an act occurs in Germany.[248] Therefore, a process patent will be infringed in Germany if the infringer performs some of the necessary steps in Germany, as long as the rest of the steps that are performed abroad may be attributed to the infringer in Germany.[249]

Localization may also be challenging when infringing acts are committed on the Internet.[250] In Germany courts view advertisements on the Internet as infringing

---

Patent Law, 82 N.Y.U. L. REV. 281 (2007). The case of *NTP v. Research in Motion* settled and was dismissed without prejudice in March 2006. NTP v. Research in Motion, U.S. District Court for the Eastern District of Virginia, case no. 3:01-cv-00767-JRS, order, docket document no. 464, March 3, 2006.

242 European patent EP 0272978 (A1).

243 *Rohrschweissverfahren*, Bundesgerichtshof, X ZR 113/04, Feb. 24, 2007.

244 *Rohrschweissverfahren*, Oberlandesgericht Düsseldorf, 2 U 18/03, June 24, 2004.

245 *Rohrschweissverfahren*, Bundesgerichtshof, X ZR 113/04, Feb. 24, 2007

246 *Prepaid-Karten II*, Oberlandesgericht Düsseldorf, 2 U 51/08, Dec. 10, 2009.

247 *Id.*

248 *Id.*

249 *Id. See also* Landgericht Düsseldorf, 4a O 235/06, Aug. 14, 2007. The decision concerned a patent on a "method for making a perfected medical model on the basis of digital image information of a part of the body" EP 0756735(B1). The defendants had one of the steps of the method performed in Sweden or the United States, but the court held that this fact did not preclude a finding of infringement of the method in Germany because "[f]or the cause of action of a use of a process it suffices when one or more steps are performed in [Germany] and others abroad, when the other necessary steps that were accomplished abroad can be attributed to the actor in [Germany]." *Id.*, para. 117.

250 As Edward Geller noted in an article from 2000, "[t]he ambiguity [of the place of infringing acts] arises out of the increasing efficacy of the media and technology." Geller, *International*, *supra* note 217, 126. The problems of enforcing patents on the Internet were thoroughly discussed as early as 1993 by Dan Burk, *supra* note 7.

offers to sell; for instance, in *Sohlen für Sportschuhe*[251] the Düsseldorf Landgericht considered as infringing an offer to sell when a U.S. manufacturer advertised a product on the Internet together with a list of German distributors. In *Einrichtung zur zentralen Notlichtversorgung*[252] the court found an offer to be localized in Germany when the Internet website was written in German. The defendant argued that it did not target distributors in Germany and that it exported its goods only to customers outside of Germany, but the court pointed out that there was no disclaimer on the website that would inform potential purchasers that the defendant would not supply goods to Germany for use in Germany.[253]

3.7 Limits on the Protection of an Invention outside the Protecting Country

The mechanisms described in this chapter provide important tools for patentees who, for whatever reason, cannot obtain patent protection in all countries of the world, or simply in a country where their invention is exploited. The mechanisms can also serve as alternatives to the parallel enforcement of multiple national patents when it is impossible to litigate the infringement of the patents in some particular country (because the patent infringements are not considered transitory causes of action or because the act of state doctrine prevents courts from deciding cases concerning foreign patents)[254] or the litigation is unlikely to succeed in that country (for example, if raising invalidity causes a removal or stay of the proceedings).[255] Although the mechanisms are often used as alternatives to multinational litigation, their existence cannot be explained only as a reaction to the high costs and complications of litigating in multiple countries simultaneously;[256] even if ways are found to make enforcement of parallel patents less complicated and costly, as discussed in Chapter 2, these mechanisms would still be needed by inventors who lack protection in countries where their invention is utilized, or who want to benefit from the

[251] *Sohlen für Sportschuhe*, Landgericht Düsseldorf, 4a O 33/01, Feb. 5, 2002.

[252] *Einrichtung zur zentralen Notlichtversorgung*, Landgericht Düsseldorf, 4a O 78/08, Mar. 26, 2009.

[253] On the role of a disclaimer, see *Arzneimittelwerbung im Internet*, Bundesgerichtshof, I ZR 24/03, Mar. 30, 2006, 2006 GRUR 513, 515.

[254] *See* Chapter 2, Section 2.1.6, for a discussion of approaches of courts in the United States and Germany to deciding cases involving foreign patents.

[255] *See, e.g.*, Chapter 2, Sections 2.1.1 and 2.1.2, for the situation in the European Union under the Brussels regime.

[256] Kendra Robins, *Extraterritorial Patent Enforcement and Multinational Patent Litigation: Proposed Guidelines for U.S. Courts*, 93 VA. L. REV. 1259, 1302 (2007). Kendra Robins suggests that "U.S. courts should look to multinational litigation before seeking to enforce U.S. patents extraterritorially." *Id.*

substantive or procedural advantages of the legal system of a particular protecting country.

This chapter shows that U.S. and German patent laws reach the exploitation of inventions beyond their countries' borders; in most respects the territorial reach of the laws is comparable, and in certain cases the extraterritorial reach of German patent law appears to be greater than that of U.S. law.[257] In most cases both laws achieve the same results, notwithstanding the differences in their statutory language; for example, despite their differing approaches to the issue of components, U.S. and German laws both seem to arrive at similar results with regard to components made domestically or offered for sale domestically for the purpose of assembly abroad.

In at least two scenarios the German approach reaches further than U.S. law: the offer to sell and the direct infringement of process patents. In Germany it has been accepted for decades that an offer to sell that is made in Germany is infringing even if the resulting sale occurs abroad, and in Germany the concept of an offer to sell includes any act that might be considered an offer to sell in an economic sense—no formal offer to sell as defined by contract law is necessary. In the United States, the U.S. Court of Appeals for the Federal Circuit has interpreted offers to sell as infringing only if they concern sales that occur or are intended to occur in the United States, and has construed an offer to sell strictly according to contract law terms. The German approach also appears to extend further in cases of cross-border infringements of process patents. In the United States under *NTP* a process patent cannot be infringed unless all of the steps of the process are performed in the United States; however, recent German decisions show that German courts have applied German patent law to a process even when the individual steps of the process are performed in multiple countries.[258]

It is remarkable that despite the similarities of U.S. and German law in their territorial reach, German law has not been subjected to the high level of criticism that is aimed at the excessive extraterritoriality of U.S. law; although not absent from the German literature,[259] criticism of the German approach is much less frequent than is

---

[257] Naturally, the fact that patent law doctrines in one country reach further than the doctrines in another country does not necessarily mean that right holders are in a better position to enforce their rights under the law of the former rather than under the law of the latter; there are other factors that influence a patent holder's success in enforcing his rights, such as procedural rules and alternatives to enforcement through litigation, such as border enforcement measures.

[258] *See supra* Section 3.6 for a discussion of infringements of process patents by acts in multiple countries.

[259] *See, for instance,* the criticism by Jens Adolphsen of the decision by the Düsseldorf Landgericht in *Rohrverzweigung*. The Düsseldorf Landgericht found that a Czech manufacturer could be held liable for infringement of a German patent because the manufacturer supplied a product to a German purchaser knowing that the purchaser intended to resell the product in Germany. *Rohrverzweigung*, 4 O 438/99, Landgericht Düsseldorf, Nov. 7, 2000, 1 Entscheidungen der Instanzgerichte zum Recht des geistigen

criticism in the literature discussing the situation in the United States.[260] One can only speculate on the origins of the more frequent criticism of the U.S. approach. It is undeniable that certain procedural differences mean that the U.S. system in general takes a more aggressive approach toward enforcement than the German litigation system does; examples are the availability in the United States of discovery and jury trials in patent infringement cases.

Two additional differences between the systems may explain the differing levels of criticism; the first is historical and the second is statutory. First, since the end of the nineteenth century, German law has developed strong tools for holders of German patents to protect their inventions; for instance, an infringing offer to sell was included in German patent law as an independent tort as early as 1877 and was applied even when offers involved foreign sales. The longer and more gradual German law tradition of reaching activities abroad may explain why the extraterritorial reach of German patent law is not as surprising to commentators as is the reach of U.S. patent law.

The second difference between the U.S. and German systems that may underlie the perception that the extraterritoriality of U.S. patent law has an excessive reach is an optical illusion resulting from the different statutory language governing certain acts of infringement. Compared to the U.S. Patent Act provisions on infringement in Section 271, the German Patent Act is very brief in describing what constitutes an infringement of a German patent; in fact, the general provisions on infringement appear only in the relatively short Article 9 and Article 10 of the Patent Act. However, what is more important is that the German Patent Act does not mention any activity outside Germany; the U.S. Patent Act, by contrast, explicitly states that it targets activities abroad in Section 271(f) (which concerns the supply of components in or from the United States) and Section 271(g) (which applies to products made outside the United States by processes that are patented in the United States).[261]

EIGENTUMS 154 (2000). The court emphasized that it was dispositive that the machines were from the beginning intended to be sold in Germany. Adolphsen criticizes the decision because of the finding of jurisdiction and insists that "the acts outside the protecting country [such as the labeling of products in the language of the protecting country, or the long-term contractual relationship with an importer in the protecting country] do *not* support jurisdiction of the court of the protecting country because these acts do not yet have the effect of infringement of the protected rights." ADOLPHSEN, EUROPÄISCHES, Chapter 2, note 47, 163.

[260] *E.g.*, Schroeder, *supra* note 8, 77–78; Holbrook, *Extraterritoriality*, *supra* note 7, 2127–28; Bradley, *supra* note 7, 584; Cameron Hutchison & Moin A. Yahya, *Infringement & the International Reach of U.S. Patent Law*, 17 FED. CIR. B.J. 241, 255 (2008); Brief for Amici Curiae Law Professors in Support of the Appellee, Jan K. Voda, M.D. v. Cordis Corporation, No. 05-1238 (Fed. Cir. July 29, 2005), 3.

[261] Dariush Keyhani, *U.S. Patent Law and Extraterritorial Reach*, 7 TUL. J. TECH. & INTELL. PROP. 51 (2005) (Noting that "[i]n recent years, the U.S. legislature and courts have expanded the extraterritorial scope of U.S. law to accommodate the growing economic importance of intellectual property." *Id.*, 52.).

These explicit extraterritorial ambitions in the U.S. Patent Act make it appear as though U.S. law attempts to reach further than the laws of other countries. Despite the general perception that the laws of civil law countries are more detailed and leave less discretion to their courts on interpretation than the laws of common law countries, on the issue of infringing acts, the German Patent Act has remained succinct, and German courts have interpreted its provisions on infringement in a manner that has avoided the need for substantial legislative changes like those that have been introduced into the U.S. Patent Act.[262]

It has been suggested that allowing patent laws to reach activities outside the protecting country has negative effects; in addition to expressing concerns over possible injury to international comity, some critics point out that the use of patent laws against conduct abroad exposes businesses to uncertainty about the legality of their activities[263] and thereby hinders the development of new businesses. However, commentators understand that many patent holders need to "stretch" the patent laws of a protecting country beyond its borders because they do not hold patents elsewhere. To reconcile the two types of interests, mitigating approaches have been proposed that would limit the application of the patent laws of one country to avoid offending other countries in their perceptions of what should be protected. For example, Timothy Holbrook proposed a system in which proof of infringement of a U.S. patent through conduct abroad would require proof "that the infringer would also infringe under the laws of the foreign country."[264]

Although they are commendable for addressing the patent policies of foreign countries and attempting harmonious international cooperation, these mitigating approaches might not be necessary. The application of any law is limited by a country's ability to enforce it; if enforcement is not feasible, any "application" of that law (meaning judicial proceedings leading to a judgment on the merits) is a useless exercise. If a country decides to adopt laws that will govern conduct abroad, the scope of those laws will be limited de facto by the country's ability to enforce its laws against those acting abroad, and the willingness of other countries to enforce the laws against those who are out of reach of the protecting country's own enforcement power. As long as an infringer is domiciled in the protecting country or has assets there that can be reached to enforce a judgment of a court of the protecting country applying its laws, the opinion of other countries about the extent of the reach of those laws is irrelevant; enforcement in the protecting country will be possible. However, once

---

[262] *See also* Moufang, *supra* note 163, 617.

[263] Hutchison & Yahya, *supra* note 260, 255.

[264] Holbrook, *Extraterritoriality*, *supra* note 7, 2120. *See also* Robins, *supra* note 256, 1309–14.

the infringer is not domiciled or has no assets in the protecting country, patent holders must take the protecting country's judgment to the country where the infringer is domiciled or where his assets are located and seek recognition and enforcement of the judgment in that country. Refusals by foreign countries to recognize the decisions by courts of protecting countries create a natural boundary to the extraterritorial application of patent laws.

The next chapter explores the potential enforcement difficulties that circumscribe the boundaries of patent laws and offers a quantitative view of the phenomena in current U.S. patent litigation.

4 Limits of Protection under the Law of the Protecting Country

WHAT TRULY DETERMINES the foreign reach of a country's patent laws is the willingness of foreign courts to recognize and enforce judgments that are rendered based on such laws.[1] Although countries may be quite ambitious when setting the territorial scope of their patent laws, without the assistance of foreign courts, patent laws, like any other laws, can be enforced only against those whose acts or assets are reachable by a domestic court. With the assistance of foreign courts no defendant will be able to escape the law by keeping assets outside the country of infringement; this fact is increasingly important today given the ease with which infringers can strategically locate their physical presence, conduct, and assets in multiple countries. This chapter provides empirical data on patent litigation[2] that has or may spawn

[1] *See* Chapter 2, Section 2.1, and Chapter 3, Section 3.6, for discussions of limitations that are set by choice of law rules.

[2] Parts of the text and some of the charts included in Chapter 4 were published in Marketa Trimble, *Cross-Border Injunctions in U.S. Patent Cases and Their Enforcement Abroad*, 13 MARQ. INTELL. PROP. L. REV. 331 (2009), and in Marketa Trimble, *When Foreigners Infringe Patents: An Empirical Look at the Involvement of Foreign Defendants in Patent Litigation in the U.S.*, 27 SANTA CLARA COMPUTER & HIGH TECH. L. J. 499 (2011). On differences between the data published in the 2009 article and the data used in this chapter, see *infra* note 6.

enforcement actions in foreign countries and analyzes the difficulties that patent holders encounter in such situations.

In many cases plaintiffs can avoid enforcement problems simply by filing a lawsuit in the jurisdiction where enforcement is anticipated; the territorial limitations are then set by the choice of law rules of the country where the lawsuit is brought, which are the gatekeeper rules used to fend off foreign laws that are deemed unacceptable to the country where the case was filed. These rules may therefore prevent adjudication of a claim under a foreign law; for instance, choice of law rules in Japan have prohibited Japanese courts from applying the U.S. patent law provision on inducement to acts committed in Japan.[3] Filing where the actual enforcement against an alleged infringer should take place is not always possible also because rules of jurisdiction can prevent the filing of a suit in the country of anticipated enforcement. Patent infringement cases are cases in which plaintiffs usually do not have a choice as to the country of litigation, as explained in Chapter 2,[4] and plaintiffs have to file in the country where their patent was granted notwithstanding the fact that an opponent's assets are located, or an opponent's actions originate, elsewhere.[5]

At first glance it might appear that cross-border enforcement problems should not even arise in patent cases; infringing conduct would seem to require that some assets be present in the protecting country, such as a manufacturing plant, warehouse, or at minimum, an office or bank account. However, this is not necessarily the case. Modern technologies permit infringers to keep assets away from the place of conduct, and as explained in Chapter 3, conduct may be found infringing even when committed outside the protecting country, in which case it is more likely that the infringer's assets will also be outside the protecting country.

There are ways in which enforcement problems may be mitigated in patent infringement cases. If a patent holder holds a parallel patent in another country where the infringer has assets and some conduct can be found infringing under the

---

[3] *E.g.*, in Fujimoto v. Neuron Co. Ltd. (Card Reader), Supreme Court of Japan, Sept. 26, 2002, *Minshu* Vol. 56, No. 7, 1551 (Japan), *available at* http://www.courts.go.jp/english/judgments/text/2002.9.26-2000.-Ju-.No..580.html (last visited Sept. 2, 2011). "To order prohibition of the act of actively inducing infringement of a U.S. patent and destruction of the infringing goods located in Japan by applying the U.S. Patent Act is contrary to the meaning of [public policy]." *Id. See also* Masato Dogauchi, *Private International Law on Intellectual Property: A Civil Law Overview*, WIPO/PIL/01/8 (Jan. 24, 2001), 10–11.

[4] Although under the Brussels regime plaintiffs can sue for patent infringement even outside the country of infringement (meaning outside the protecting country), such choice of forum by the plaintiffs may be easily defeated by defendants if the defendants raise the issue of patent validity. *See supra* Chapter 2, Section 2.1.1. Therefore, even though filing outside the protecting country may be possible under the Brussels regime, it is inadvisable in light of a likely counterattack by defendants based on patent validity that will result in the court dismissing, or at least staying, the infringement proceedings.

[5] *See* Chapter 2, Section 2.1.6, for examples of the rare cases in which courts were willing to entertain cases concerning foreign patents.

law of that country, a remedy in that country—injunctive or monetary relief—may be possible. The remedy awarded in the country where the infringer has assets, which should be readily enforceable, may not be sufficient for the patent holder to recover all of his damages for infringement in both protecting countries, but it may inflict enough pain on the infringer to cause him to stop infringing in both countries and create an opportunity for a negotiated solution. However, it may also happen that the patent holder holds no parallel patent in a country where the infringer has assets, since the patent holder might have insufficient resources to patent everywhere and the infringer might have purposefully located its assets in a country where no parallel patent has issued.

Another option for alleviating the enforcement problem is for the patent holder to sue in the protecting country both the foreign infringer and a domestic company that has participated in the infringement with the foreign infringer; domestic distributors, parents, or subsidiaries located in the protecting country are the typical examples. Even if the patent holder fails to secure enforcement abroad of the remedy awarded against the foreign co-defendant, the relief granted against the domestic co-defendant may be sufficient to prevent infringements, at least through the same distribution channels.

This chapter analyzes the problems that patent holders face when they sue an entity that is outside the reach of the enforcement power of the court that adjudicates the patent infringement. Section 4.1 presents the results of a quantitative analysis of a population of patent cases filed in the United States that was conducted to investigate the involvement of foreign entities in patent litigation in U.S. courts, and to demonstrate the magnitude of the phenomenon and the related potential for cross-border enforcement problems. Particular enforcement difficulties are discussed in Sections 4.2 and 4.3, which focus on injunctive and monetary relief, respectively. Finally, Section 4.4 summarizes the enforcement difficulties identified in this chapter and offers observations on the impact of these difficulties on the territorial scope of patent laws.

4.1 Foreign Parties before U.S. Courts—A Quantitative View of the Enforcement Problem[6]

While the qualitative aspect of the problem of cross-border enforcement in patent litigation is described in subsequent sections, this section offers an insight into the

[6] Data in this chapter that concern patent cases filed in U.S. district courts in 2004 differ from the data that were published previously in Marketa Trimble, *Cross-Border Injunctions in U.S. Patent Cases and Their Enforcement*

quantitative magnitude of the problem. It is very difficult to quantify the cases in which cross-border enforcement problems arise or may arise because there are no existing court statistics or survey results that provide data on right holders attempting to enforce judgments issued in patent cases against infringers in other countries. Surveying the data where they should be readily available—at the courts that recognize and enforce foreign judgments—is impossible; the courts responsible for recognition and enforcement of judgments, typically the lowest courts of a country's judicial system, do not publish statistics on such matters, and even if some court decisions are published and include some decisions in cases of recognition and enforcement, other pertinent decisions remain unpublished.

Instead of looking at the conclusion of the process, meaning decisions by foreign enforcing courts, the research presented in this section focuses on the beginning of the process: the filing of a suit that may eventually generate a judgment that would require recognition and enforcement in another country. An ab initio research approach is not without difficulties because comprehensive databases of court dockets that are accessible and searchable in toto are rarely available. However, for U.S. patent litigation a resource exists that provides access to all patent cases filed in U.S. district courts: the Lex Machina database, originally begun under the auspices of Stanford Law School as the Stanford IP Litigation Clearinghouse.[7]

While Lex Machina makes possible the comprehensive research of U.S. patent cases that is presented in this section,[8] no database is available to conduct research on German patent cases that would support a mirror-image comparison. Although access to court information in Germany has improved in the past decade and selected

Abroad, 13 Marq. Intell. Prop. L. Rev. 331 (2009). There are two reasons for the differences: 1) The Lex Machina database (*see infra* note 7) is being updated continuously; false positives are being removed from and false negatives are being added to the database. The data presented in this chapter are based on the database as of July 2010. 2) The data published in the above-mentioned article concerned a nonrandom convenience-based sample that was defined by the author's ability to determine the domicile of the parties at that time. *Id.*, 337. Because of improvements in the database since the publication of the article the author was able to determine the parties' domiciles in the remainder of the cases, with the result that the data in this chapter cover the entire population of patent cases filed in U.S. district courts in 2004 (as of July 2010), as defined by the listing in the Lex Machina database.

[7] The Genesis of Lex Machina, *available at* https://lexmachina.com/about/genesis (last visited Sept. 2, 2011).

[8] Databases that served as supporting resources in the research were the following: the Bloomberg Law database, the USPTO Patent Full-Text and Full-Page Image Databases, and the database of the University of Houston Law Center Institute for Intellectual Property and Information Law. Bloomberg Law, *available at* http://www.bloomberglaw.com/ (last visited Sept. 2, 2011); USPTO Patent Full-Text and Full-Page Image Databases, *available at* http://patft.uspto.gov/ (last visited Sept. 2, 2011); the University of Houston Law Center Institute for Intellectual Property and Information Law, *available at* http://www.law.uh.edu/ipil/ (last visited Sept. 2, 2011).

court decisions are available,[9] including on the Internet,[10] accessibility is still limited and no project on the scale of Lex Machina exists today in Germany or any other country in Europe.[11] Therefore, this section focuses solely on U.S. patent litigation and U.S.-filed cases that have the potential to generate cross-border enforcement problems.

For the purposes of the present study the cases that have the potential to create cross-border recognition and enforcement problems are defined as cases that were filed against at least one foreign defendant. In the vast majority of cases, these cases are patent infringement cases in which a patent holder, either U.S. or foreign, sues a foreign entity for infringing a U.S. patent; the foreign defendant may be sued alone, or together with other foreign or U.S. defendants. The research defines a foreign defendant—a defendant with a foreign domicile—to include either a person residing outside of the United States or an entity incorporated or having its principal place of business outside of the United States.[12] Of course, domicile is a rough proxy for potential cross-border enforcement problems, which are more likely to be associated with an absence of assets in the country of litigation, but the use of the proxy is unavoidable, given the significant difficulties associated with determining the location of a defendant's assets at any given time. Domicile appears to be a reasonable substitute for approximating the likelihood of cross-border enforcement problems.

It is clear that not all patent cases filed against foreign defendants will result in cross-border enforcement problems; in fact, many patent cases will not generate any kind of enforcement problems, regardless of whether or not the defendant is foreign. There will be cases in which parties, regardless of domicile, decide to comply with court decisions voluntarily—because they want to either restore a preexisting business relationship or build a new business relationship with the opposing party, or establish a business presence in the country of litigation. Compliance may also be

---

[9] *E.g.*, Gewerblicher Rechtsschutz und Urheberrecht (including GRUR-RR and GRUR International); Entscheidungen der Instanzgerichte zum Recht des geistigen Eigentums (Thomas Kaess & Thomas Kuehnen eds.). *See also* Juris and Beck databases.

[10] *See, e.g.*, Düsseldorfer Archiv, *available at* http://www.duesseldorfer-archiv.de/ (last visited Sept. 2, 2011); Rechtsprechung Nordrhein-Westfalen, *available at* http://www.justiz.nrw.de/Bibliothek/nrwe2/index.php (last visited Sept. 2, 2011).

[11] Technical and personnel conditions in the Düsseldorf Landgericht and the Munich Landgericht and strict personal data protection rules in Germany did not permit mirror-image research of German cases through direct access to court archives. As a consequence, the research of German cases was limited to published decisions. *See* Straus, Chapter 2, note 30. ("Comprehensive and reliable information on the numbers and nature of cases litigated involving validity or infringement of European patents in the [then] 19 EPC Contracting States is not available." *Id.*, 407).

[12] A U.S. subsidiary of a foreign corporation is treated as a U.S.-domiciled entity, not as a foreign entity. Foreign parent corporations are often sued as co-defendants with their U.S. subsidiaries.

motivated by public relations concerns or by a defendant's broader litigation strategy involving other cases. Finally, the defendant may simply be a law-abiding entity that has no ulterior motives when it complies with a court's decision.

The fact that the defendant and its assets are not located in the country of the issuing court will not necessarily negate any of the reasons for voluntary compliance; the reasons do not disappear simply because the defendant and its assets are unreachable by the issuing court's enforcement power. For instance, if a party is concerned about its reputation, it may comply with an injunction regardless of the court and country of issuance. However, the reasons for voluntary compliance may be less compelling in a cross-border scenario; for instance, merely the greater physical distance from the original litigation may be enough for a party to cease being concerned about damage to its reputation among its domestic customers. Similarly, complying with a foreign court order might be outside the scope of a defendant's litigation strategy that is focused on purely domestic disputes.

A presumption that the reasons for voluntary compliance arise with less frequency or a lower degree of intensity in cross-border scenarios, if correct, would suggest an increased need for effective enforcement of court decisions against foreign defendants. Even if such a presumption is incorrect and parties in fact have incentives just as strong to comply voluntarily with foreign court orders as they do with domestic court orders, cross-border enforcement still merits particular attention because of the significant difficulties that it poses to a plaintiff when a defendant does not comply voluntarily.

Some critics may argue that looking at all court cases filed may be overinclusive because such an approach disregards the fact that most patent cases settle. According to a study that covered U.S. patent cases closed in 2005–2007, 85 percent of cases settled;[13] typically only about 5 percent of all patent cases proceed to trial and result in adjudication by a court.[14] Including cases that eventually settle is not detrimental to the research because the research presented in this section focuses on the *potential* for cross-border enforcement difficulties, and therefore the research deliberately includes all cases against foreign defendants—even if in particular instances the

---

[13] Patstats, Settlement Rates for Patent Cases, *available at* http://liveweb.archive.org/http://www.patstats.org/2005-2007_FY_PATENT_CASE_DISPOSITIONS_(corrected).doc (last visited Sept. 2, 2011). According to a study of patent cases filed in 1995, 1997, and 2000, nearly 70 percent of patent cases settled. Jay P. Kesan, *Taking Stock of the U.S. Patent System*, *in* INTELLECTUAL PROPERTY AND INFORMATION WEALTH: PATENTS AND TRADE SECRETS (Peter K. Yu, 2007), 227–47, at 233.

[14] A study shows that only about 5 percent of patent cases filed in 1995, 1997, and 2000 went to trial. Kesan, *supra* note 13, at 233. According to Kimberley Moore, of cases terminated in 1999 and 2000 only 5.3 percent entered the trial stage. Kimberley A. Moore, *Xenophobia in American Courts*, 97 NW. U. L. REV. 1497, 1512 (2003).

cases might have settled. The fact that the cases arise at all indicates the potential that the present study is attempting to identify.

It would be ideal if the research could include not only cases filed in court but also disputes that never resulted in a lawsuit—cases that might have not been filed because the prospective plaintiffs were aware of cross-border enforcement problems that would complicate and perhaps prevent any final adjudication and enforcement that they might otherwise achieve. Unfortunately, it is impossible to determine the number of cases in which the deterrent of cross-border enforcement problems dissuades potential plaintiffs from filing suits against foreign defendants. Therefore, reviewing cases filed is the best available approach.

The research focuses on patent cases filed in U.S. district courts in 2004 and 2009. Although the resulting statistics offer only two data points, and therefore cannot prove a trend, they indicate the direction that the involvement of foreign defendants and the potential for cross-border enforcement problems might take in the future. It is difficult to assess whether the 2009 global economic downturn significantly impacted patent litigation; the statistics do not show a dramatic increase or decrease in the number of patent suits filed, and experts disagree on how the downturn did or might have affected patent litigation in the United States.[15] However, with the economic recovery now progressing slowly, we may assume that the 2004 and 2009 statistics are indicative of what a future trend might look like.

4.1.1 PATENT CASES FILED IN 2004 AND 2009

Patent cases in the United States may be filed in either federal or state courts, which have concurrent jurisdiction in patent matters; however, most cases are filed directly in federal courts or are removed to federal courts on a petition by the defendant. In federal courts, patent cases may be filed in any one of the ninety-four U.S. federal district courts where venue is proper, but in practice, patent cases are not distributed

[15] *Cf.* Robert Aronoff, *The State of the US IP Marketplace 2009–2010*, 1004 PLI/Pat 477 (2010). "Litigation watchers like Patent Freedom and RPX publish statistics that suggest that litigation increases in bad economic times as traditional operating means for achieving needed revenue become more limited. Compared to so many other investment options, an investment in patent assets and monetization through litigation is emerging in the eyes of many as a strong counter-cyclical investment opportunity with very real upside." *Id.*, 486–87. *Cf.* a recent study by Bradley D. Riel and Paul T. Meiklejohn, in which they claim that "considering long term litigation trends and the constantly increasing US economy, there appears to be no correlation between changes in the US economy and patent litigation activity. On a micro-scale, however, when extreme fluctuations in the US economy are recognized—in particular, contractions in the economy—patent litigation activity in the district courts tends to increase substantially." Bradley D. Riel & Paul T. Meiklejohn, *A Correlation Between the State of the US Economy and Patent Litigation Activity*, 92 J. PAT. & TRADEMARK OFF. SOC'Y 71, 103 (2010).

evenly among the courts. The disproportionate patent case load results both from natural circumstances (some districts may have less industry than others) and from flexible jurisdictional and venue rules that allow plaintiffs a certain degree of forum shopping to choose the district in which they wish to litigate.[16]

Figure 1 presents the two populations of this study—patent cases filed in U.S. federal district courts in 2004 and 2009;[17] the populations include not only patent infringement cases but also cases in which plaintiffs sought a declaration of patent invalidity and noninfringement and also the rare cases concerning disputes over inventorship. Figure 1 shows that there were fewer patent cases filed in 2009 than in 2004; 2,772 cases were filed in 2004, but only 2,635 cases in 2009. The difference of 137 cases was 4.9 percent fewer cases filed in 2009 than in 2004. This difference in the number of patent cases filed does not appear unusual; according to the Lex Machina database, which covers patent cases filed since 2000, 2004 had the second-highest number of filings (only 2007 had more) in the first decade of the twenty-first century.[18]

Patent cases in 2004 and 2009 were filed in eighty-four and eighty-five federal district courts, respectively, out of the total of ninety-four federal district courts,[19] which might suggest a fairly evenly distributed workload among the courts. However, almost half of all U.S. patent cases filed in 2004 were filed in only eight district courts (which each had more than 100 patent cases filed in their district that year):[20] the district courts for the Southern District of New York, the District of Delaware, the District of New Jersey, the Eastern District of Pennsylvania, the Eastern District of Texas,[21] the Northern District of Illinois, the Northern District of California, and

[16] *See infra* Section 4.1.4 on venue transfer rules.

[17] These populations were defined by the Lex Machina database as available in July 2010. On possible differences between the data reported in this study and the data currently available in Lex Machina, *supra* note 6.

[18] Lex Machina, as of April 17, 2011. Only three more cases were filed in 2007 than in 2004. In 2010 about 3 percent more cases were filed than in 2004, which was an increase of about 8 percent over the number of cases filed in 2009. *Id.*

[19] The U.S. districts with no patent litigation in 2004 were the following: the District of The Virgin Islands, the Southern District of West Virginia, the Northern District of Mississippi, the District of Alaska, the District of Guam, the District for the Northern Mariana Islands, the Middle District of Alabama, the Southern District of Alabama, the Middle District of Georgia, and the Southern District of Georgia. In 2009 no patent cases were reported in the Southern District of West Virginia, the Middle District of Louisiana, the District of North Dakota, the District of South Dakota, the District of Montana, the District of Guam, the District for the Northern Mariana Islands, the District of Alaska, and the Southern District of Alabama.

[20] The eight district courts handled 44.8 percent of all patent cases filed in U.S. federal courts in 2004.

[21] In 2004 the Eastern District of Texas was becoming a popular plaintiff's venue because it was perceived as favoring plaintiffs, and that year was the first year in which the popularity of the court became highly visible statistically—the number of cases filed almost doubled from the previous year. The rising trend in the district continued until 2007, when the numbers peaked; data from 2008 and 2009 showed a gradual

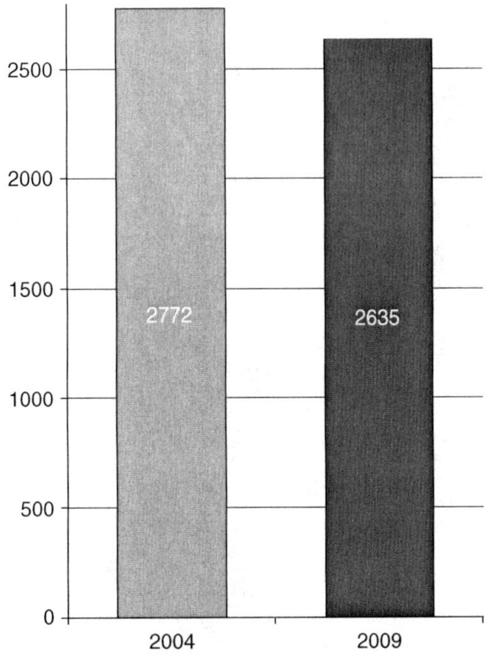

FIGURE 1: Patent cases filed in U.S. federal district courts in 2004 and 2009.

the Central District of California. Based on case filings, these courts, with the exception of the Eastern District of Pennsylvania, were also the busiest patent litigation venues in 2009.[22]

4.1.2 CASES INVOLVING FOREIGN PARTIES

Coding for the domicile of parties allows for a statistical view of the involvement of foreign parties in U.S. patent litigation in 2004 and 2009.[23] Figure 2 shows that although fewer cases were filed in 2009 than in 2004, the number of cases in which

decline in the numbers of cases filed in the district but in 2010 the number of cases rose again. Lex Machina, as of April 16, 2011.

[22] In the Eastern District of Pennsylvania the number of patent cases filed each year never reached 100 before or after 2004, and in fact since 2004 never exceeded 45; the spike of 106 cases in 2004 was caused by a single plaintiff who filed 48 cases in the district. The plaintiff was Laughlin Products, Inc., a manufacturer of heating equipment headquartered in Texas and a holder of 21 U.S. patents (according to the USPTO database as of Feb. 17, 2010). As of Feb. 17, 2010, the IPLC indicated that the company was involved in 170 patent cases filed since the beginning of 2000. The company is also among the holders and litigators of the most litigated U.S. patents. John R. Allison, Mark A. Lemley, & Joshua Walker, *Extreme Value or Trolls on Top? The Characteristics of the Most-Litigated Patents*, 158 U. PA. L. REV. 1, 33 ff. (2009).

[23] *See supra* introduction to Section 4.1 for the definition of a "foreign party."

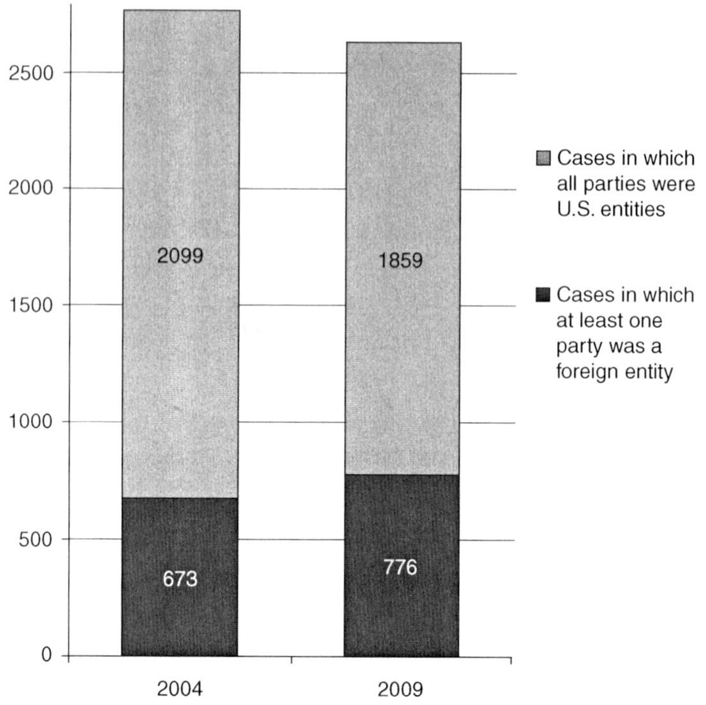

FIGURE 2: Patent cases filed in U.S. federal district courts in 2004 and 2009, by domicile of the parties.

at least one foreign party was involved—either as one of the plaintiffs or as one of the defendants—increased from 673 to 776 cases. While the number of all patent cases dropped 4.9 percent in 2009 compared to 2004, the number of cases involving foreign entities rose 15.3 percent.

Figures 3 and 4 provide good visualizations of the proportion of cases that involved at least one foreign party and cases that involved only U.S. parties in 2004 and 2009, respectively, and the change in the proportion from 2004 to 2009. While in 2004 24.3 percent of all U.S. patent cases involved foreign parties (Figure 3), in 2009 the percentage was 29.4 percent (Figure 4).

A comparison of Figures 3 and 4 indicates the growing internationalization of patent litigation. Although no comparable studies exist that would show the level of internationalization in patent litigation in earlier years,[24] one study suggests that there might be a steady level of involvement of foreign parties in recent years, or perhaps even an increase. The study covered patent cases terminated in federal

[24] For a discussion of the relevant statistical studies, see Trimble, *When Foreigners, supra* note 1, Part III.

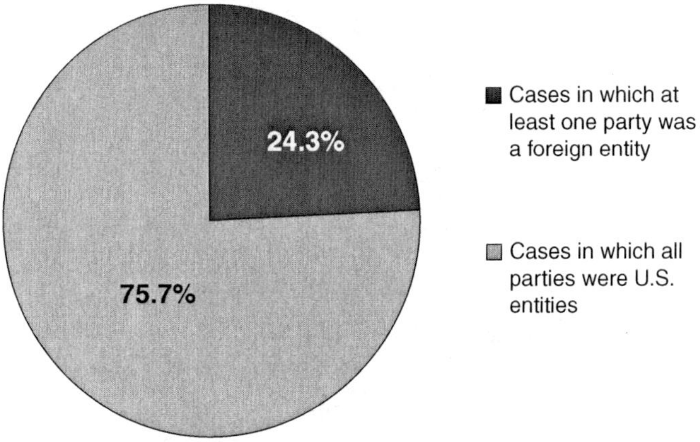

FIGURE 3: Patent cases filed in U.S. federal district courts in 2004, by domicile of the parties.

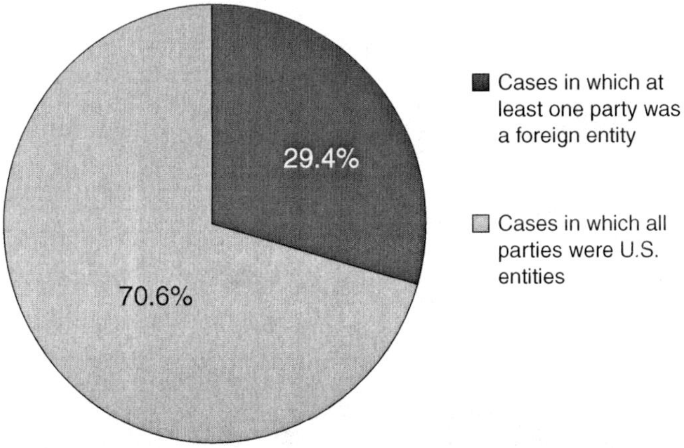

FIGURE 4: Patent cases filed in U.S. federal district courts in 2009, by domicile of the parties.

district courts in 1999–2000, and it showed that in 9.7 percent of cases foreign plaintiffs sued U.S. defendants, and in 13.0 percent of cases U.S. plaintiffs sued foreign defendants.[25]

Figure 5 shows the number of cases brought by only U.S. plaintiffs, only foreign plaintiffs, or foreign plaintiffs together with U.S. co-plaintiffs that were filed in 2004 and 2009. The number of cases in which no foreign plaintiffs were involved dropped

[25] Moore, *supra* note 14, 1527–28. Although there were likely additional cases that involved both foreign defendants and foreign plaintiffs in the same lawsuit, such cases were probably rare.

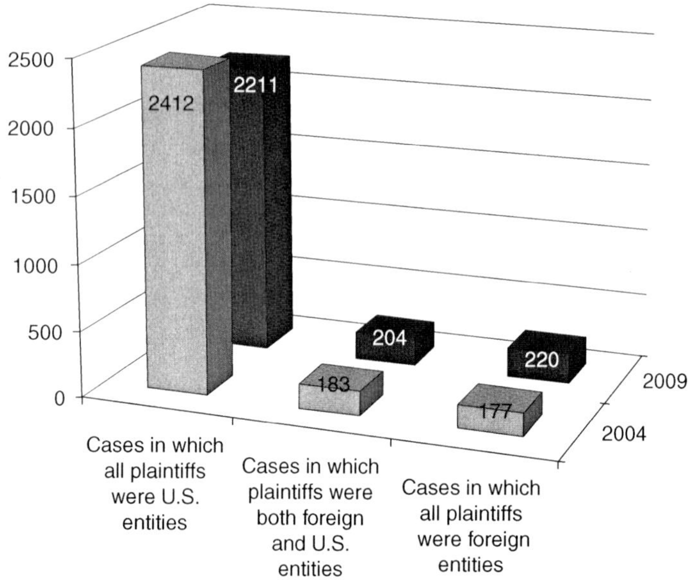

FIGURE 5: Patent cases filed in U.S. federal district courts in 2004 and 2009, by domicile of the plaintiffs.

from 2,412 in 2004 to 2,211 in 2009, or an 8.3 percent decrease. This decrease in the number of cases filed by only U.S. plaintiffs was slightly offset by an increase in the number of cases filed by plaintiffs that included at least one plaintiff who was a foreign party. As shown in Figure 5, the number of cases in which U.S. and foreign parties acted as co-plaintiffs grew from 183 in 2004 to 204 in 2009, or an 11.5 percent increase. An even greater increase occurred in cases that were brought by one or multiple foreign plaintiffs with no U.S. co-plaintiffs; in 2009 a total of 220 of such cases were filed, compared to 177 filed in 2004. The increase was 24.3 percent.

As for the proportion of cases involving foreign plaintiffs with respect to the total number of cases filed each year, in 2004 foreign plaintiffs were involved in 360 cases, or 13.0 percent of the 2,772 cases filed; in 2009 they were involved in 424 cases, or 16.1 percent of the 2,635 cases filed. The higher number of cases filed by at least one foreign plaintiff in 2009 is the result of an increase in both the category of cases in which plaintiffs were foreign and U.S. and the category of cases in which plaintiffs were only foreign; the proportion in the number of cases filed jointly by foreign and U.S. co-plaintiffs grew from 6.6 percent in 2004 to 7.7 percent in 2009, and in cases filed by only foreign plaintiffs the proportion increased from 6.4 percent in 2004 to 8.4 percent in 2009.

The increase in the number of patent cases filed by foreign plaintiffs may be explained by the growing number of foreign holders of U.S. patents, who are increasingly likely to appear as plaintiffs in U.S. patent infringement suits. The percentage of patent applications filed in the United States by foreign applicants grew dramatically in the past five decades—from 23.3 percent in 1963 to 50.7 percent in 2009.[26] The percentage of patents granted to foreign applicants surpassed the percentage of patents granted to U.S. applicants one year earlier; 50.9 percent of patents issued in 2008 were granted to foreign applicants, and the percentage remained above 50 percent in 2009 and 2010.[27] This too is a significant change since 1963, when only 18.6 percent of patents were granted to foreign applicants.[28] As the percentage of patents that are held by foreign parties increases, it will be more likely that foreign parties will appear as plaintiffs suing in patent infringement cases; additionally, the increase in patenting by foreign parties suggests their greater interest in the U.S. market, and therefore the likelihood that they will more often contest the validity of U.S. patents in declaratory judgment suits.

4.1.3 CASES INVOLVING AT LEAST ONE FOREIGN DEFENDANT AND CASES WITH ONLY FOREIGN DEFENDANTS

As the percentage of cases grew in which foreign parties were plaintiffs, so did the percentage of cases in which foreign parties were defendants. This increase is important because cases involving foreign defendants may generate recognition and enforcement problems if defendants do not comply voluntarily with court decisions and have no assets in the United States to satisfy a judgment. Enforcement can be particularly difficult when only foreign defendants are sued; if enforcement becomes necessary, plaintiffs must rely on cross-border enforcement, and there will be no U.S. assets to attach if the cross-border enforcement fails.

Figure 6 presents statistics on the involvement of foreign defendants in patent cases filed in 2004 and 2009. The number of cases against only U.S. defendants dropped from 2,357 in 2004 to 2,138 in 2009, a 9.3 percent decrease. The percentage decrease in this category of cases (9.3 percent) was greater than the percentage decrease in the numbers of all patent cases filed (4.9 percent) from 2004 to 2009. There was also a decrease from 2004 to 2009 in the number of cases filed against only foreign defendants—from 143 to 97, or a decrease of 32.2 percent. By contrast, the number of cases in which foreign defendants were sued together with U.S. co-defendants grew from 272 in 2004 to 400 in 2009, an increase of 47.1 percent.

[26] U.S. Patent Statistics, Calendar Years 1963–2010, USPTO, *available at* http://www.uspto.gov/web/offices/ac/ido/oeip/taf/us_stat.pdf (last visited Sept. 2, 2011).

[27] *Id.*

[28] *Id.*

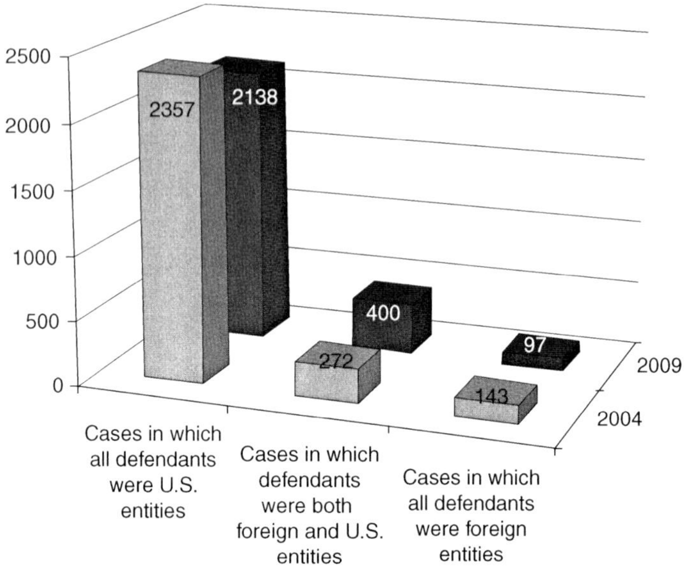

FIGURE 6: Patent cases filed in U.S. federal district courts in 2004 and 2009, by domicile of the defendants.

The increase in the number of cases filed against at least one foreign defendant (which rose from 415 in 2004 to 497 in 2009, and as a percentage of all cases filed in those years grew from 15.0 percent in 2004 to 18.9 percent in 2009) was caused only by the growth in the number of cases filed against foreign and U.S. co-defendants; the number of such cases as a percentage of all cases filed grew from 9.8 percent in 2004 to 15.2 percent in 2009. Figure 7 shows the relative magnitudes of the percentage increase in the number of cases filed against foreign and U.S. co-defendants and the percentage decrease in the number of cases in which all defendants were foreign. As a percentage of all cases filed against at least one foreign defendant, the number of cases filed against foreign and U.S. co-defendants grew from 65.5 percent in 2004 to 80.5 percent in 2009, while the number of cases filed against only foreign defendants dropped from 34.5 percent in 2004 to 19.5 percent in 2009.

Figures 8 and 9 provide a picture of the landscape at the district court level. The statistics are for the years 2004 and 2009 for the seven federal district courts having the highest number of patent cases filed in those two years: the district courts of the Southern District of New York (SDNY), the District of Delaware (DDEL), the District of New Jersey (DNJE), the Eastern District of Texas (EDTX), the Northern District of Illinois (NDIL), the Northern District of California (NDCA), and the Central District of California (CDCA).[29] In 2004 the Eastern District of

[29] *See supra* Section 4.11 for a discussion of the busiest federal district courts.

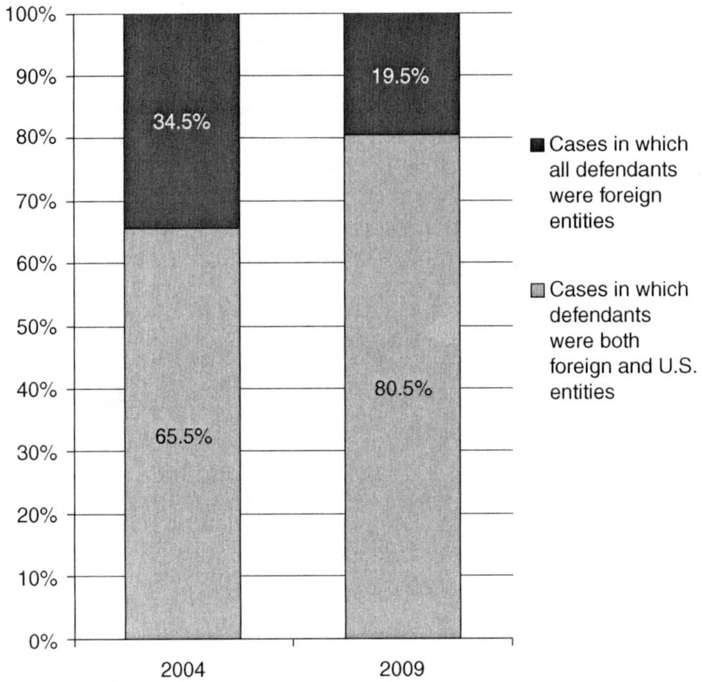

FIGURE 7: Patent cases filed in U.S. federal district courts in 2004 and 2009 against foreign defendants, by domicile of the defendants.

Pennsylvania was one of the top seven courts and had the same number of cases as the District of New Jersey (106 cases), which was more cases than were filed in the Eastern District of Texas that year (102 cases). However, because the 2004 spike in the Eastern District of Pennsylvania was caused by extraordinary circumstances,[30] the number is treated as an outlier and the District is not included in Figures 8 and 9.

Patent cases filed in these seven district courts were 40.9 percent and 49.7 percent of all patent cases filed in federal district courts in 2004 and 2009, respectively. Cases that were filed in these seven courts in which at least one foreign defendant was sued were 47.7 percent and 58.6 percent of all such cases filed in federal district courts in 2004 and 2009, respectively. The figures show that neither patent cases that were filed against only U.S. defendants, nor patent cases that were filed against at least one foreign defendant, were evenly distributed among all federal district courts.

As is shown in Figures 8 and 9, the Central District of California had the highest numbers of patent cases filed against only U.S. defendants in both 2004 and 2009

[30] On the reason for the spike in the number of patent cases filed in the Eastern District of Pennsylvania in 2004, see *supra* note 22. The plaintiff (Laughlin Products, Inc.) who caused the spike did not sue any foreign entities in the court in 2004.

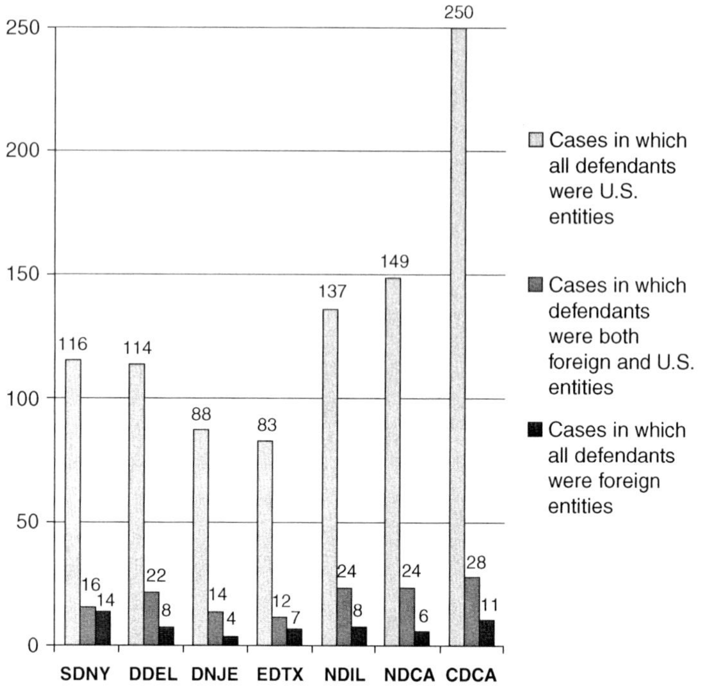

FIGURE 8: Patent cases filed in 2004 in the seven most frequented patent litigation venues, by domicile of the defendants.

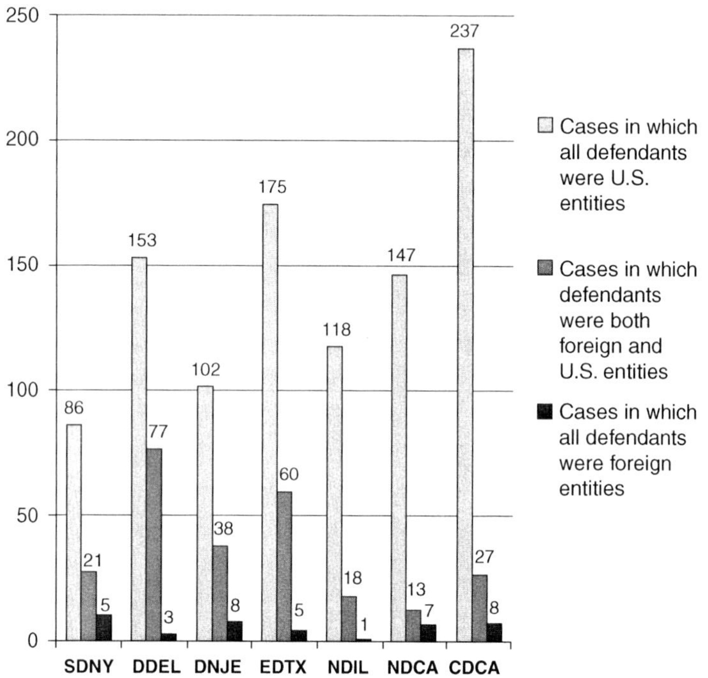

FIGURE 9: Patent cases filed in 2009 in the seven most frequented patent litigation venues, by domicile of the defendants.

(250 and 237 cases, respectively); it also had the highest total numbers of patent cases filed among all federal district courts, with a total of 289 patent cases filed in 2004 and 272 in 2009, figures that in both years were more than 10 percent of all patent cases filed in U.S. federal district courts.

The Central District of California was also the busiest court in 2004 for patent cases filed against at least one foreign defendant; in 2004 a total of 39 cases were filed in the District against defendants that included at least one foreign party, which was 13.5 percent of all cases filed in that district court. However, the Central District of California was surpassed in the number of such cases in 2009 by other courts, including the District of Delaware, where 80 cases against at least one foreign defendant were filed that year, or 34.3 percent of the total of 233 patent cases filed in that district court. Stated in another way, every third patent case filed in the District of Delaware in 2009 involved at least one foreign defendant.

The increase per district court in the number of cases in which foreign defendants were sued together with U.S. co-defendants is notable. As shown in Figure 8, the highest number of such cases in 2004 was filed in the Central District of California (28 cases); however, as Figure 9 indicates, in 2009 the filings of such cases in three courts surpassed those of the Central District of California (27 cases): the District of New Jersey had 38 cases, the Eastern District of Texas had 60 cases, and the District of Delaware had 77 cases. The data for the busiest district courts suggest possible explanations for the increase in the number of such cases, which is discussed below in Section 4.1.4.

Figure 10 offers another interesting perspective on patent litigation involving foreign defendants; it summarizes information about the numbers of cases in which defendants from certain countries appear. Countries of domicile are either countries of residence, of incorporation, or of principal place of business;[31] each foreign party was coded for only one country of domicile (depending on the data from lawsuits or from supporting sources),[32] and each case was coded for all the countries of domicile of the defendants sued in the case. For example, for a hypothetical case filed against three defendants from Canada and two defendants from Germany, the case would appear in the statistics as one case filed against Canadian defendants and one case filed against German defendants.

Figure 10 lists the following seventeen countries of domicile grouped by their geographical location: Canada (CA), Germany (DE), Switzerland (CH), the

---

[31] *See supra* the introduction to Section 4.1 for an explanation of the definition of a foreign party for the purposes of this research.

[32] *See supra* note 8 for supporting resources utilized for this research.

Netherlands (NL), Great Britain (GB), France (FR), Sweden (SE), Italy (IT), Finland (FI), Japan (JP), Korea (KR), Taiwan (TW), China (CN), Hong Kong (HK), India (IN), Israel (IL), and Australia (AU). These seventeen countries appeared in more than 10 cases in either 2004 or 2009 or in both years, but they were not the only countries represented: in 2004 cases were filed against defendants from twenty-six different countries, and in 2009 cases were filed against defendants from thirty-two different countries.[33]

Figure 10 reveals that the most represented country of domicile of foreign defendants was Canada, with 97 cases filed against at least one Canadian defendant in 2004 and 93 in 2009; in 2004 cases against at least one Canadian defendant were 23.4 percent of all cases filed against at least one foreign defendant, and in 2009 the proportion was 18.7 percent. This might be surprising to those who expect countries traditionally perceived as breeding grounds for infringing activities to appear at the top of the list; although Canada was on the Priority Watch List of the Special 301 Reports in 2009, 2010, and 2011, and was listed in the Reports even prior to 2009,[34] it is usually not considered by the American public as one of the notorious source countries for intellectual property rights infringements. However, it is important to

---

[33] Even more countries are involved if the countries of plaintiffs' domiciles are added; for instance in 2004 a total of thirty-three different countries appeared as the domiciles of either plaintiffs or defendants.

[34] 2009 Special 301 Report, Apr. 30, 2009, *available at* http://www.ustr.gov/sites/default/files/Full%20Version%20of%20the%202009%20SPECIAL%20301%20REPORT.pdf (last visited Sept. 2, 2011), 17–18; 2010 Special 301 Report, Apr. 30, 2010, *available at* http://www.ustr.gov/webfm_send/1906 (last visited Sept. 2, 2011), 25; 2011 Special 301 Report, April 2011, *available at* http://www.ustr.gov/webfm_send/2841 (last visited Sept. 2, 2011), 27. Canada has been a permanent feature of Section 301 Reports; for instance, Canada was on the Watch List in 2000, 2001, 2002, 2003, 2006, 2007, and 2008 and on the Special Watch List in 2004 and 2005. *See* 2008 Special 301 Report, *available at* http://www.ustr.gov/sites/default/files/asset_upload_file553_14869.pdf, (last visited Sept. 2, 2011), 39; 2007 Special 301 Report, *available at* http://www.ustr.gov/sites/default/files/asset_upload_file230_11122.pdf (last visited Sept. 2, 2011), 30; 2006 Special 301 Report, *available at* http://www.ustraderep.gov/assets/Document_Library/Reports_Publications/2006/2006_Special_301_Review/asset_upload_file473_9336.pdf (last visited Sept. 2, 2011), 33; 2005 Special 301 Report, *available at* http://www.ustraderep.gov/assets/Document_Library/Reports_Publications/2005/2005_Special_301/asset_upload_file195_7636.pdf (last visited Sept. 2, 2011), 37; 2004 Special 301 Report *available at* http://www.keionline.org/sites/default/files/ustr_special301_2004.pdf (last visited Sept. 2, 2011), 23; 2003 Special 301 Report, May 1, 2003, *available at* http://www.keionline.org/sites/default/files/ustr_special301_2003.pdf (last visited Sept. 2, 2011), 18–19; 2002 Special 301 Report, *available at* http://www.keionline.org/sites/default/files/ustr_special301_2002.pdf (last visited Sept. 2, 2011), 26; 2001 Special 301 Report, *available at* http://www.keionline.org/sites/default/files/ustr_special301_2001.pdf (last visited Sept. 2, 2011), 25; 2000 Special 301 Report, *available at* http://www.keionline.org/ustr/2000special301 (last visited Sept. 2, 2011).

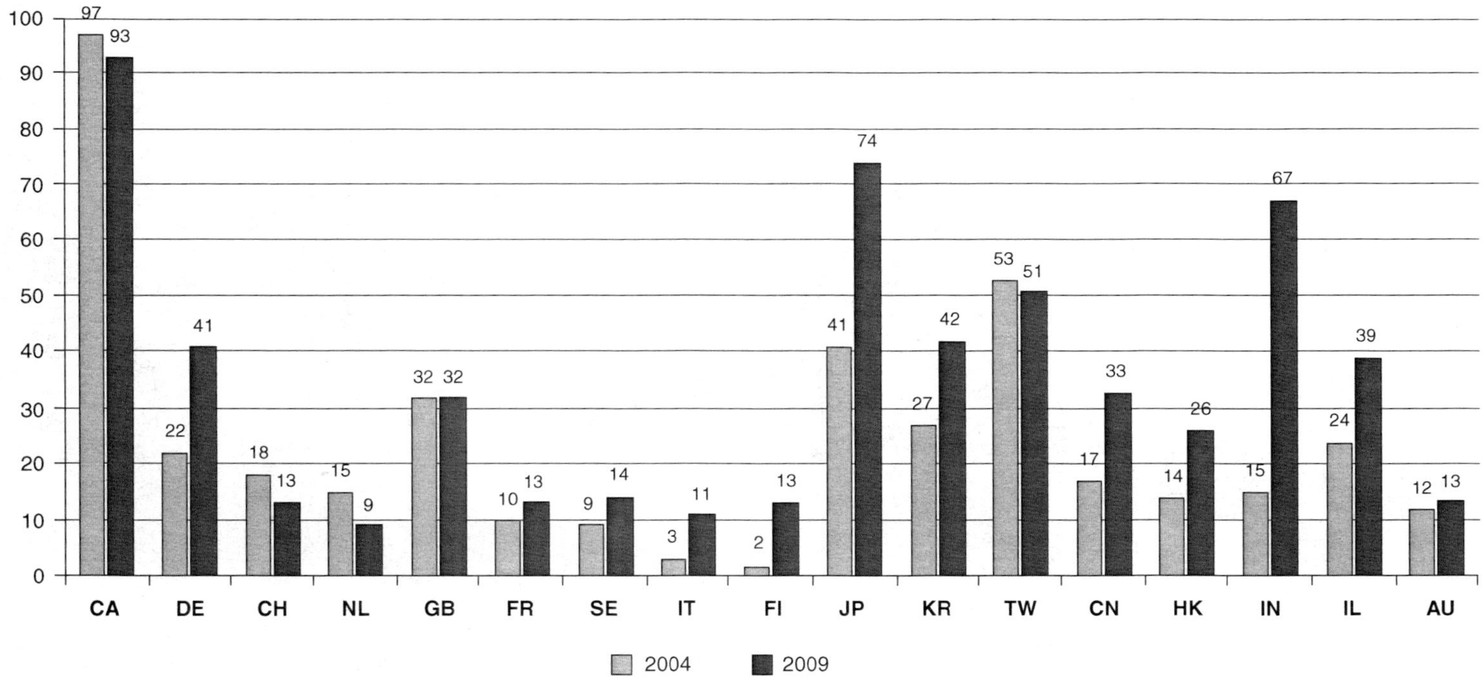

FIGURE 10: Countries represented in the most patent cases filed in U.S. federal district courts in 2004 and 2009, by domiciles of the defendants.[35]

[35] The numbers in Figure 10 do not correspond to the number of parties from a particular country but indicate the numbers of cases in which a country appeared as the domicile of one or more parties to the suit.

remember that Canada and the United States share a close trading relationship,[36] which explains the higher incidence of patent cases involving Canadian parties. In fact, it is not realistic to expect that all countries that are reported to have significant intellectual property infringement problems, such as Indonesia and other countries listed either on the Priority Watch List or the Watch List in the Special 301 Reports,[37] will be at the very top of the list; many of these countries have problems with their judicial systems that are likely to deter plaintiffs from filing suits in the United States that would eventually require recognition and enforcement of final judgments in those systems.

Although the number of countries from which defendants originate is high, with as many as thirty-two countries represented in 2009, many cases involve defendants from only a limited number of these countries. In fact, in both 2004 and 2009 more than 50 percent of cases involving at least one foreign defendant involved only four countries: Canada (97 cases), Taiwan (53 cases), Japan (41 cases), and Great Britain (32 cases) in 2004 (53.7 percent); and Canada (93 cases), Japan (74 cases), India (67 cases), and Taiwan (51 cases) in 2009 (57.3 percent). If we add only four additional countries in 2004 (Korea, Israel, Germany, and China) and three additional countries in 2009 (Korea, Germany, and Israel), the percentages of cases involving defendants from those top eight and top seven countries, respectively, exceed 75 percent of all cases filed against at least one foreign defendant in both years (75.4 percent and 81.9 percent, respectively).

4.1.4 SOME OBSERVATIONS ABOUT THE DATA ON THE INVOLVEMENT OF FOREIGN DEFENDANTS IN PATENT LITIGATION IN 2004 AND 2009

The statistics in the preceding sections are illuminating, and an even richer picture emerges when the data are analyzed in greater detail. The statistics presented so far have shown the growing internationalization of patent litigation in the United States, with more cases filed that involved at least one foreign party in 2009 than were filed in 2004. Although plaintiffs filed fewer cases against only foreign defendants, in cases with U.S. and foreign co-defendants more cases were filed in 2009 than in 2004. Notwithstanding the growing numbers of cases involving U.S. and

[36] According to the brief by the Canadian government filed in *Research in Motion v. NTP* in January 2006, "Canada and the United States share the largest bilateral trading relationship in the world, with trade in goods and services of over $1.2 billion crossing the border every day." Brief for the Government of Canada as Amicus Curiae in Support of the Petition, Research in Motion, Ltd. v. NTP, Inc., (No. 05-763), 3.

[37] 2010 Special 301 Report, April 30, 2010, *available at* http://www.ustr.gov/webfm_send/1906 (last visited Sept. 2, 2011), 3.

foreign co-defendants, there appears to be no large increase in the number of defendants' countries of domiciles. In 2004 more than three-fourths of cases filed against at least one foreign defendant involved only eight foreign countries, and in 2009 a similarly large portion of cases involved only seven foreign countries. A closer look at the data reveals some possible explanations for the statistics.

The data for cases filed in the District of Delaware, for example, as shown in Figures 8 and 9 in the preceding section, show that the District recorded an increase from 2004 to 2009 in the number of cases filed against foreign defendants. The numbers of cases by countries of defendants' domicile for the District, which are shown in Figure 11, reveal that most of the increase consisted of cases filed in the District against defendants from India (from 2 cases in 2004 to 25 cases in 2009) and Israel (from 3 cases in 2004 to 23 cases in 2009). Cases that involved defendants from the two countries accounted for 86.0 percent of the increase from 2004 to 2009 in the number of cases filed in the District against at least one foreign defendant.[38]

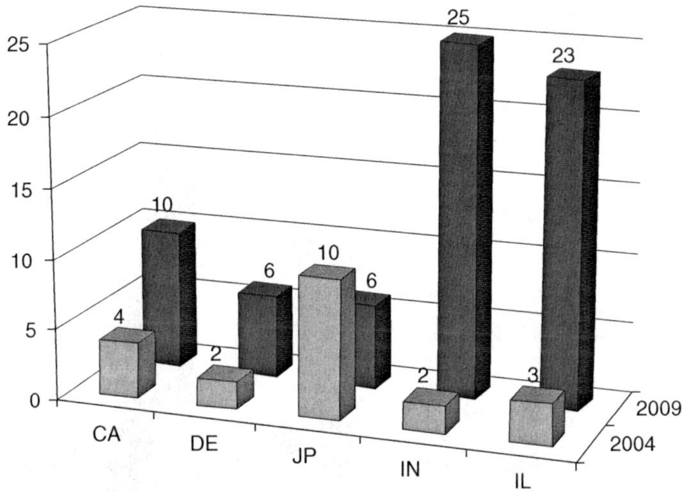

FIGURE 11: Patent cases filed in the U.S. District Court for the District of Delaware in 2004 and 2009 against foreign defendants, by domiciles of the defendants.[39]

[38] The number of cases filed in the District of Delaware against at least one foreign defendant grew by 50 cases—from 30 in 2004 to 80 in 2009 (*see supra* Figures 8 and 9). The number of cases filed in the District against defendants from India and Israel grew by 43 cases—from 5 in 2004 to 48 in 2009.

[39] Figure 11 shows only the five countries that were represented most often in cases that were filed in the District of Delaware in 2004 and 2009.

The fact that so many defendants originated in these two particular countries is revealing for those familiar with the patent litigation landscape in the United States; India and Israel are both countries with a number of large generic drug manufacturers—pharmaceutical companies that manufacture drugs that are not covered by any patents at all, drugs that were covered by patents that expired, or drugs that are claimed by right holders to be covered by existing patents.[40] It is therefore foreseeable that cases filed against defendants from these countries are likely to involve pharmaceutical patents.

An analysis of the claims raised in these cases confirms that the cases involve pharmaceutical patents; as Figure 12 illustrates, the entire growth from 2004 to 2009 in the number of cases filed in the District of Delaware against foreign defendants consisted of NDA/ANDA actions—New Drug Application actions and Abbreviated New Drug Application actions—filed by pharmaceutical patent holders under Section 271(e)(2) of the Patent Act[41] against generic drug manufacturers that were preparing to launch generic drugs into the U.S. market and had filed an application for Food and Drug Administration approval of the generic drugs. Figure 12 indicates that in 2004 only one action filed in the District of Delaware against at least one

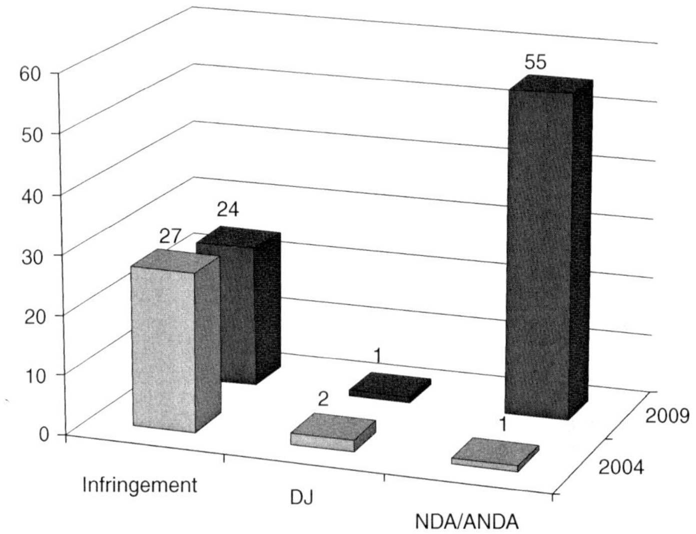

FIGURE 12: Patent cases filed in the U.S. District Court for the District of Delaware in 2004 and 2009 against foreign defendants, by type of claim.

---

[40] *E.g.*, Dr. Reddy's, Torrent Pharmaceuticals Ltd., Sun Pharmaceuticals, Teva Pharmaceuticals.

[41] 35 U.S.C. §271(e)(2).

foreign defendant was an NDA/ANDA action. However, in 2009 a total of 55 NDA/ANDA actions were filed in the District against at least one foreign defendant, which was an increase that contrasted with the decrease in the number of infringement actions and declaratory judgment actions filed against at least one foreign defendant, which both slightly declined from 2004 to 2009.

The observations drawn from the statistics presented in Figures 11 and 12 have significance for the study of cross-border enforcement problems. Decisions in NDA/ANDA actions, even if rendered against foreign defendants, are unlikely to present recognition and enforcement difficulties because defendants involved in NDA/ANDA actions are usually parties who want to maintain a business presence in the United States and therefore have significant incentives to comply with court decisions voluntarily.[42]

A similar picture to that in the District of Delaware emerges in the District of New Jersey, which was another of the three districts in Figures 8 and 9 that recorded substantial growth from 2004 to 2009 in the number of cases filed against at least one foreign defendant. While only 18 such cases were filed in the District of New Jersey in 2004, the number in 2009 jumped to 46 cases. Figure 13 shows that most of the "additional" cases filed in 2009 were NDA/ANDA actions, or actions filed

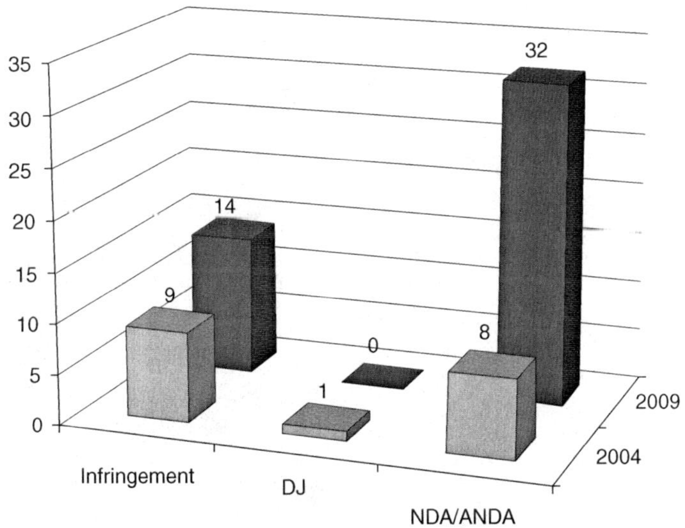

FIGURE 13: Patent cases filed in the U.S. District Court for the District of New Jersey in 2004 and 2009 against foreign defendants, by type of claim.

[42] *See supra* the introduction to Section 4.1 for a discussion of the reasons for voluntary compliance.

against defendants with strong incentives for voluntary compliance. In 2009, 32 NDA/ANDA actions were filed against at least one foreign defendant in the District, representing 69.6 percent of all patent cases filed against at least one foreign defendant in the District that year, and accounting for 85.7 percent of the increase recorded from 2004 to 2009 in the number of cases filed against at least one foreign defendant in the District.[43]

Another interesting observation concerning the presence of foreign defendants in patent litigation can be derived from the statistics from the Eastern District of Texas—the third district in Figures 8 and 9 in which the number of cases involving at least one foreign defendant rose from 2004 to 2009. While only 19 of these cases were filed in the District in 2004, the number increased to 65 cases in 2009. Because the total number of patent cases filed in the District, which has been popular with plaintiffs,[44] grew from 102 in 2004 to 240 in 2009, it might also be expected that the number of cases involving at least one foreign defendant would rise; however, the increase in the number of cases involving at least one foreign defendant was disproportionately greater than the increase in the total number of patent cases. While the increase in the total number of patent cases was 135.3 percent from 2004 to 2009, in cases involving at least one foreign defendant the increase was 242.1 percent.

Figure 14 shows that the growth from 2004 to 2009 in cases involving at least one foreign defendant occurred in cases in which foreign defendants were sued together with U.S. co-defendants. In 2009 five times as many cases involving U.S. and foreign co-defendants were filed in the Eastern District of Texas than were filed in 2004, which contrasted with the slight decrease in the number of cases filed against only foreign defendants.

One phenomenon that might explain the disproportionate growth in cases involving U.S. and foreign co-defendants is the popularity of the Eastern District of Texas as a patent litigation venue among plaintiffs; the District has been perceived as a plaintiff-friendly venue for some time, and plaintiffs were able to secure venue in the district by suing geographically diverse defendants, including foreign defendants.[45] However, in 2008 and 2009 appellate courts rendered decisions on transfer of venue motions that attacked the District's interpretation of the transfer of venue rules and its reluctance to transfer venue to other districts. In October 2008 the U.S. Court of Appeals for the Fifth Circuit rejected the District's broad interpretation of

[43] The number of cases filed in the District of New Jersey against at least one foreign defendant grew by 28 cases—from 18 in 2004 to 46 in 2009 (*see supra* Figures 8 and 9). The number of NDA/ANDA actions filed in the District grew by 24 cases—from 8 in 2004 to 32 in 2009.

[44] *See supra* note 21.

[45] *Id.*

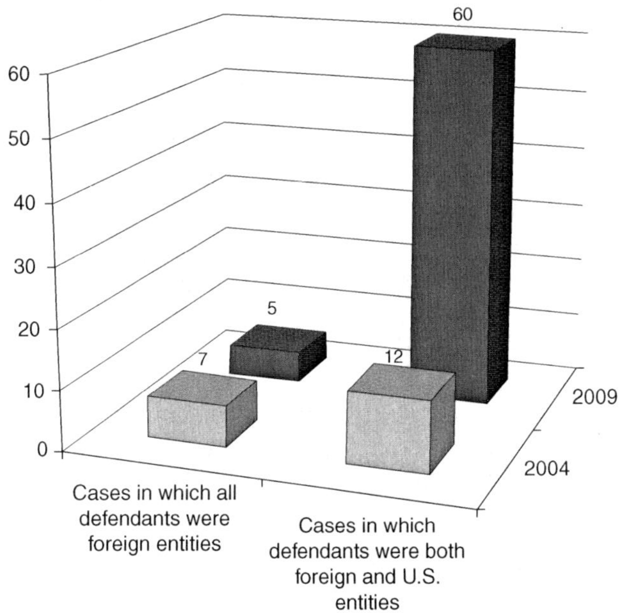

FIGURE 14: Patent cases filed in the U.S. District Court for the Eastern District of Texas in 2004 and 2009 against foreign defendants, by domicile of the defendants.

"public interest" in *In re Volkswagen of America, Inc.*;[46] the District's interpretation of "public interest" had led it to conclude that a product liability case should be tried in the District merely because the product was available for sale in the District. In December 2008 the U.S. Court of Appeals for the Federal Circuit found that the District abused its discretion when it denied a motion to transfer venue in the patent case *In re TS Tech USA Corp.*[47] Although the defendants in that case were from Ohio and Ontario, Canada, and the plaintiff was from Michigan, the District had maintained venue in Texas based on the general "substantial interest" that the citizens of the District had "in having the case tried locally."[48] The Circuit Court disagreed, and after weighing the relevant factors, including the location of evidence,[49] ordered that venue be transferred.

To maintain venue in the Eastern District of Texas after *In re TS Tech USA Corp.* plaintiffs attempted to ensure that no other district was more convenient for their litigation than the Eastern District of Texas, or at least that all other districts were

[46] In re Volkswagen of America, Inc., 545 F.3d 304 (5th Cir. 2008).

[47] In re TS Tech USA Corp., 551 F.3d 1315 (Fed. Cir. 2008).

[48] *Id.*, 1318.

[49] *Id.*, 1321. "[A]ll of the physical evidence [was] far more conveniently located near the Ohio venue." *Id.*

just as inconvenient for their litigation as the Eastern District of Texas. Plaintiffs did this by bringing suits against geographically decentralized defendants, which was initially a successful approach because the district court denied venue transfer in 2009 in several cases such as *MHL Tek, LLC v. Nissan Motor Co.*,[50] in which defendants were sued who were from New Jersey, Michigan, Tennessee, Alabama, Georgia, South Carolina, Indiana, Virginia, California, Germany, Japan, and South Korea.[51] In March 2009 the court denied a motion to transfer venue out of the District in *Novartis Vaccines and Diagnostics, Inc. v. Hoffman-La Roche Inc.*;[52] in that case the plaintiff was located in California and the defendants were located in Colorado, North Carolina, and New Jersey.[53]

Although the District's venue transfer decisions changed at the end of 2009 when the U.S. Court of Appeals for the Federal Circuit reversed the *Novartis* decision,[54] throughout 2009 plaintiffs continued to have an incentive to sue foreign defendants together with U.S. co-defendants as part of any strategy they might have had to maintain venue in the Eastern District of Texas. Of course, the situation in the Eastern District of Texas might not necessarily have resulted in plaintiffs "fabricating" additional defendants—adding foreign defendants solely for purposes of venue; it is also possible that plaintiffs who would have filed against foreign defendants in any case, perhaps even in another district, opted to file in the Eastern District of Texas because venue in the District was possible.

Figure 15 illustrates the situation in the Eastern District of Texas in 2009. Out of the 60 cases in which foreign defendants were sued together with U.S. co-defendants, 17 cases had no party involved in the litigation—either as plaintiff or defendant—who was from the Eastern District of Texas. In an additional 25 cases there was at least one plaintiff but no defendants from the District. These numbers are consistent with a hypothesis that either 1) including foreign defendants in the suits might have been a tactic to secure venue in the District, or 2) because foreign

---

50 MHL Tek, LLC v. Nissan Motor Co., Slip Copy, 2009 WL 440627 (E.D.Tex. 2009).

51 *Id.*, *1.

52 Novartis Vaccines and Diagnostics, Inc. v. Hoffman–La Roche Inc., 2:07-CV-507 (DF), docket document No. 90, February 3, 2010.

53 *Id.*, *5.

54 Novartis Vaccines and Diagnostics, Inc. v. Hoffman–La Roche Inc. In re Hoffman–La Roche Inc., 587 F.3d 1333 (Fed. Cir. 2009). The Federal Circuit Court had already issued an important decision on venue transfer in May 2009 in *In re Genentech, Inc.*, 566 F.3d 1338 (Fed. Cir. 2009); however, that case concerned two California defendants (sued by a German plaintiff) and not the scenario of decentralized defendants. The decision did suggest that a decentralization of plaintiffs (or plaintiffs combined with otherwise centralized defendants) would not suffice to protect plaintiffs' choice of the Eastern District of Texas from being subjected to a transfer to another venue.

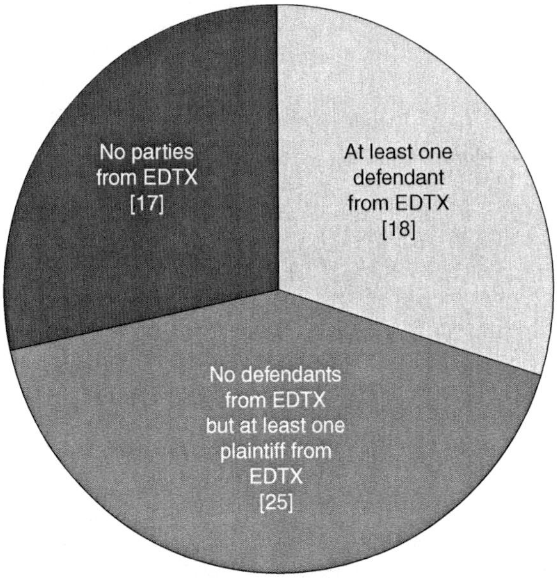

FIGURE 15: Patent cases filed in the U.S. District Court for the Eastern District of Texas in 2009 against both foreign and U.S. defendants.

defendants were to be sued, plaintiffs could file in the District and be reasonably assured that they could maintain venue in the District because foreign defendants were included in the suit.

Finally, Figure 16 shows that it is not only the number of cases that matters, but also the nature of patents at stake. Figure 16 shows the number of cases filed in all federal district courts in which at least one defendant from China or Hong Kong was sued. The cases are categorized by the types of patents that were being litigated in each case. There was a small or no increase in half of the categories of patents—patents in the areas of machine industry, apparel, and furniture. Another category that also registered only a small increase from 2004 to 2009 is entitled "other" and encompasses patents such as an "inflatable wedge for diving onto a water slide"[55] or a "tree stand"[56] (as in a Christmas tree stand). The categories with substantial increases are electronic, electric, software, and telecommunications patents (from 9 cases in 2004 to 28 cases in 2009) and chemical patents (from 0 cases in 2004 to 5 cases in 2009).

The finding presented by Figure 16 is significant because it suggests that the growth in the number of cases concerns patents that are potentially of great economic

[55] U.S. Patent 6,558,264.

[56] U.S. Patent 6,572,068.

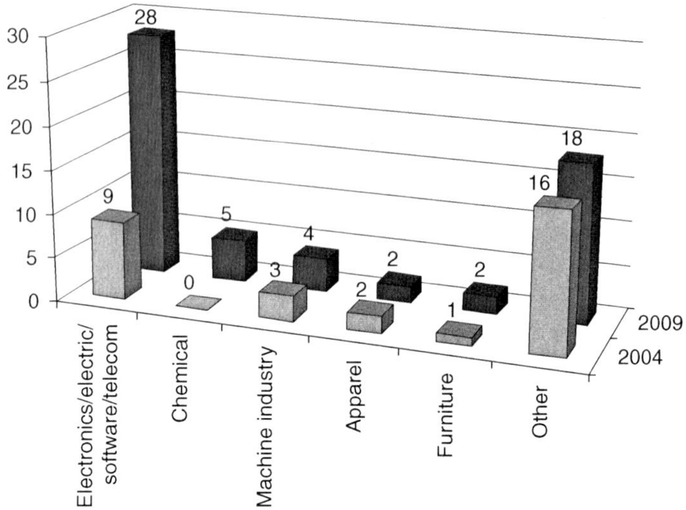

FIGURE 16: Patent cases filed in U.S. federal district courts in 2004 and 2009 against defendants from China and Hong Kong, by subject matter of the patent.

significance to the United States; effective enforcement of these categories of patents is likely to be very important for the U.S. economy.

4.2 Injunctions

The preceding section demonstrates the extent to which foreign entities are sued in patent cases. In the United States in 2004, 9.8 percent of all patent cases filed involved both foreign and U.S. co-defendants, and an additional 5.2 percent of cases were filed against foreign defendants only; in 2009 these two categories of cases were 15.2 percent and 3.7 percent, respectively, of the total number of patent cases filed.[57] In other countries, foreign entities are also being sued in patent infringement cases, either with or without domestic co-defendants. Because foreign entities may have no assets in the country of litigation, enforcement of remedies awarded in the litigation against these parties can be particularly difficult. This section reviews the difficulties connected with the enforcement of injunctions; of the remedies that may be awarded against patent infringers, injunctions pose the greatest enforcement difficulties if they must be enforced abroad.

---

[57] *See supra* Figure 6 in Section 4.1.3.

The difficulties associated with the enforcement of injunctions are not insignificant, particularly in patent infringement cases, because injunctions play such an important role in patent enforcement. As the U.S. Court of Appeals for the Federal Circuit pointed out in *Smith Intern., Inc. v. Hughes Tool Co.* in 1983, "[w]ithout the right to obtain an injunction, the right to exclude granted to the patentee would have only a fraction of the value it was intended to have, and would no longer be as great an incentive to engage in the toils of scientific and technological research."[58] Although in the United States it has become clear since then that the right to an injunction may not always function as an incentive but may actually inhibit inventing activity, and in Europe the experiences with injunctions have been similar,[59] the injunction has not lost its pivotal position as a frequent remedy in patent infringement cases; patent holders almost always request injunctions, courts regularly issue them,[60] and courts occasionally enforce them if they are not complied with voluntarily.

The following sections examine the problems of enforcement of "cross-border injunctions." The analysis is not limited to the kind of injunctions that Fawcett and Torremans termed "cross-border injunctions"; they use the term to describe injunctions "which operate[. . .] extra-territorially in respect of infringement abroad of *foreign* intellectual property rights."[61] Such injunctions have been at the center of lively discussions in Europe, and Section 4.2.2 explains the European experience. The analysis here focuses primarily on injunctions that do not concern foreign patent rights but instead are issued to enforce *domestic* patent rights while being directed at activities outside of the protecting country. Chapter 3 explained that instances exist in which conduct outside the protecting country may be deemed infringing; this section looks at how injunctions targeting such conduct may or may not be enforced.

---

[58] Smith Intern., Inc. v. Hughes Tool Co., 718 F.2d 1573, 1578 (Fed. Cir. 1983).

[59] The increasingly strong perception that injunctions are inhibitors of inventive activity can be attributed to the activities of nonpracticing entities in the United States. There have also been the first sightings of U.S.-style nonpracticing entities in Europe. *See* Philippa Maister, *German Court Sees First Signs of European Patent Trolls*, IP Law & Business, Oct. 2, 2008, *available at* Law.com, http://www.law.com/jsp/article.jsp?id=1202424954133 (last visited Sept. 2, 2011). In the first reported case an injunction was issued—*see Unterlassungsansprüche einer Patentverwertungsgesellschaft*, Landgericht Mannheim, 7 O 94/08, Feb. 27, 2009. Although the defendants apparently tried to convince the court that it should adopt an approach to injunctions comparable to the one used in the United States, the court rejected such suggestions, issued the injunction, and emphasized that it was bound by German law. *Id.*, para. 94. On appeal the Oberlandesgericht Karlsruhe stayed the injunction pending the decision on the merits. Oberlandesgericht Karlsruhe, 6 U 38/09, May 11, 2009. *See also* Nokia GmbH v. Ipcom GmbH & Co KG [2009] EWHC 3482 (Pat) (Ch D (Patents Ct)).

[60] On the situation under German law, see *Unterlassungsansprüche einer Patentverwertungsgesellschaft*, Landgericht Mannheim, 7 O 94/08, 27 Feb. 2009, paras. 95–97. *See also* Oberlandesgericht Karlsruhe, 6 U 38/09, May 11, 2009.

[61] James J. Fawcett & Paul Torremans, Intellectual Property and Private International Law 218 (1998) (emphasis added).

4.2.1 CROSS-BORDER INJUNCTIONS IN U.S. COURTS

Injunctions prohibiting future infringements are a classical feature of patent infringement cases and tend to be frequently requested in U.S. courts. Although there were concerns about whether plaintiffs would stand as high a chance of obtaining injunctive relief as they did before the Supreme Court in *eBay Inc. v. MercExchange, L.L.C.*[62] rejected the practice of almost automatic awards of such relief in patent cases,[63] injunctions continue to be issued frequently; according to the University of Houston Law Center Institute for Intellectual Property and Information Law, in 118 post-*eBay* rulings entered before January 11, 2010, courts awarded permanent injunctions in 89 cases, or in 75 percent of the cases in which they were requested.[64]

It is interesting to view the data on injunctions from the perspective of the involvement of foreign defendants. Of the 89 cases in which injunctions were issued after *eBay*, 20 involved foreign defendants together with U.S. co-defendants, and in 18 of these cases injunctions were awarded against both the U.S. and foreign defendants; in the two remaining cases the injunctions were issued only against the U.S. defendants. Additionally, in four cases out of the total of 89 cases foreign entities alone were sued, and in all four cases injunctions were issued.

As for the rate of success in obtaining injunctions against foreign as opposed to U.S. defendants, the data show very small differences in the success rates. In the 118 post-*eBay* cases in which injunctions were requested, the country of domicile of the defendants seemed to have no particular impact on court decisions to issue injunctions. Injunctions were issued in 83 percent of cases that involved a foreign defendant compared to 72 percent of cases in which no foreign defendants were involved; injunctions were issued in 100 percent of cases in which defendants were only foreign entities, but no conclusions can be drawn from the percentage because it is based on a population of only four cases. Given the relatively small difference in the percentages it does not seem to be reasonable to suggest that it was slightly easier for plaintiffs to obtain permanent injunctions in cases that involved foreign defendants than it was in cases involving only U.S. defendants. Apparently, though, it seems it was not *more* difficult to obtain an injunction against a foreign entity than against a U.S. entity, and that courts have not hesitated to issue such injunctions. This finding

---

[62] eBay Inc. v. MercExchange, L.L.C., 547 U.S. 388 (2006).

[63] Mitchell G. Stockwell, *Implementing* eBay*: New Problems in Guiding Judicial Discretion and Enforcing Patent Rights*, 88 J. PAT. & TRADEMARK OFF. SOC'Y 747 (2006); Douglas Ellis, John Jarosz, Michael Chapman, & L. Scott Oliver, *The Economic Implications (and Uncertainties) of Obtaining Permanent Injunctive Relief After* eBay v. MercExchange, 17 FED. CIR. B.J. 437 (2008).

[64] Post-eBay Perm. Injunction Rulings by District Courts, Patstats, U.S. Patent Litigation Statistics, *available at* http://www.patstats.org/Patstats2.html (last visited Sept. 2, 2011).

necessarily raises the question of whether injunctions against foreign entities are targeting acts outside U.S. borders, and if so, what the success rate of the enforcement of such injunctions might be.

The assessment of the territorial scope of an injunction is not as simple as it might initially appear to be; it requires a detailed review not only of the text of the injunction but also of the facts of the particular case. This section gives examples of injunctions that were issued in cases that were identified either from the 2004 population described earlier in Section 4.1 or in the post-*eBay* dataset by the University of Houston Law Center Institute for Intellectual Property and Information Law.[65]

Most injunctions issued in patent infringement cases follow the wording typical for injunctive relief in patent cases by simply reiterating the statutory language of the Patent Act that prohibits acts of infringement. For instance, in *Lumitex, Inc. v. Sheffmed Trade Services LTD*[66] the U.K. defendant was ordered not to "make, have made, use, sell or offer for sale in the United States any Illuminated surgical refractor covered by the claims of the [. . .] patent, including but not limited to Sheffmed's 'Neon' Illuminated surgical retractor."[67]

Injunctions that concern acts of inducement may also follow statutory language; for instance, the consent decree in *Prima Tek II LLC v. Leong*[68] targeted both inducement and contributory infringement under Section 271(b) and (c). The acts of inducement were prohibited by the court as it enjoined the Canadian defendants "against, directly or indirectly, making, using, selling, offering for sale or importing, or aiding or encouraging others, directly or indirectly, in the making, using, selling, offering for sale or importing any [products] that would infringe, [. . .] or induce or contribute to the infringement of any claim of Plaintiff's [valid patents]."[69]

Other injunctions have targeted infringement under Section 271(g); for example, in *3M Company* et al. *v. Asia Sun (Taiwan) Inc.*[70] the district court enjoined the Taiwanese defendant from "importing into or selling in the United States its [infringing product] or similar product made by the same method."[71] In the same injunction the court used sweeping language prohibiting the defendant "from otherwise

[65] Post-eBay Perm. Injunction Rulings by District Courts, Patstats, U.S. Patent Litigation Statistics, as of Jan. 11, 2010, *available at* http://www.patstats.org/Patstats2.html (last visited Sept. 2, 2011).

[66] Lumitex, Inc. v. Sheffmed Trade Services LTD, case No. 1:04-cv-02225-AA, N.D. Ohio.

[67] Consent Judgment and Stipulated Permanent Injunction, docket document 16, filed June 21, 2005, p. 2.

[68] Prima Tek II LLC v. Leong, case No. 3:04-cv-00214-MJR-CJP, S.D. Ill.

[69] Consent Decree, docket document 4, filed May 3, 2004, pp. 4–5.

[70] 3M Company et al. v. Asia Sun (Taiwan) Inc., case No. 2:04-cv-00417-TJW, E.D. Tex.

[71] Final Judgment, docket document 10, filed June 20, 2005, p. 3.

infringing" the patent;[72] the same language also appeared in *O_2 Micro Int'l v. Beyond Innovation* et al.[73] despite criticism by the U.S. Court of Appeals for the Federal Circuit that such injunctions are contrary to Rule 65(d) of the Federal Rules of Civil Procedure and the relevant U.S. Supreme Court interpretation, which require a higher level of specificity for an injunction.[74] One injunction concerned infringement under Section 271(e), and thus the injunction paralleled the wording of Section 271(e)(4)(B).

In addition to prohibiting acts of infringement, courts may also order defendants to affirmatively act in a certain manner. For instance, in *O_2 Micro Int'l* the court required very specific conduct by the Taiwanese defendants, who were sued for their infringement of two of plaintiff's patents for high efficiency adaptive DC/AC converters. Following a trial in which the jury found that the defendants induced and contributed to the infringement,[75] the court entered a permanent injunction against the defendants not only prohibiting infringing acts ("manufacturing, using, selling, offering to sell or importing into the United States") but also ordering the defendants to "label prominently their respective inverter controller or module products covered by this order and their accompanying product literature 'Not for Sale in, Use in, or importation into the United States.'"[76]

In this last example, the cross-border nature of the injunction is obvious; the foreign defendants are ordered to act in a certain way when manufacturing their products outside the United States. However, the extraterritorial reach of an injunction may not always be so explicit; for instance, if the order imposes the obligation "to deliver" infringing products to the plaintiff in the United States and "to buy" original products from the plaintiff in the United States, the wording might seem to suggest that only behavior in the United States is governed and expected, but such language encompasses the defendant's behavior abroad when in order "to deliver" in the United States the defendant has to package and arrange for the delivery from abroad. Similarly, a defendant may make purchases in the United States but use assets located abroad to do so.

---

[72] *Id.*

[73] O_2 Micro Int'l v. Beyond Innovation et al., case No. 2:04-cv-00032-TJW, E.D.Tex.

[74] KSM Fastening Systems, Inc. v. H.A. Jones Co., Inc., 776 F.2d 1522, 1526 (Fed. Cir. 1985). On the need for specificity of injunctions, see also *Abbott Laboratories v. Torpharm, Inc.*, 503 F.3d 1372, 1382 (Fed. Cir. 2007), and *Tivo Inc. v. Echostar Corp.*, 646 F.3d 869, 884 ff. (Fed. Cir. 2011).

[75] Verdict Form, docket document 367, filed May 15, 2006.

[76] Final Judgment and Permanent Injunction, docket document 425, filed Mar. 21, 2007. The injunction was vacated by the U.S. Court of Appeals for the Federal Circuit once it vacated the jury verdict and the final judgment of infringement and remanded the case to the district court for further proceedings. O_2 Micro Intern. Ltd. v. Beyond Innovation Technology Co., Ltd., 521 F.3d 1351 (Fed. Cir. 2008).

The extraterritorial reach of an injunction might be less obvious in a case involving the classical negative injunction that prohibits infringing behavior. In the abstract, to the extent that the text of the injunction parallels the statutory language, one might expect the extraterritorial reach of the injunction to extend as far as the extraterritorial scope of the statute. If inducement of patent infringement is prohibited by an injunction, the extraterritorial reach of the injunction depends on the extent to which the statute applies to conduct abroad that induces infringement of a U.S. patent.[77] As a practical matter, the injunction should be designed primarily to prevent prior infringing acts from recurring; therefore, if the infringing acts such as the acts of inducement that led to the injunction occurred outside the United States, the injunction should target such extraterritorial conduct as long as the conduct would continue to infringe or induce infringement.[78] *Litecubes, L.L.C.* et al. *v. Northern Light Products*[79] provides a good example of prior extraterritorial acts that were considered infringing; the negative injunction issued in the case is extraterritorial, as it targets such acts by the defendant.

The injunction issued in *Litecubes* prohibited the defendant from engaging in certain acts in Canada that the court considered as infringing plaintiff's U.S. patent. The defendant, a Canadian company, sold a product to U.S. customers that infringed the plaintiff's U.S. patent for an "illuminatable novelty item that can be placed in beverages." After a jury entered a verdict of willful infringement, the defendant moved for dismissal for lack of subject matter jurisdiction, claiming that jurisdiction should be limited to acts committed within the United States and arguing that its acts were purely extraterritorial because it had no physical presence in the United States and shipped the products to its clients free on board, thereby passing legal title to the goods in Canada and not in the United States.[80] However, the U.S. Court of Appeals for the Federal Circuit disagreed and rejected the notion that an inquiry concerning the place of infringement should have any impact on subject matter jurisdiction. Additionally, the court pointed out that when goods are shipped free

---

[77] *See* Chapter 3, Section 3.5, on the territorial scope of the inducement provision in the U.S. Patent Act. 35 U.S.C. §271(b).

[78] However, courts cannot be expected to later interpret such injunctions as prohibiting some other extraterritorial conduct that does not constitute infringement under U.S. patent law. For instance, in *International Rectifier Corporation v. Samsung Electronics Co., Ltd. et al.*, 361 F.3d 1355 (Fed. Cir. 2004), the Court refused to extend the scope of a permanent injunction to defendant's activities outside the United States. *See also* Robert J. Benson, *Beyond Borders: How U.S. Patent and Copyright Laws Can Reach Transactions That Occur Entirely Outside U.S. Borders*, 18 INTELL. PROP. & TECH. L.J. 15, 18 ff. (2008).

[79] Litecubes, L.L.C. et al. v. Northern Light Products, case No. 4:04-cv-00485-ERW, E.D. Mo.

[80] *See* Chapter 3, Section 3.6, for a discussion of the "free on board" argument in localizing a sale for purposes of the Patent Act.

on board, "the sale also occurred at the location of the buyer";[81] therefore, under these circumstances, by enjoining the defendant from "selling in the United States," the court actually enjoined the defendant from acting in Canada.

The case of a free on board shipment is not the only scenario in which a patent may be infringed by acts committed abroad or in multiple locations simultaneously;[82] patents may also be infringed by activities on the Internet that are initiated from abroad.[83] Offers to sell, or the sale and use of a patented product or method may occur on the Internet and result in liability, either for the direct acts or for inducement or contributory infringement. For instance, a foreign company offering distance learning packages on the Internet may sell its products to U.S. customers in the form of software downloadable from the Internet that operates in conjunction with online services provided by the company. The sale of the software and the related online services may constitute direct infringements of U.S. patents, or the sale of the software and the related online services may be deemed acts of inducement or contributory infringement. In all such instances, an injunction aimed at acts committed online impacts the defendant's behavior regardless of the jurisdiction from which he initiates his activities; even if injunctions target only the activities that have effects inside the territory of the United States, they have to require or prohibit certain conduct by defendants outside the United States to prevent such effects in the United States.[84]

Given the extraterritorial reach of U.S. patent law it is not surprising that U.S. courts issue cross-border injunctions; when asked to enforce the law in its full territorial scope, courts may prohibit conduct beyond U.S. borders to the same extent that the law itself prohibits such conduct. Thus, if U.S. patent law views shipping free on board from abroad to U.S. customers as conduct that infringes a U.S. patent, a U.S. court may prohibit such conduct through an injunction. Even if packaging the products in Canada and handing them in Canada to a Canadian shipping

---

[81] Litecubes, LLC v. Northern Light Products, Inc., 523 F.3d 1353, 1369 (Fed. Cir. 2008); cert. denied on Nov. 10, 2008.

[82] *See* Chapter 3, Section 3.6, on acts committed in multiple locations.

[83] Burk, Chapter 3, note 7, 38 ff.

[84] Mark A. Lemley & Philip J. Weiser, *Should Property or Liability Rules Govern Information?*, 85 TEX. L. REV. 783, 803, 805 (2007). Naturally, before an inquiry into potentially infringing activities may begin, courts must establish personal jurisdiction; this may entail weighing additional characteristics of defendants' Internet activities unless other facts warrant the exercise of personal jurisdiction over the defendants. On the issue of establishing personal jurisdiction on the basis of activity on the Internet, see, for instance, *Trintec Industries, Inc. v. Pedre Promotional Products, Inc.*, 395 F.3d 1275 (Fed. Cir. 2005). For an overview of the development of the approaches of U.S. courts to jurisdiction on the Internet, see Michael Geist, *The Shift Toward "Targeting" for Internet Jurisdiction*, *in* WHO RULES THE NET? 91 (Adam Thierer & Clyde Wayne Crews, Jr. eds., 2003), 94–105.

company for shipment free on board to U.S. customers is completely legal under Canadian law, a U.S.-issued injunction will target such activity as conduct that constitutes infringement under U.S. patent law.

U.S. courts do not necessarily limit their cross-border interventions only to conduct that is infringing under U.S. patent law when they attempt to prevent infringement of U.S. patents. As the U.S. Court of Appeals for the Federal Circuit opined in *Johns Hopkins University v. CellPro, Inc.*, "[a]n injunction [. . .] can reach extraterritorial activities [. . .], even if these activities do not themselves constitute infringement" as long as the injunction is designed to "*prevent infringement* of a United States patent."[85] The order requiring a Taiwanese company to attach certain labels to its products in Taiwan is an example of such an injunction; it is aimed at conduct abroad that has nothing to do with infringing U.S. activity per se, but the court ordered the conduct nevertheless because it considered it to be an appropriate tool to "prevent infringement of a U.S. patent."[86]

Whether a cross-border injunction targets foreign conduct actually found to infringe a U.S. patent or conduct that is noninfringing under U.S. patent law, the injunction clearly intrudes into another state's sovereign territory. If the defendant does not comply voluntarily and enforcement becomes necessary, the enforcement power of U.S. courts extends outside the U.S. de facto only if the defendant is a U.S. entity, or a foreign entity that has some physical presence in the United States or assets located in the United States that can be reached by U.S. courts. Such defendants may be ordered by U.S. courts to act in a certain manner abroad, but the successful enforcement of an injunction against a foreign entity with no presence or assets in the United States depends entirely on the degree to which the courts of other countries are willing to lend their power to enforce U.S.-issued (or, in general, foreign-issued) injunctions pertaining to the jurisdiction of foreign courts.

4.2.2 CROSS-BORDER INJUNCTIONS IN EUROPE

U.S. courts are not alone in granting injunctions in patent cases that reach beyond domestic borders; in fact, Europe has actually been the hotbed of debates about cross-border relief in patent cases for the past two decades, although the cross-border injunctions that have generated the debates among European patent practitioners, judges, and academics were of a different type than the U.S. injunctions

[85] Johns Hopkins University v. CellPro, Inc., 152 F.3d 1342, 1366–67 (Fed. Cir. 1998).

[86] *Cf.* the dissenting opinion in *Tivo Inc. v. Echostar Corp.*,646 F.3d 869 (Fed. Cir. 2011) questioning whether a court "would even have the authority to issue an injunction barring design-arounds" in light of the strong policy favoring encouragement of design-arounds. *Id.*, 893.

discussed above in Section 4.2.1; they were the so-called "pan-European" injunctions that targeted infringements of foreign patents.[87]

The European practice of issuing cross-border injunctions based on infringements of foreign patent rights was widely criticized,[88] and commentators expressed hopes that the Court of Justice of the European Union (CJEU) would find a way to stop the practice. Indeed, the fact that the injunctions pertained to other countries' patents made them much more intrusive to the sovereignty of foreign countries than are the U.S.-issued cross-border injunctions, because the pan-European injunctions were based on the premise that the issuing courts could adjudicate the infringement of foreign countries' patents. The CJEU decisions in *GAT*[89] and *Roche*,[90] which were expected to extinguish the practice of pan-European injunctions, did not go that far;[91] Lord Justice Jacob noted in a qualified observation that the CJEU "virtually" "put an end" to the practice,[92] but the rulings did leave some limited space for cross-border relief concerning foreign patents.[93]

Injunctions such as the pan-European injunctions that target infringements of foreign patent rights are unlikely to appear any time soon in the United States. As explained earlier in Chapter 2, Section 2.1.6.1, although isolated cases have been reported in the United States in which considerations of infringements of foreign

---

[87] *See supra* note 61 for the definition of "cross-border injunctions" by Fawcett & Torremans.

[88] Pitz & Meibom, Chapter 2, note 53, 478; Remco E. P. De Ranitz, *Jan Brinkhof in Conversation with Remco De Ranitz*, 21 EUR. INTELL. PROP. REV. 142, 142 (1999); Franzosi, *Germany*, Chapter II, note 74, N174; Véron, *Thirty Years*, Chapter 2, note 53, 441; Bruno Vandermeulen, *Harmonization of IP Litigation Practice—Still a Long Road Ahead*, 1 J. INTELL. PROP. L. & PRAC. 30 (2005), 34.

[89] *GAT*, Chapter 2, note 57.

[90] *Roche*, Chapter 2, note 58.

[91] Commentators' predictions have ranged from positions that such injunctions will become "much more limited" and possible only "in certain circumstances," because their availability will be "severely curtaile[d]," to predictions that cross-border injunctions will be rendered "effectively dead." *Bettacare*, Chapter 2, note 101.

Döring & van Velsen, Chapter 2, note 98, 860; Jochen Bühling, *Cross-Border Injunctions in Patent Infringement Cases: Paradise Lost?*, *in* BUILDING AND ENFORCING INTELLECTUAL PROPERTY VALUE (Krieger Mes & Grad v. der Groeben, 2007), 172–75, 174 ("Paradise has not been lost for patentees, but it has become a little shady."); *ECJ Ruling Against European Cross-Border Relief Will Provide Further Impetus for a European Patents Court*, Simmons & Simmons, *available at* http://www.simmons-simmons.com/docs/ipupdateaug06ecjrulingdetailedanalysis.pdf (last visited Sept. 2, 2011), 1. Alastair J. McCulloch & Neil Coulson, *The (Cross) Border Is Closed: ECJ Rules on Patent Injunctions*, *available at* http://www.jonesday.com/pubs/pubs_detail.aspx?pubID=S3557 (last visited Sept. 2, 2011); Steven Warner & Susie Middlemiss, *Patent Litigation in Multiple Jurisdictions: An End to Cross Border Relief in Europe*, 28 EUR. INTELL. PROP. REV. 580 (2006), 580. Pertegas, *EC: Patents*, Chapter II, note 106; Joseph, Chapter II, note 91, 857; Radcliffe, Chapter II, note 91 ("[T]his will effectively end cross-border injunctions in patent cases.").

[92] Jacob, *The Judge's Perspective*, Chapter II, note 55, 4.

[93] *See* Chapter 2, Section 2.1.2.

patents were entertained by U.S. courts,[94] the current approach of the U.S. Court of Appeals for the Federal Circuit, as outlined in *Voda*, seems to indicate that the court is not inclined to agree with the assertion of jurisdiction over foreign patents.[95]

While pan-European injunctions have no counterpart in U.S. case law, the U.S. cross-border injunctions analyzed above in Section 4.2.1 do have mirror images in Europe; the European injunctions, which cover conduct by foreign entities but pertain to domestic patents, have not been specifically discussed in the European literature. These injunctions have been mentioned only if they were issued as pan-European injunctions, which often encompass not only conduct involving foreign patents but also activities that infringe domestic patents. However, outside the context of pan-European injunctions, the lack of literature on the point, combined with a limited availability of court decisions in patent cases, makes the inquiry into the injunction practice in Europe much more difficult than it is in the United States.[96]

Even from the limited information available in Europe one can still observe that European courts issue cross-border injunctions similar to those issued by U.S. courts. Jurisdiction over foreign companies in such cases was confirmed, for instance, when the Swiss Federal Supreme Court decided that Swiss courts had jurisdiction over a U.S. defendant in an action for a Swiss patent infringement in Switzerland in which the plaintiff requested an injunction against the U.S. defendant who had no physical presence in Switzerland. The court noted that the manufacturing abroad of the products by the U.S. defendant was "of itself not sufficient to establish patent infringement within the territory of Switzerland," but if the defendant "[took] measures that facilitate[d] the sale of these products in Switzerland, its participation in infringement ultimately occurring in Switzerland [was] to be upheld."[97]

Referring to the same decision by the Swiss Supreme Court, the Mannheim Landgericht stated that although "the effect of the patent protection is limited to the territory of the protecting country [. . .i]t does not exclude civil liability of the participators (inducers, indirect infringers, joint infringers or contributors) for infringement committed within the country when the participators acted exclusively abroad but from there induced or supported the use of the patent [in the

---

[94] *See* Brief for Amici Curiae Law Professors in Support of the Appellee, Jan K. Voda, M.D. v. Cordis Corporation, No. 05-1238 (Fed. Cir. July 29, 2005), 12.

[95] Jan K. Voda, M.D. v. Cordis Corporation, 476 F.3d 887 (Fed. Cir. 2007). *See* Chapter 2, Section 2.1.6.1, for a more detailed discussion of the case.

[96] *See supra* the introduction to Section 4.1 for a discussion about the accessibility of European patent decisions and case files.

[97] *Test Cassettes*, Bundesgericht, No. 4C. 196/2002, Oct. 7, 2002, reported in IIC Vol. 35, 2/2004, 206–09, 208.

protecting country]."[98] Neither the Mannheim Landgericht nor the Swiss Supreme Court suggested that injunctions could not be issued against the defendants in these cases, and injunctions, even if worded to target only actions in Switzerland or Germany, would in fact cover defendants' conduct abroad and theoretically could require enforcement outside the countries of the issuing courts.

An example of an injunction issued against a foreign entity for its actions abroad that resulted in infringement of a domestic patent is provided in the decision of the Düsseldorf Landgericht in *Elektrisches Steckergehäuse*.[99] The Italian defendant supplied a Slovenian company with electrical connector housings covered by plaintiff's German patent[100] with the understanding that the housings would be installed by the Slovenian company in washing machines destined for the German market. The court found the defendant to be a participator in infringement under German patent law and enjoined the defendant from "in the Federal Republic of Germany offering, introducing into the stream of commerce, using, or for such purposes importing or owning" the product infringing the German patent at issue. Again, although formulated as being strictly limited to German territory, the injunction clearly regulated defendant's behavior outside Germany.

An injunction with the same wording was issued in *Sohlen für Sportschuhe*,[101] a case involving infringement by a foreign entity on the Internet. The Düsseldorf Landgericht granted an injunction against a U.S. entity that advertised on the Internet athletic shoes that included a "multilayered athletic shoe sole" covered by a German patent.[102] The U.S. entity claimed that it did not sell any shoes directly to German customers, but its website provided a list of distributors in Germany to which the entity supplied its shoes and from which the customers could purchase them. The U.S. entity argued that its website did not target German customers but was oriented only toward the U.S. market (it was apparently available only in English), that not all of its shoe models were sold outside the United States, and that a German customer could not actually order and purchase the shoes at issue from the U.S. entity. Additionally, it claimed that it prohibited the retailers to which it linked on its website from selling or shipping any of its products to customers outside the United States. However, the court dismissed these arguments, concluding from the use of the word "worldwide" in defendant's domain name that the defendant was ready to serve customers anywhere, including in Germany; the court

[98] *Kondensatore für Klimaanlage*, Chapter 3, note 210, para. 37.

[99] Landgericht Düsseldorf, Juli 31, 2007, Az. 4b O 199/06—*Elektrisches Steckergehäuse*.

[100] German patent DE3912730, published May 23, 1990. The plaintiff held no patents for the invention in countries other than Germany.

[101] *Sohlen für Sportschuhe*, Chapter 3, note 251.

[102] European patent EP0548475, published June 30, 1993. The plaintiff held no U.S. patent for this invention.

further found that the U.S. defendant targeted the German market by virtue of its listing of a German distributor on the website. Additionally, there was proof that a person authorized by the plaintiff actually used the website to order a pair of the shoes at issue and the pair was indeed delivered in Germany. The court therefore agreed with the plaintiff that the U.S. entity offered the shoes for sale in Germany and that it supplied the shoes to Germany or "caused them to be supplied" there, and issued the injunction, which clearly had an extraterritorial aim despite its formulation in purely domestic terms.

4.2.3 CHALLENGES TO ENFORCEMENT OF INJUNCTIONS ABROAD

Courts should refrain from issuing injunctions that require conduct abroad simply out of respect for other countries' sovereignty. However, as indicated in the previous sections, patent cases provide an interesting pool of instances in which courts reach defendants' activities outside the protecting country; in the U.S. courts may even target behavior that is not considered infringing per se if they deem it necessary to prevent infringement of a U.S. patent.[103] Injunctions that target conduct abroad could be perceived as unreasonably intrusive by foreign countries; for instance, when a U.S. court prohibits a Canadian company from shipping products free on board from Canada to U.S. customers, it clearly affects the behavior of the company in Canada and the company's Canadian revenue and tax contribution as a Canadian taxpayer. If a U.S. court prohibits a Canadian company from selling a downloadable Internet product to customers located in the United States, it will again be in Canada where the company will have to take action to comply with the injunction, and Canada may lose tax revenue stemming from such cross-border trade.

Any economic interest that Canada or another foreign country has might be outweighed by its desire to follow the principle of international comity, which leads courts of different countries to recognize and enforce each other's decisions unless an exception applies. The principle of comity promotes the notion that a court will enforce a foreign court's decision today with the expectation that the foreign court will reciprocate when the situation reverses in the future. However, foreign courts may be highly critical of injunctions that aim to prohibit conduct that is actually legal from the point of view of the foreign countries where such injunctions should be enforced.[104]

---

[103] Johns Hopkins University v. CellPro, Inc., 152 F.3d 1342, 1366–67 (Fed. Cir. 1998).

[104] Lucasfilm Limited et al. v. Andrew Ainsworth et al., [2009] EWCA Civ 1328, para. 176 (Eng.). Justice Jacob pointed out the potential "clash of the IP policies of different countries." He noted that "[t]he effect of the injunction [based on U.S. copyright law] is that the defendant is restrained from doing acts in [England] which by the laws [of England] are lawful. This is because American law says they are not lawful."

4.2.3.1 Enforcement of an Injunction

A plaintiff who seeks enforcement of a cross-border injunction abroad against a foreign defendant with no presence in the country where the injunction was issued has two options for "exporting" such an injunction: The plaintiff may request recognition and enforcement by a foreign court of the final decision containing the injunction, or the plaintiff may proceed with an enforcement action before the court that issued the injunction, obtain a contempt order, and then seek recognition and enforcement of the contempt order abroad. Either option might be possible, and the two can even be utilized in tandem; however, both present certain difficulties that plaintiffs should be aware of and consider, not only when seeking enforcement but also when designing their litigation strategies. In addition to their high costs and complicated logistics, both methods of enforcement are likely to expose plaintiffs to two problems associated with recognition and enforcement, namely the requirement of finality and the public policy exception.

Principles of private international law require that a foreign decision be final before a country's courts may recognize and enforce the foreign decision. Although the concept of finality may vary in detail from country to country,[105] the requirement is likely to eliminate preliminary injunctions or temporary restraining orders from enforcement outside the protecting country.[106] The requirement also postpones the enforcement of a permanent injunction abroad until after a nonappealable decision is issued or the statute of limitations for an appeal expires. This may lead to a significant gap between the points in time when the injunction becomes effective in the protecting country and enforceable abroad because, unless stayed pending appeal,[107] the injunction will be effective in the protecting country as of the date of issue in the protecting country but be on hold abroad for several years until an appellate decision is issued. Naturally, in this interim period a court of the protecting country may attempt to secure compliance by issuing contempt orders against a noncompliant defendant, but since the enforcement of contempt orders is likely to be delayed as well, or even be impossible for public policy reasons, as explained later

---

[105] Arthur T. von Mehren & Donald T. Trautman, *Recognition of Foreign Adjudications: A Survey and a Suggested Approach*, 81 HARV. L. REV. 1601, 1656–58 (1967–1968).

[106] On enforcement of foreign provisional remedies in the United States, see Lawrence W. Newman & Michael Burrows, *Enforcement of Foreign Provisional Remedies*, 212 INTERNATIONAL LITIGATION (1994); Lawrence W. Newman, *Orders In Support of Foreign Proceedings*, 226 INTERNATIONAL LITIGATION (2001).

[107] On stays of injunctions pending appeal, see George M. Sirilla, William P. Atkins, & Stephanie F. Goeller, *Will* eBay *Bring Down the Curtain on Automatic Injunctions in Patent Cases?*, 15 FED. CIR. B.J. 587, 607–14 (2005–2006).

in this section, the plaintiff may be without an effective remedy for a lengthy period of time.

The time gap in foreign enforceability may be mitigated by a provisional measure granted by a foreign court in support of the domestic proceedings if the foreign court is willing to award the measure. For instance, interim relief in support of foreign proceedings is available in England[108] under Article 25 of the Civil Jurisdiction and Judgments Act 1982, which provides for interim relief in support of not only commenced foreign proceedings but also prospective foreign proceedings.[109] Where foreign patent infringement proceedings have not yet been brought, Article 50(6) of the TRIPs Agreement requires that the defendant be allowed to request that the provisional measure "be revoked or otherwise cease to have effect, if proceedings leading to a decision on the merits of the case are not initiated within" the required period.[110] The issue of provisional measures in support of foreign patent infringement proceedings is another topic that yet awaits an empirical inquiry.[111]

In addition to the problem of finality, authors of proposals for an international instrument on the recognition and enforcement of court decisions in intellectual property matters have addressed the problem that occurs when the content of an injunction is incompatible with a foreign country's laws or the enforcement abilities of that country's courts. This type of case might arise if the issuing court ordered certain conduct that foreign courts would not recognize as enforceable by a court action in their own country. Although in theory such a problem could arise, it does not appear that the injunctions that are typically issued in the United States in patent infringement cases[112] are likely to generate any serious content-related concerns that

---

[108] Article 25 of the Civil Jurisdiction and Judgments Act 1982.

[109] The availability of interim relief is not limited to proceedings commenced in a country of the Brussels I Regulation; it can also be granted in proceedings commenced in a country outside the Brussels regime, as long as the proceedings' "subject-matter is within the scope of the Regulation as determined by Article 1 of the Regulation (whether or not the Regulation has effect in relation to the proceedings)." Article 25.1.b) of the Civil Jurisdiction and Judgments Act 1982. Patent matters are within the scope of the Regulation.

[110] Defendants may request revocation of such measures if proceedings on the merits are not initiated within twenty working days or thirty-one calendar days, whichever is longer. TRIPs, Chapter 1, note 19, Article 50(6).

[111] In 2000 Steffen Schwarz commented on a lack of cases concerning one specific type of interim relief: "Though Mareva injunctions have never been issued in cases related to infringement of IPRs there is no reason why this should not be a subject matter in the future." Steffen Schwarz, *Freezing Orders in the Context of the Lugano Convention and the TRIPs Agreement* (2004) (MAS-IP Diploma Papers & Research Reports, No. 13), 31. On provisional measures in support of foreign proceedings in general, see, for instance, Newman, *Orders, supra* note 106; David Westin & Peter Chrocziel, *Interim Relief Awarded by U.S. and German Courts in Support of Foreign Proceedings*, 28 COLUM. J. TRANSNAT'L L. 723 (1990); George Bermann, *Provisional Relief in Transnational Litigation*, 35 COLUM. J. TRANSNAT'L L. 553 (1997).

[112] *See supra* Section 4.2.1 for a discussion of injunctions issued in U.S. patent cases.

would require a foreign court to seek alternative remedies. However, difficulties may arise if injunctions target conduct occurring simultaneously in multiple countries, such as on the Internet. These difficulties may sometimes be eliminated by the application of mechanisms that can localize the effects of injunctions so that they are comparable to the effects that are achieved in cases of injunctions concerning other media.[113]

It is unclear whether an injunction issued by a foreign court that is based on the patent law of the enforcing country will trigger the public policy exception; the cases involving pan-European injunctions in which the public policy exception was raised provide guidance only inside the countries that are bound by the Brussels regime, which has not been replicated anywhere else in the world. Isolated instances of enforcement of pan-European injunctions have been reported but none of them have resulted in a finding of repugnancy to the public policy of the enforcing country. In 1994 the Paris Court of Appeal chose to recognize and enforce a pan-European injunction in the territory of France,[114] although the opposing party argued that the Dutch injunction was contrary to French public policy because 1) French law did not provide for preliminary injunctions in patent cases, and 2) Dutch rules concerning the burden of proof differed from French rules. The court rejected both arguments and concluded that the recognition of the Dutch order was not contrary to French public policy.[115] Similarly, in 2004 the Köln Oberlandesgericht faced a question of enforcement of a pan-European injunction issued by The Hague District Court in which the defendant was prohibited from indirectly infringing certain European patents in multiple countries.[116] The Oberlandesgericht rejected the argument that the injunction would be contrary to German public policy; it reiterated that only if "the recognition of the foreign decision appears absolutely unacceptable according to the evaluation of the German legal order" would it be held to be repugnant to German public policy.[117] If an injunction concerns infringement of a

---

[113] *See, e.g.*, Dan Jerker B. Svantesson, *Geo-Location Technologies and Other Means of Placing Borders on the "Borderless" Internet*, 23 MARSHALL J. COMPUTER & INFO. L. 101 (2004). For a rather skeptical view of currently available technological means, see Kimberlee Weatherall, *Can Substantive Law Harmonisation and Technology Provide Genuine Alternatives to Conflict Rules in Intellectual Property?*, 11 MEDIA & ARTS L. REV. 393 (2006). *See also* Marketa Trimble, *The Future of Cybertravel: Legal Implications of the Evasion of Geolocation*, manuscript, on file with the author.

[114] Braillecellen II, [1994] B.E.E. 394, No. 111, Jan. 28, 1994 (Fr.), reported in Tony Huydecoper, *Netherlands: Extra-Territoriality: French Appeal Court Recognises and Enforces Netherlands Decision Having Extra-Territorial Effect*, 17 EUR. INTELL. PROP. REV. D73 (1995); Pitz & Meibom, Chapter 2, note 53, 476.

[115] Huydecoper, *supra* note 114; Véron, *Thirty Years*, Chapter 2, note 53, 436.

[116] Oberlandesgericht Köln, 16 W 2/04, Mar. 17, 2004.

[117] *Id.*

patent of the country where the injunction was issued, the public policy exception should pose no difficulty as long as the scope of the injunction is limited.

An injunction will be denied enforcement if it is not defined with a degree of precision expected by the foreign court that is asked to enforce it;[118] vaguely formulated injunctions will cause difficulties in enforcement abroad.[119] For instance, injunctions with the all-encompassing language prohibiting defendants "from otherwise infringing" the patents at issue, such as the injunctions issued by a U.S. court in two of the cases reviewed in Section 4.2.1,[120] would likely create great enforcement difficulties if enforcement of such injunctions were to be requested abroad. In Germany, for instance, a lack of sufficient specificity in the wording of an injunction will lead to rejection of enforcement[121] since courts consider unspecific injunctions to be contrary to public policy.[122]

A problem related to the issue of specificity of injunctions in patent infringement cases is the problem of interpretation of the scope of the injunction. This problem is actually present any time plaintiffs seek to enforce classical negative injunctions, whether or not cross-border, that prohibit further infringement, and the problem will likely be accentuated in a cross-border scenario. When a plaintiff requests enforcement of a negative injunction, the defendant typically argues a design-around; in other words, the defendant claims that he has modified the originally infringing products or methods sufficiently so that they no longer infringe the patents in the original suit. The question in enforcement proceedings then becomes

---

[118] As noted in the dissenting opinion in *Tivo Inc. v. Echostar Corp.*, 646 F.3d 869 (Fed. Cir. 2011), "[a]n accused party cannot be held in contempt for violating an injunction which does not clearly reach the accused conduct." *Id.*, 894. *See id.*, 894 ff., for a discussion of the issue of clarity of injunctions.

[119] See a discussion of the need for foreign-granted injunctions to be precisely formulated in *Elektrothrombose*, Oberlandesgericht Köln, 16 W 2/04, Mar. 17, 2004, GRUR-RR 2005, Heft 1, 34–36, at 35–36. *See also* Martin Fähndrich, Arne Ibbeken, *Gerichtzuständigkeit und anwendbares Recht im Falle grenzüberschreitender Verletzungen (Verletzungshandlungen) der Rechte des geistigen Eigentums (Q174)—Bericht für die deutsche Landesgruppe*, 2003 GRUR INT. 616, 622.

[120] 3M Company et al. v. Asia Sun (Taiwan) Inc., case No. 2:04-cv-00417-TJW, E.D. Tex.; O_2 Micro Int'l v. Beyond Innovation et al., case No. 2:04-cv-00032-TJW, E.D. Tex.

[121] *E.g., Gesetzeswiederholende Unterlassungsanträge*, Bundesgerichtshof, I ZR 189/07, Nov. 24, 1999, GRUR 2000, Heft 5, 438–41 (in the context of unfair competition); *Unbestimmter Unterlassungsantrag*, Bundesgerichtshof, I ZR 35/89, Oct. 11, 1990, NJW 1991, Heft 1, 1114–16 (in the context of unfair competition). On the need to specify patent infringement claims as a basis for future enforcement, see *Blasfolienherstellung*, Bundesgerichtshof, X ZR 126/01, Mar. 30, 2005, GRUR 2005 Heft 7, 569–72.

[122] *See, e.g.*, Oberlandesgericht Köln, 16 W 2/04, Mar. 17, 2004. (The Oberlandesgericht noted that in this particular case the injunction issued by The Hague District Court was adequately specific and therefore did not trigger the public policy exception. The Oberlandesgericht explained that "for the reasons of the rule of law, the debtor must be able to determine from the injunctive relief without any doubts which conduct is prohibited." *Id.*).

whether the altered product is indeed a sufficient design-around or whether it still falls within the scope of the injunction.

Enforcement of injunctions is an exercise that is more complicated in patent infringement cases than in other cases. In the United States, for instance, the decision by the U.S. Court of Appeals for the Federal Circuit in *KSM Fastening Systems, Inc. v. H.A. Jones Co., Inc.*[123] has been blamed for introducing a test for design-arounds that made it even more difficult than before for courts to find contempt and easier for defendants to escape contempt.[124] Judge Newman in her partially concurring opinion in *KSM* criticized the rules imposed by the U.S. Court of Appeals for the Federal Circuit as an unnecessary curtailment of court discretion in finding contempt, and warned that "harassing litigation will be harder to control"[125] than previously.

The perception that significant enforcement difficulties are connected with contempt proceedings involving design-arounds in the United States was reflected in the decision in *MercExchange, L.L.C. v. eBay, Inc.* rendered in 2003, in which the District Court for the Eastern District of Virginia discussed potential contempt proceeding problems (contempt proceedings were foreseeable in this case since the parties by that stage had already disagreed on whether a future design-around was feasible or not), factored them into the balance of hardships test, and explained that by issuing an injunction in the case it would "essentially be opening a Pandora's box of new problems"[126] as "contempt hearing after contempt hearing [would require] the court to essentially conduct separate infringement trials to determine if the changes to the defendants' systems violates the injunction."[127] However, and perhaps not surprisingly, the U.S. Court of Appeals for the Federal Circuit did not consider

---

[123] KSM Fastening Systems, Inc. v. H.A. Jones Co., Inc., 776 F.2d 1522 (Fed. Cir. 1985).

[124] "*KSM* crafted a special rule for patent infringement cases, in that it required a threshold inquiry on the propriety of initiating a contempt proceeding." Tivo Inc. v. Echostar Corp., 646 F.3d 869, 881 (Fed. Cir. 2011). John E. Tsavaris II, *Proceedings after KSM: Has the Federal Circuit Infringed Patentee's Rights*, 54 FORDHAM L. REV. 1005, 1006 (1985–1986) ("This holding places the burden of potentially protracted and expensive relitigation on the patent owner and effectively deprives him of the remedy of the summary contempt proceeding.") *Id.*, 1012, 1014. William H. Mandir, John F. Rabena, & Mark C. Davis, *Invited to an ITC Party? Bring Your Redesigns*, Sughrue Mion, PLLC, Sept. 20, 2005, *available at* http://www.sughrue.com/files/Publication/8a6b4a5c-a0ea-4d02-9bde-2c238430233f/Presentation/PublicationAttachment/39268144-b4a2-4b6f-8f00-355357d3c526/InvitedtoanITCarticle(1).pdf (last visited Sept. 2, 2011), 22. ("[I]f any factual disputes are raised, or any testimony or significant evidence must be introduced, contempt proceedings are not allowed." *Id.*).

[125] KSM Fastening Systems, Inc. v. H.A. Jones Co., Inc., 776 F.2d 1522, 1536 (Fed. Cir. 1985).

[126] MercExchange, L.L.C. v. eBay, Inc., 275 F. Supp. 2d 695, 714 (E.D.Va. 2003); rev'd, 401 F.3d 1323 (Fed. Cir. 2005), rev'd, 126 S. Ct. 1837 (2006).

[127] *Id.*

the possibility of future disputes to constitute "a sufficient basis for denying a permanent injunction."[128]

Whether contempt proceedings in the United States under the *KSM* analysis in any way favored defendants who argued modifications would be a topic for a separate empirical study;[129] the U.S. Court of Appeals for the Federal Circuit eventually held the *KSM* analysis "unsound"[130] and "unworkable"[131] and introduced a revised standard for contempt proceedings in *Tivo Inc. v. Echostar Corp.*[132] However, the reality is that a finding of contempt continues to be a difficult exercise,[133] and it seems warranted to conclude that courts facing foreign-issued injunctions are likely to have even greater difficulties in finding contempt when design-arounds are used as a defense.

Most importantly, courts may be reluctant to find contempt when it is based on any foreign-issued injunction; just as they refrain from adjudicating the validity of foreign patents because they deem it improper to second-guess a foreign patent authority, they might also refuse to identify what the foreign patent covers and what it does not in the context of contempt proceedings.[134] The design-around argument

---

[128] MercExchange, L.L.C. v. eBay, Inc., 401 F.3d 1323, 1339 (Fed. Cir. 2005); rev'd, 126 S. Ct. 1837 (2006). The U.S. Supreme Court did not comment on the argument when it vacated the judgment of the U.S. Court of Appeals for the Federal Circuit.

[129] ITC proceedings appear to offer a significantly easier avenue to patent holders who are fighting design-arounds than do federal district court proceedings. Before the ITC, it is upon the alleged infringer to prove that the design-around does not infringe; until it is held noninfringing, it is covered by the exclusion order. William H. Mandir, John F. Rabena, & Mark C. Davis, *Invited to an ITC Party? Bring Your Redesigns*, Americas Enforcement Focus 2005, *available at* http://www.sughrue.com/files/Publication/8a6b4a5c-a0ea-4d02-9bde-2c238430233f/Presentation/PublicationAttachment/39268144-b4a2-4b6f-8f00-355357d3c526/InvitedtoanITCarticle(1).pdf (last visited Sept. 2, 2011) ("A lesser-known yet powerful advantage of the ITC is the post-judgment treatment of new products developed by respondents." *Id.*, 21).

[130] Tivo Inc. v. Echostar Corp., 646 F.3d 869, 876 (Fed. Cir. 2011).

[131] *Id.*, 881.

[132] Tivo Inc. v. Echostar Corp., 646 F.3d 869 (Fed. Cir. 2011). The analysis under *Tivo* continues to consist of two steps: In the first step, a court has to establish "whether the newly accused product is so different from the product previously found to infringe that it raises 'a fair ground of doubt as to the wrongfulness of the defendant's conduct.'" *Id.*, 882 (internal citation omitted). If there "are no more than colorable differences between the adjudged infringing product and modified product," the court continues to the second step of the analysis to determine whether "the newly accused product continues to infringe the relevant claims." *Id.*, 883.

[133] On the so-called "Kerntheorie" applicable in German law, see, e.g., Reinhardt Schuster, *Das Gebot der Anpassung an die konkrete Verletzungsform im Patentrecht—eine unendliche Geschichte*, *in* Festschrift für Jochen Pagenberg 57, 64 ff. (Dietrich Beier, Laurence Brüning-Petit, & Christopher Heath eds., 2006); Jörg Fritzsche, Unterlassungsanspruch und Unterlassungsklage 237 (2000).

[134] For a comparison of the rules for interpretation of patent claims in the European Patent Office, Japan Patent Office and the USPTO, see Jinseok Park, *Interpretation of Patent Claims in the EPO, USPTO and JPO—In the Context of the Doctrine of Equivalents and Functional Claims*, 27 Eur. Intell. Prop. Rev. 237 (2005).

may thus be very successful at preventing enforcement of negative injunctions not only in the United States but also abroad.

4.2.3.2 Enforcement of a Contempt Order

An alternative to the export of an injunction is to obtain a contempt order in the protecting country and then seek enforcement of the order in the foreign country where the defendant's assets are located. The primary problem of enforcement of a contempt order lies in the public policy concern, as explained below, but the issue of finality complicates the enforcement of the order as well, in two respects: first, the contempt order itself must be a final (nonappealable or not timely appealed) order for it to be recognized, and second, a foreign court is likely to require that the contempt order follow a recognizable injunction, i.e., there must be a final decision on the merits. The finality requirement leads to the same substantial delay that the plaintiff would face if it had attempted to enforce the injunction instead of the contempt order.

The public policy problem with enforcement of contempt orders abroad is that foreign courts may consider them to be decisions that are penal in nature and therefore refuse to recognize and enforce them for that reason; just as courts do not recognize and enforce foreign criminal judgments, they also give no effect to other courts' decisions that may be interpreted as punishing the defendant, such as awards of punitive damages.[135] In Europe, within the Brussels regime, contempt orders may be enforced as long as they determine a specific amount;[136] however, outside the Brussels regime, there is no internationally uniform rule that would govern the enforcement of foreign contempt orders.

It may not even matter whether the contempt order is issued as a civil or criminal contempt order under domestic law, even when such a distinction is made by domestic law. In a decision by the Supreme Court of Canada in *Pro Swing Inc. v. Elta Golf Inc.*[137] concerning the enforcement of a U.S.-issued judgment and contempt order in

---

But cf. Brief for Amici Curiae Law Professors in Support of the Appellee, Jan K. Voda, M.D. v. Cordis Corporation, No. 05-1238 (Fed. Cir. July 29, 2005), 23–25.

[135] *See, for instance*, Symeon C. Symeonides, *Resolving Punitive-Damages Conflicts*, 5 Y.B. PRIVATE INT'L L. 3 (2003). *But cf.* the Spanish Supreme Court in *Miller Import Corp. v. Alabastres Alfredo, S.L.*, translation by Scott R. Jablonski, 24 J.L. & COM. 225, 242; John Y. Gotanda, *Charting Developments Concerning Punitive Damages: Is the Tide Changing?*, 45 COLUM. J. TRANSNAT'L L. 507, 508–09 (2007). *See also infra* Section 4.3.1.

[136] Brussels I Regulation, Chapter 2, note 25, Article 49. *See also* Oberlandesgericht Köln, 16 W 2/04, Mar. 17, 2004, in which the court declined to recognize and enforce a contempt order that set a monetary penalty per future infringement.

[137] Pro Swing Inc. v. Elta Golf Inc., [2006] 2 S.C.R. 612, 2006 SCC 52 (Can.).

a trademark infringement matter, the Canadian Supreme Court found the U.S. contempt order to be "quasi-criminal in nature." The Court observed that U.S. law differentiates between civil and criminal contempt orders but still concluded that a U.S. contempt order, even if considered civil in nature by U.S. law, becomes "quasi-criminal" once it crosses the Canadian border: "[I]t becomes a Canadian contempt order that has a quasi-criminal nature" because "[i]n Canadian law, a contempt order is first and foremost a declaration that a party has acted in defiance of a court order,"[138] and that such an action "exposes the offender to imprisonment."[139] The dissenting justices, led by the Chief Justice, disagreed, pointing out the existence of both civil and criminal contempt under Canadian law, and urged that foreign civil contempt orders be treated as decisions noncriminal in nature and potentially recognizable and enforceable in Canada.[140]

In *Pro Swing* the plaintiff submitted both the U.S.-issued injunction and the U.S.-issued contempt order but relied primarily on the contempt order because Canadian law does not provide for recognition and enforcement of foreign nonmonetary relief. Not all countries agree with the rule that is followed in Canada; even in common law countries that have traditionally followed the same principle, laws have been adopted that enable "importation" of foreign injunctions, and Canada might soon follow suit.[141] When plaintiffs can request enforcement of injunctions directly it saves them the time and effort connected with persuading foreign courts of the civil nature of a contempt order. However, the fact that a problem concerning recognition and enforcement of injunctions exists in Canada is not insignificant in U.S. patent infringement cases, given the relatively high number of cases that are being filed in the United States against Canadian entities.[142]

4.3 Monetary Relief

Enforcement abroad of monetary relief should not pose the difficulties and serious questions presented by the foreign enforcement of injunctions. Certainly, the issue of delay is still present because the enforcement of monetary relief also cannot occur

[138] *Id.*, 29.

[139] *Id.*, 33.

[140] For a discussion of the *Pro Swing* case and its implications, see Stephen G. A. Pitel, *Enforcement of Foreign Non-Monetary Judgments in Canada (and Beyond)*, J. PRIVATE INT'L L. 241 (October 2007).

[141] On recent trends in Canada and other common law jurisdictions toward enforcement of nonmonetary judgments, see Pitel, *supra* note 140, 253–57.

[142] *See supra* Figure 10 in Section 4.1.3.

until a final decision is rendered; however, with a final decision and absent any unusual circumstances, an award of monetary relief should be viewed simply as a debt of the defendant that should be enforceable outside the country where the decision awarding the relief was rendered. However, two kinds of monetary relief may pose difficulties when it is necessary to enforce them abroad: punitive damages and ongoing royalties.

4.3.1 PUNITIVE DAMAGES

As explained earlier, countries do not recognize and enforce relief that they consider to be penal in nature; punitive damages, including the increased civil damages available under U.S. patent law,[143] are considered in other countries to be monetary relief of a penal nature. The strict opposition to awards that include punitive damages may, however, be weakening, making enforcement easier, at least to a limited extent.

One example of the weakening opposition to punitive damages is in the courts in Germany, which are willing to recognize U.S. judgments even when the judgments include awards of increased damages; the enforcement in such cases will be limited to the compensatory amount and the increased part of the award will not be enforced. This approach was recently confirmed by the Stuttgart Oberlandesgericht when it enforced a 2007 U.S. federal court decision that arose from a patent infringement case originally filed in the Northern District of Georgia in 2004.[144] The plaintiffs in the case asked the German court to enforce the U.S. decision that awarded attorneys' fees and other costs; the defendant, an Austrian national domiciled in Germany, raised a number of arguments usually used in contesting U.S. decisions, including the argument that the decision could not be enforced in Germany because it awarded punitive damages and therefore was repugnant to German public policy.[145] The Stuttgart Oberlandesgericht decided that the U.S. decision was enforceable notwithstanding the award of increased damages and referred to a 1992 decision by the

[143] 35 U.S.C. §284.

[144] Oberlandesgericht Stuttgart, 5 U 39/09, July 27, 2009. The U.S. case was Keg Technologies et al. v. Laimer et al., N.D.Ga., 1:04-cv-00253-RWS; one foreign and two U.S. parties were sued in the case. The plaintiff filed for enforcement in the Heilbronn Landgericht, which declared the U.S. decision enforceable. The defendant appealed to the Stuttgart Oberlandesgericht.

[145] The defendant argued that 1) the reciprocity required for enforcement in Germany did not exist, 2) the decision awarded punitive damages and therefore was against German public policy, 3) the plaintiffs sued in the United States specifically because they knew that the costs were higher there and they were trying to ruin the defendant financially, 4) the U.S. judge denied the parties the right to be heard when it ignored the parties' agreement, and 5) the U.S. decision had a penal character. Oberlandesgericht Stuttgart, 5 U 39/09, July 27, 2009.

Bundesgerichtshof[146] that confirmed that an award of punitive damages does not make the entire judgment unenforceable; instead, only the portion of the judgment that awards punitive damages will be ignored, and the rest of the decision may be enforced in Germany.[147]

Other countries have agreed with the German approach to recognition and enforcement of awards that include punitive damages. The Japanese Supreme Court in 1997 confirmed that punitive damages awarded by a California court were unenforceable because they had "the same function as a fine and other criminal punishment" in Japan; however, while it denied enforcement of the punitive portion of the award, it affirmed a lower court decision to enforce compensatory damages and costs.[148] In 2010 the French Supreme Court opined that if an award of punitive damages is not principally against public policy and disproportional to the harm suffered, the award may be recognized and enforced in France.[149] In the particular case before it the Court decided that punitive damages awarded in the United States were disproportional.

A 2001 decision by the Supreme Court of Spain suggests that some courts could go even further in accepting punitive damages. In *Miller Import Corp. v. Alabastres Alfredo, S.L.*[150] the Spanish Supreme Court recognized a U.S. judgment awarding punitive damages in a trademark and unfair competition case. Although the defendant also raised the public policy argument, the Supreme Court enforced the U.S. judgment; the Court explained that "the idea of compensation for injuries is part of the process and is not totally foreign" to the Spanish legal system, and suggested that "punitive damages cannot be considered as a concept that is (completely) counter to [Spanish] public policy."

Some commentators argue that the recent decisions indicate a change in the former hostile approach in many countries to punitive damages and that the hurdles to enforcing awards of increased damages may be disappearing. John Y. Gotanda,

---

146 Bundesgerichtshof, IX ZR 149/91, June 4, 1992, NJW 1992, Heft 48, 3096–3106.

147 The court also explained that a U.S. decision on costs is not automatically against German public policy merely because U.S. courts apply the "American rule" instead of exclusively awarding costs to the winning party. The court reviewed federal and Georgia rules on costs and explained that in Germany—where the winning party is usually awarded costs—there are also exceptions that can lead to a result similar to the one dictated by the "American rule." Oberlandesgericht Stuttgart, 5 U 39/09, July 27, 2009.

148 Mansei Kogyo, Supreme Court of Japan, July 11, 1997, *Minshu* Vol. 51, No. 6, p. 2537 (Japan), *available at* http://www.courts.go.jp/english/judgments/text/1997.07.11-1993-O-No.1762.html (last visited Sept. 2, 2011). "[P]art of the foreign judgment in the present case which ordered the appellee company to pay punitive damages for the purpose of deterrence and sanction in addition to compensatory damages and the cost is against public order of Japan and therefore, has no effect." *Id.*

149 Judgment No. 1090 of Dec. 1, 2010 (09-13.303), Cour de cassation.

150 Miller Import, *supra* note 135.

for instance, noticed that recent developments "point toward greater receptivity toward punitive damages and the enforcement of these foreign awards."[151] As the text of the decision by the Spanish Supreme Court suggests, the critical approach to reviewing awards of punitive damages that has been adopted by U.S. courts is being noticed outside the United States and may be part of the reason that attitudes seem to be changing in foreign courts toward enforcement of U.S. awards outside the United States.[152] Inroads may eventually be made to the enforcement of punitive awards,[153] particularly in the intellectual property area, where countries have become receptive to the idea of introducing increased damages.[154]

4.3.2 ONGOING ROYALTIES

The second problem of enforcement of monetary relief is posed by the so-called "ongoing royalties" that U.S. courts have awarded in some cases.[155] The concept of an

---

[151] Gotanda, *supra* note 135. *See also* Yves P. Piantino, *Switzerland's Treatment of U.S. Money Judgments*, 46 AM. J. COMP. L. 181 (1998) ("Swiss case law is [. . .] tilting toward a liberal approach with regard to foreign judgments to the point where even U.S. punitive damages awards have a fairly reasonable chance to be granted recognition." *Id.*, 200). *But cf.* Ronald A. Brand, Punitive Damages Revisited: Taking the Rationale for Non-Recognition of Foreign Judgments Too Far (2005) (University of Pittsburgh School of Law Working Paper Series, Paper 26).

[152] *E.g.*, BMW of North America, Inc. v. Gore, 517 U.S. 559 (1996); State Farm Mutual Automobile Insurance Company v. Campbell, 438 U.S. 408 (2003); Exxon Shipping Company v. Baker, 128 S. Ct. 2605 (2008). *See also, e.g.*, Torsten Schwarze, *"Das Ende des Schreckens?"—Beschränkung der punitive damages durch den US-Supreme Court*, 2003 NEUE ZEITSCHRIFT FÜR GESELLSCHAFTSRECHT 804; Volker Behr, *Punitive Damages in American and German Law—Tendencies Towards Approximation of Apparently Irreconcilable Concepts*, 78 CHI.-KENT L. REV. 105 (2003) ("Despite apparent differences between German and American blackletter doctrine, recent developments suggest that the gap is narrowing for practical purposes." *Id.*, 148).

[153] There was an attempt to introduce increased damages in the European Union Enforcement Directive, Chapter 1, note 83. Recital 26 of the Directive is carefully phrased to emphasize that no provision of the Directive was aimed at introducing punitive damages. In the provision on damages the original proposal for the directive—COM(2003) 46 final (Jan. 30, 2003)—included an option for a court to award either compensatory damages or "damages set at double the royalties or fees which would have been due if the infringer had requested authorisation to use the intellectual property right in question" (Article 17.1 of the proposal). This wording was opposed by the representatives of member states in the Council working group and was eventually changed to order courts to set damages either while "tak[ing] into account all appropriate aspects [. . .] including [. . .], in appropriate cases, elements other than economic factors, such as the moral prejudice caused to the rightholder" or calculating "a lump sum on the basis of elements such as at least the amount of royalties or fees" (Article 13.1 of the Directive).

[154] In Slovenia, for instance, "[t]he Copyright Act introduced concept of punitive damages for infringement of copyrights (art. 168 of Copyright Act). A punitive damages [*sic*] might be awarded as triple damages." *Slovenia, Report Q186, Punitive Damages as a Contentious Issue of Intellectual Property Rights*, AIPPI, *available at* https://www.aippi.org/download/commitees/186/GR186slovenia.pdf (last visited Sept. 2, 2011).

[155] The majority in *Paice LLC v. Toyota Motor Corp.* distinguished between the grant of an "ongoing royalty" and a "compulsory license," arguing that "'compulsory license' implies that *anyone* who meets certain criteria has congressional authority to use that which is licensed." Paice LLC v. Toyota Motor Corp., 504 F.3d 1293, 1313,

ongoing royalty as an alternative to an injunction existed before the landmark decision in *eBay*[156] but gained even greater significance thereafter in cases in which injunctions were not issued.[157] The concept is not limited to cases in which no injunctions are issued; even in cases where permanent injunctions have been granted, courts sometimes have decided to impose a royalty for a transitional period during which they have stayed the permanent injunction. The stays were designed to support the strong public interest in having the products at issue available until noninfringing alternatives could be introduced; such strong public interest has been found in the medical field,[158] but instances of transitional royalties also exist outside of the medical field.[159]

The concept of an ongoing royalty is not without its critics; some have suggested that such a remedy has no basis in law[160] and that it ignores the willfulness of an infringer who continues to infringe after a verdict finding infringement is entered.[161] It has been argued that such willfulness has not been factored into the ongoing royalty and thus the plaintiffs have been deprived of the increase for willfulness that would be available to them in the form of treble damages if they had filed another suit for post-verdict infringement. Others have expressed concerns that the ongoing

---

fn. 13 (Fed. Cir. 2007). This book makes no such distinction and uses the term "ongoing royalty" for both. For another theory distinguishing between "ongoing royalty" and "compulsory license," see George M. Newcombe, Jeffrey E. Ostrow, Patrick E. King, & Gabriel N. Rubin, *Prospective Relief for Patent Infringement in a Post-eBay World*, 4 N.Y.U. J. L. & Bus. 549 (2008).

156 eBay Inc. v. MercExchange, L.L.C., 547 U.S. 388 (2006).

157 Paice LLC v. Toyota Motor Corp., 504 F.3d 1293, 1314 (Fed. Cir. 2007).

158 For instance, in *Shiley, Inc. v. Bentley Labs., Inc.* the court imposed a royalty increasing gradually from 12 percent to 18 percent on sales of the infringing bubble blood oxygenators during a six-month transitional period. Shiley, Inc. v. Bentley Labs., Inc., 601 F.Supp. 964, 971 (C.D.Ca. 1985). In *Schneider (Europe) AG v. SciMed Life Systems, Inc.*, the court set a gradually increasing royalty rate of 15–24 percent for infringing balloon dilatation catheters sold within a one-year transitional period. Schneider (Europe) AG v. SciMed Life Systems, Inc., 852 F.Supp. 813, 869 (D.Minn. 1994).

159 For instance, in *Broadcom Corp. v. Qualcomm Inc.*, the court awarded "sunset royalties" to be paid while the injunction was temporarily stayed. Broadcom Corp. v. Qualcomm Inc., C.D.Ca., No. 8:05-cv-00467-JVS-RNB. Qualcomm made two payments of the "sunset royalties" to Broadcom before the U.S. Court of Appeals for the Federal Circuit found one of the patents in the suit invalid. Broadcom Corp. v. Qualcomm Inc., 543 F.3d 683 (Fed. Cir. 2008). The matter was thus returned to the U.S. District Court for the Central District of California where Qualcomm successfully requested repayment of the royalties paid to Broadcom. Broadcom Corp. v. Qualcomm Inc 585 F.Supp.2d 1187 (C.D.Ca. 2008).

160 Bernard H. Chao, *After* eBay, Inc. v. MercExchange*: The Challenging Landscape for Patent Remedies*, 9 Minn. J. L. Sci. & Tech. 543, 545, 567–68 (2008).

161 Stockwell, *supra* note 63, 756; Newcombe et al., *supra* note 155. Mark Lemley in his remarks at the conference "The Federal Circuit Visits the Valley," organized by the Stanford Program in Law, Science and Technology, Santa Clara Law School and the Federal Circuit Bar Association, Palo Alto, CA, Nov. 5, 2008.

royalty might be in conflict with U.S. obligations stemming from the TRIPs Agreement.[162]

The question is whether the argument contending that the ongoing royalty is contrary to U.S. obligations under TRIPs could persuade a foreign court not to enforce a debt arising from unpaid ongoing royalties. It seems that even if the foreign court shared the critics' doubts about the compatibility of the concept of the ongoing royalty with the TRIPs Agreement, those doubts would still not warrant a decision of nonrecognition of a U.S. decision awarding such a royalty; the process of recognition and enforcement of foreign judgments is not an avenue for enforcing a foreign country's obligations under international treaties. Although it is difficult for a plaintiff to find a positive side of an ongoing royalty (since the plaintiff either did not want to license his invention to begin with or hoped to use a permanent injunction as powerful leverage in licensing negotiations), the good news for the plaintiff might be that an ongoing royalty should be enforceable across borders if enforcement becomes necessary. However, before enforcement abroad can be attempted, a decision of a foreign court specifying the particular amount due will likely be necessary.[163]

4.4 Additional Requirements of Recognition and Enforcement

Sections 4.2 and 4.3 review the obstacles to recognition and enforcement by focusing on particular forms of remedies, but the obstacles are not necessarily limited to issues concerning remedies. The requirements that countries set for foreign judgments to meet in order for the judgments to be recognizable tend to be similar;[164] in addition to the requirement mentioned earlier that the recognition of the judgment or the judgment itself not be against the public policy of the enforcing country,[165]

---

[162] *For instance*, Charlene A. Stern-Dombal, *Tripping Over TRIPs: Is Compulsory Licensing Under* eBay *at Odds With U.S. Statutory Requirements and TRIPs?*, 41 SUFFOLK U. L. REV. 249 (2007); Paul M. Schoenhard, *Who Took My IP? Defending the Availability of Injunctive Relief for Patent Owners*, 16 TEX. INTELL. PROP. L. J. 187 (2008).

[163] Oberlandesgericht Köln, 16 W 2/04, Mar. 17, 2004. Although the case concerned a contempt order and not an ongoing royalty, it raised the same point. The Hague District Court ordered the defendant to pay €100,000 for each future breach of the injunction. The plaintiff asked for enforcement of the injunction in Germany but the Köln Oberlandesgericht rejected the enforcement of the contempt order because the final amount due was not specified.

[164] For general requirements of recognition, see, e.g., Samuel P. Baumgartner, *How Well Do U.S. Judgments Fare in Europe?*, 40 GEO. WASH. INT'L L. REV. 173, 191 (2008).

[165] Brussels I Regulation, Chapter 2, note 25, Article 34.1 ("manifestly contrary to public policy"); Zivilprozessordnung, §328(1)(4); Unif. Foreign-Country Money Judgments Recognition Act §4(c)(3) ("the judgment or the [cause of action] [claim for relief] on which the judgment is based"). On the public policy

countries require that the foreign proceedings in which the judgment was issued comply with basic due process requirements,[166] that the judgment not be irreconcilable with an existing decision,[167] and that it comply with jurisdictional requirements.[168] Some countries require reciprocity; they will not recognize and enforce a foreign judgment unless the courts of the issuing country recognize and enforce judgments from the enforcing country.[169] In the United States, in addition to the mandatory grounds it lists for nonrecognition, the Uniform Foreign-Country Money Judgments Recognition Act includes a number of discretionary grounds for which courts may deny recognition and enforcement.[170]

The provisions that set the requirements for recognition are expressed similarly in the laws of various countries, but they may have varying meanings in practice, as can be documented in jurisdictional requirements. All countries require that the enforcing court verify that the foreign court had jurisdiction over the defendant; a lack of jurisdiction on the part of the issuing court will lead to nonrecognition of the decision. However, the jurisdictional inquiry is not guided by the law of the issuing court but by the requirements set by the law of the enforcing court. In some countries, these requirements are identical to their regular jurisdictional rules, as is the case in Germany, where the same provisions on jurisdiction that apply for German courts will be used to verify that the foreign issuing court had jurisdiction over the defendant.[171] In other jurisdictions, such as England and the United States, special jurisdictional requirements exist that must be met by the foreign court for its decision to be enforceable in the other jurisdiction.[172] In one recent decision an English court held that it was inconsistent with these special rules when a U.S. court claimed jurisdiction

---

exception, see Marketa Trimble Landova, *Public Policy Exception to Recognition and Enforcement of Judgments in Cases of Copyright Infringement*, 40 IIC 642 (2009).

[166] Brussels I Regulation, Chapter 2, note 25, Article 34.2 (sufficient service of process if judgment in default); Zivilprozessordnung, §328(1)(2); Unif. Foreign-Country Money Judgments Recognition Act §4(b)(1) (impartial tribunals and procedures); Unif. Foreign-Country Money Judgments Recognition Act §4(c)(1) (service of process); Unif. Foreign-Country Money Judgments Recognition Act §4(c)(2) (absence of fraud).

[167] Brussels I Regulation, Chapter 2, note 25, Article 34.3; Zivilprozessordnung, §328(1)(3); Unif. Foreign-Country Money Judgments Recognition Act §4(c)(4).

[168] Brussels I Regulation, Chapter 2, note 25, Article 35; Zivilprozessordnung, §328(1)(1); Unif. Foreign-Country Money Judgments Recognition Act §4(b)(2) and (3) (both personal and subject matter jurisdiction).

[169] Absent a treaty provision to the contrary, Germany imposes the requirement of reciprocity in Zivilprozessordnung, §328(1)(5). This requirement does not apply to judgments from the Brussels regime countries. Brussels I Regulation, Chapter 2, note 25; Lugano II Convention, Chapter 2, note 24.

[170] Unif. Foreign-Country Money Judgments Recognition Act §4(c).

[171] The rule is based on the so-called "Spiegelbildgrundsatz." Zivilprozessordnung, §328(1)(1).

[172] Unif. Foreign-Country Money Judgments Recognition Act §5. The provision gives courts discretion to "recognize bases of jurisdiction other than those" specifically listed in the provision. *Id.*, §5(b).

over an English defendant based solely on the contacts that the defendant had with the United States through Internet sales.[173]

Decisions by U.S. courts may encounter problems related to certain specifics of U.S. law that are deemed repugnant to the public policies of some other countries. For instance, pre-trial discovery has been viewed as overly "intrusive" and inconsistent with other countries' public policies.[174] A lack of agreement as to what countries consider to be proper service of process or adequate notice may also disqualify U.S. decisions from enforceability outside the United States; decisions in U.S. class action suits are likely to fall victim to the problem of inadequate notice in many countries.[175] Absence of sufficient reasoning in a court decision may also render the decision unenforceable abroad.[176]

Additionally, specific public policy concerns have been voiced in the context of intellectual property. For example, Justice Jacob expressed his concern about a possible "clash of [intellectual property] policies in different countries" in his decision in *Lucasfilm v. Ainsworth*.[177] Injunctions or damages may be granted in the issuing country, as was the case in *Lucasfilm*, to remedy acts that infringed intellectual property rights (in this case, copyright) in the issuing country, even though those acts were completely legal in the enforcing country where the acts were committed. The problem will be most prominent in cases such as *Lucasfilm*, in which the laws of the issuing and enforcing countries are at odds as to whether the subject matter at issue should be protectable by an intellectual property right at all. Though the same problem arises in cases involving inventions that are patented in the issuing country but not in the enforcing country because the inventor did not file for a patent in the enforcing country, the problem becomes even more pressing when the invention could not be patented in the enforcing country because the enforcing country does not consider the invention to be patentable.

---

[173] *Lucasfilm, supra* note 104; Lucasfilm Ltd & Ors v Ainsworth & Anor [2011] UKSC 39, July 27, 2011 (U.K.).

[174] *E.g.*, Alessandro Barzaghi, *Recognition and Enforcement of United States Judgments in Italy*, 18 N.Y. Int'l L. Rev. 61, 93 (2005); Baumgartner, *How Well, supra* note 164, 201–02 and 208–11.

[175] Class action suits seemed to be outside the interest of intellectual property experts; however, the Google Books settlement case shows that even the area of intellectual property is not immune to class actions. Although various forms of collective actions exist today in many countries around the world, countries' requirements for service of process are unlikely to change in the near future. For the outcome of the proceedings concerning the Google Books settlement see Authors Guild v. Google, Inc., 770 F.Supp.2d 666 (SDNY 2011). On problems associated with service of process in general, see, e.g., Baumgartner, *How Well, supra* note 164, 201–02 and 217.

[176] *E.g.*, Barzaghi, *supra* note 174; Baumgartner, *How Well, supra* note 164, 222.

[177] Lucasfilm Limited et al. v. Andrew Ainsworth et al., *supra* note 104.

U.S. injunctions may also be questioned if they target acts not infringing U.S. patents but concern other acts, not deemed infringing even under U.S. law, for the purpose of preventing infringements of U.S. patents.[178] What may appear indispensible to a court in the United States to prevent infringements of a U.S. patent will not necessarily comport with other countries' views of the degree to which U.S. law should influence the otherwise legal behavior of entities in other countries. It is questionable whether the clash of intellectual property-related policies will constitute a sufficient basis for finding a foreign decision contrary to the public policy of the enforcing country.[179] However, a foreign court's perception of a clash may cause that court to consider very critically some other requirements for recognition and enforcement and seek an alternative reason to deny recognition of the decision.

4.5 Obstacles to Enforcement Abroad

This chapter shows that patent cases do exist in which courts issue decisions that may require enforcement abroad; it demonstrates that concerns about the issues of cross-border enforcement of decisions in patent infringement cases are real. In the United States, patent cases against foreign defendants are not unusual; the present study shows that 15.0 percent of all patent cases filed in 2004 and 18.9 percent of cases filed in 2009 involved foreign defendants, many of which may have no assets in the United States. When remedies are awarded against such defendants and if enforcement of the remedies becomes necessary, plaintiffs must seek recognition and enforcement of the U.S. decisions outside the United States. The review of the cases and enforcement difficulties in this chapter suggests that civil enforcement abroad in general is a lengthy and difficult exercise, but that patent cases present additional challenges.

The detailed empirical study in this chapter of patent cases filed in the United States reveals the potential magnitude of the problem that is suggested by the current litigation landscape. However, we may expect that the number of cases that reach across national borders will increase in the future. As countries' economies become even more interconnected and the dispersion of research and development, patent holding, and manufacturing capabilities continues, more cases will likely arise in which foreign entities with no assets in protecting countries are involved in infringements of intellectual property rights in protecting countries.

---

[178] *See supra* Section 4.2.1 for a discussion of injunctions that address noninfringing conduct.

[179] For a general discussion of the public policy exception, see, e.g., Trimble Landova, *supra* note 165.

Many of the obstacles that patent holders face when they try to enforce abroad decisions in infringement cases are not specific to patent litigation; the obstacles arise when cross-border enforcement is sought for any court decision. Certainly the issues of delay due to the lack of finality of a decision are present in many types of cases, and punitive or increased damages face the same public policy challenges regardless of the types of cases in which they are granted. However, in addition to their exposure to general enforcement problems, such as limitations on enforcement of punitive awards, patent holders may also be exposed to problems that are specific to the enforcement of remedies in patent infringement cases, problems that often involve the enforcement of injunctions abroad.

As explained in Section 4.2.3, there are two aspects of injunctions that are likely to cause significant difficulties when injunctions are enforced in foreign courts: level of specificity and design-around as a defense to enforcement. An injunction will have to be worded with a level of specificity sufficient to satisfy the requirements of the enforcing country; courts in that country will look to their own laws to determine whether the injunction issued abroad is specific enough to be enforced in their country. Litigants should keep this requirement in mind when they request injunctions and there is a possibility that the injunctions will have to be enforced abroad.

The second great challenge associated with injunctions issued in patent infringement cases is posed by design-around arguments that may be, and often are, used by defendants to defeat the enforcement effort. Whether the enforcing court chooses to apply its own law or the law of the issuing court to determine what the injunction covers and what it does not, the court will have to conduct a complicated inquiry into the scope of the patent. Courts may hesitate to embark on such an exercise, particularly if they normally refrain from interpreting the scope of foreign patents in other contexts, namely in disputes over patent validity and infringement. The situation will be different, of course, and an enforcing country's court will have no problem in acting if asked to decide on design-around arguments and patent scope for a patent granted by its own country. Whether many decisions concerning foreign patents will issue from courts in the United States and Europe remains to be seen; as explained in Chapter 2, Section 2.1.6, recent jurisprudence by the U.S. Court of Appeals for the Federal Circuit and the CJEU suggests that adjudications of foreign patent infringements and the issuance of injunctions concerning foreign patents will be extremely limited.

It is important to note that some of the general enforcement obstacles that are not specific to the enforcement of decisions in patent infringement cases may have effects that are particularly damaging to patent holders. Time is of the essence in patent cases because the right at issue is always time-limited. In cases of time-limited rights, a prospective remedy, be it an injunction or an ongoing royalty, loses its efficacy if it is enforced late in the life of the right; late enforcement of an injunction means that the injunction will not effectively prevent infringements of the right. In a cross-border enforcement scenario the length of the enforcement process, combined with the complete lack or limited availability of a preliminary remedy, diminishes the usefulness of the injunction.

With patents, little time is left when a substantial number of years is subtracted from the twenty-year patent term for prosecuting a patent, litigating an infringement to a final nonappealable decision, and recognizing and enforcing the decision abroad. Even if recognition and enforcement has not been foreclosed because of one or more of the general hurdles of foreign enforcement, such as insufficient grounds of jurisdiction of the issuing court, the various problems discussed above may complicate and protract the recognition and enforcement process to a point at which the remedy is too late to be of practical use. The ineffectiveness of an injunction negatively impacts the patent holder in the particular case but also harms the patent system; if patent holders cannot use the system to threaten defendants with the enforcement of injunctions, defendants have one less incentive to comply "voluntarily" with court-ordered injunctions in the future.

The ALI and CLIP proposals discussed in Chapter 2 attempt to eliminate the problems associated with cross-border enforcement;[180] the drafters of the proposals offer tools that plaintiffs can utilize to avoid or mitigate problems. First, the proposals allow for litigation in the country of the defendant's domicile, even if the patent at issue was granted by another country.[181] Second, the proposals provide for preliminary measures that can be requested and awarded in the country where the infringing activity is initiated, even if it is not where the infringement is litigated.[182] Third, the proposals facilitate easier recognition and enforcement abroad of any remedies that are awarded.[183] For instance, both proposals endorse the German approach to punitive damages by stipulating that the enforcement of a damage award that includes a punitive component may not be denied in its entirety on public policy grounds; only the noncompensatory portion of the damages may be denied enforcement.[184]

Although the proposals address all of the general problems of recognition and enforcement of court decisions concerning intellectual property rights, they do not

---

[180] *See* Chapter 2, note 10 for additional proposals.

[181] ALI Principles, Chapter 2, note 123, §201 and §204; CLIP Principles, Chapter 2, note 140, Article 2:101 and 2:203.

[182] ALI Principles, Chapter 2, note 123, §214; CLIP Principles, Chapter 2, note 140, Part 2, Section 5.

[183] ALI Principles, Chapter 2, note 123, Part IV; CLIP Principles, Chapter 2, note 140, Part 4.

[184] ALI Principles, Chapter 2, note 123, §411; CLIP Principles, Chapter 2, note 140, Article 4:402.

discuss the two issues particular to the enforcement of injunctions in patent infringement cases, namely the issues of specificity of injunctions and design-arounds. The proposals also do not tackle the problem of contradictory patent policies. Perhaps the drafters expect that these problems will largely disappear once countries consent to foreign court decisions on the validity (albeit inter partes) and infringement of their patents; this consent is the precondition that underlies the proposals and the one on which they rely.

The problem, as noted in Chapter 2, Section 2.3, is that countries are unlikely to agree to having their patents adjudicated abroad without also accepting the concept of continuous harmonization of their patent laws with those of other countries; absent an agreement on harmonized patent laws or acceptance of the fact that judicial interpretations will gradually and continuously lead toward harmonized patent laws, no cross-border enforcement of decisions in patent infringement cases will be possible. "Halfway" solutions—solutions that allow for cross-border enforcement while attempting to preserve differences in national patent laws—do not seem to work; the Brussels regime, which attempted this solution, created several problems and eventually was significantly curtailed by the CJEU. The fact that European countries are now linking their search for a unified litigation framework with a proposal for a uniform regional patent suggests that this solution is where the future lies. With no agreement among countries that patent laws may be shaped by foreign courts and no acknowledgment that harmonization may be gradually and at least partially achieved judicially, cross-border enforcement of decisions in patent infringement matters will continue to suffer the problems described in this chapter.

Conclusions

THE PROCESS OF patent law internationalization that began 140 years ago is ripe for the next stage of its development. Patent law internationalization has made tremendous progress, which has improved the position of inventors who strive to protect their inventions in multiple countries or worldwide. Despite the undeniable progress, however, the process has fallen short of providing viable worldwide protection that will reward inventors for the global disclosure of their inventions. In theory, the existing patchwork of national patent systems allows for global patent protection through country-by-country patenting, but in practice the high costs associated with obtaining and enforcing patents in multiple countries make global protection effectively unavailable, particularly for an individual inventor or a small or medium-sized enterprise (SME). It is questionable whether having regional or global protection available for only the inventions of the largest multinational corporations is good policy.

The next stage in patent law internationalization should address the tension between the territoriality of existing national patent systems and the global nature of trade and exchange of information, both of which facilitate global and instantaneous disclosure of inventions. While there is little doubt about the goal of the stage, its character and the approach that should be adopted for achieving the goal are yet to be determined. The detailed analysis in this book of the various facets of the current limitations of cross-border enforcement of patents should be helpful in defining the features of the next stage of patent law internationalization.

Patent law internationalization to date has developed in three stages. The first stage began in the 1870s and resulted in countries giving foreigners the right to obtain patents under the same conditions as their own nationals; also, some countries that had prohibited their own nationals from obtaining patents in other countries abolished these prohibitions. In the second stage of patent law internationalization countries created mechanisms for obtaining patents in multiple countries. The first indications of the second stage emerged at the beginning of the twentieth century, but because of the world wars and devastating economic circumstances in the first half of the century, the stage faltered and bore no fruit until the early 1970s, when the Patent Cooperation Treaty and the European Patent Convention (EPC) were created to assist inventors in securing parallel patents to protect their inventions in the signatory countries.

The current (third) stage of patent law internationalization evidences the recognition by countries that international cooperation in the area of intellectual property cannot stop at granting rights in multiple countries; cooperation must embrace the effective enforcement of rights as well. The desire to secure minimum standards for enforcement resulted in recent international instruments on intellectual property; Part III of the 1994 TRIPs Agreement is directed entirely toward issues of enforcement of intellectual property rights through civil litigation, criminal law, and customs measures. In the European Union, the uniform customs measures that were created in 1994 to fight piracy and counterfeiting[1] were redesigned in 2003 to include instances of patent infringements, and several aspects of enforcement through civil litigation have been harmonized among the European Union member states by the 2004 European Union Enforcement Directive.[2] Free trade agreements

[1] *See* Chapter 3, note 54.

[2] The European Commission pushed for criminal law enforcement to be included in the 2004 Enforcement Directive but many member states objected; one of the reasons given for the objections was uncertainty about the legislative competence of the European Union to adopt a directive (within the First Pillar of the European Union) that would concern criminal law. Because competence within the First Pillar was later confirmed for limited cases by the Court of Justice of the European Union (CJEU) in the context of environmental policy, the proposal for a framework decision on criminal enforcement of intellectual property rights that had been submitted as an alternative within the Third Pillar was withdrawn in March 2009. *Proposal for a Council Framework Decision to Strengthen the Criminal Law Framework to Combat Intellectual Property Offences*, COM(2005) 276–2 (July 12, 2005). A separate proposal for a directive concerning criminal enforcement of intellectual property rights was submitted in 2005 and amended in 2006, but ultimately withdrawn in September 2010. *Proposal for a European Parliament and Council Directive on Criminal Measures Aimed at Ensuring the Enforcement of Intellectual Property Rights*, COM(2005) 276-1 (July 12, 2005); *Amended Proposal for a Directive of the European*

concluded by the United States and other countries include provisions on enforcement of intellectual property rights,[3] as does the proposed Anti-Counterfeiting Trade Agreement.[4]

The three stages of patent law internationalization to date have ultimately addressed not only procedural aspects of patent law but also certain substantive patent law issues. For example, the Paris Convention established the rule that importation of a patented device should not result in forfeiture of the patent.[5] The EPC not only created a mechanism for applying for patents in multiple European countries, it also harmonized the requirements of patentability.[6] Similarly, the TRIPs Agreement, in addition to advancing measures for effective enforcement of rights, took important steps in substantive patent law harmonization: TRIPs defined patentable subject matter,[7] rights conferred by a grant of a patent,[8] term of protection,[9] and limitations of patent protection.[10] However, major differences still persist among countries' visions of substantive patent law, and the differences hinder further agreement on more deeply harmonized or unified patent law.

What is remarkable about the recent instruments that embody the achievements of the current stage of patent law internationalization is that they approach enforcement of intellectual property rights through civil litigation as if those rights were strictly confined within national borders—the instruments do not address any cross-border difficulties that may arise in civil litigation. The instruments instruct countries to adopt certain procedures and measures to make rights readily enforceable in civil courts; for example, countries have since agreed to make provisional measures available in their courts to prevent a continuing infringement of an intellectual property right and to preserve evidence in support of proceedings on the merits in

Parliament and of the Council on Criminal Measures Aimed at Ensuring the Enforcement of Intellectual Property Rights, COM(2006) 168 final (April 26, 2006).

[3] *E.g.*, North American Free Trade Agreement, Dec. 17, 1992, Articles 1714–1718; U.S.-Australia Free Trade Agreement, May 18, 2004, Article 17.11.

[4] Anti-Counterfeiting Trade Agreement, Dec. 3, 2010, *available at* http://www.ustr.gov/webfm_send/2417 (last visited Sept. 2, 2011).

[5] Paris Convention, Chapter 1, note 63, Article 5. Other provisions concerning substantive law, such as Article 4*ter* concerning patentability when sale of the patented invention is restricted by law, were added by later revisions of the Convention. For example, Article 4*ter* was introduced by the 1958 revision. BODENHAUSEN, Chapter 1, note 68, 65.

[6] EPC, Chapter 1, note 114, Part II.

[7] TRIPs, Chapter 1, note 19, Article 27.

[8] *Id.*, Article 28.

[9] *Id.*, Article 33.

[10] *Id.*, Articles 30–31.

the same country.[11] However, no provisions have been negotiated to resolve the cross-border problems of provisional measures, such as the issuance of these measures in support of foreign court proceedings or the recognition and enforcement of measures outside the country of the issuing court. The instruments approach intellectual property as if the patchwork of national rights had well-defined borders and no territorial overlap, even though that image is far from reality. Given the failure that countries experienced in negotiating a general convention on jurisdiction, recognition, and enforcement of judgments,[12] it is understandable that the instruments of the current stage of internationalization omit such issues in intellectual property treaties; however, the absence of discussions of the issues at the international level cannot be taken to mean that the issues do not arise in intellectual property cases, including patent cases.

Patent laws have extraterritorial reach, and a number of doctrines were developed to reach activities that harm the economic interests of patent holders outside protecting countries. The doctrines are used not only by patent holders who lack protection for their inventions in the countries where the harmful activities take place; they are also used by litigants who either cannot or do not want to litigate outside a particular protecting country. Often, high costs will prevent litigants from litigating abroad; in other cases they will engage in forum shopping to benefit from more advantageous substantive or procedural rules in a particular protecting country. The doctrines that reach beyond the borders of a protecting country sometimes allow them to draw the foreign conduct into the litigation in the protecting country.

The statistics presented in this book show that there are cases in which foreign entities are sued in patent cases; for such entities there is a likelihood that some or all of their assets are located outside the protecting country, and the potential exists for difficulties to arise when a court decision against a foreign entity needs to be enforced. The enforcement requires that the decision be recognized and enforced by a court in a foreign country—the country where the entity is domiciled or where it holds assets—in a process that is lengthy and probably subject to multiple cross-border enforcement difficulties. In patent cases these difficulties may completely frustrate enforcement of the patent, or at a minimum significantly diminish the effectiveness of the enforcement effort.

In reaction to the increasingly frequent problems of cross-border enforcement that the statistical data reveal, a number of proposals emerged to offer private

[11] Articles 7 and 9 of the European Union Enforcement Directive, Chapter 1, note 83; North American Free Trade Agreement, Dec. 17, 1992, Article 1716.

[12] *See* Chapter 2, Section 2.1.3, for a discussion of The Hague Convention proposal.

international law solutions to mitigate enforcement problems; currently, these proposals are important candidates to shape the next stage of patent law internationalization. Based on the European Union experience with the Brussels regime, the proposals seek to provide for centralization of patent litigation in one national, regional, or supranational court, and to provide rules on jurisdiction, choice of law, and recognition and enforcement of court decisions that would facilitate a smooth process of enforcement of intellectual property rights in multiple countries. The rules would also assist patent holders who utilize the laws of one country to reach activities that occur outside that country.

The existing proposals for improving cross-border enforcement face several problems: First, the procedure that they propose would require an international treaty rather than nonbinding principles; a unilateral adoption of a set of principles by any given country would not suffice. Second, the proposals require significant concessions from national governments; countries would have to consent to a great degree of coordination among their judiciaries, including allowing courts to decide questions of foreign patent validity. Finally, despite their comprehensiveness, the proposals fail to address some substantial hurdles to recognition and enforcement of court decisions in patent cases, such as the difficulties associated with design-around arguments that are raised in contempt proceedings concerning foreign patents.

Europeans appear to be close to adopting a patent-specific institutional solution to cross-border enforcement; the original proposal was developed by the European Patent Organization but was taken over by the European Union, and despite some roadblocks that the proposal encountered, it might still be on track to become the first institutional solution ever tested. The proposal is being propelled by disappointment with the Brussels regime, which was not designed specifically for patent litigation and which created numerous problems for cross-border patent litigation; additionally, the regime's ability to provide for concentration of patent litigation was significantly curtailed by recent CJEU decisions.

For countries that are not ready to agree on institutional solutions, private international law solutions may appear to be an attractive alternative, particularly if the lessons learned from the Brussels regime are applied to shape the new private international law solutions. However, the question is whether such solutions can provide answers to all the shortcomings of fragmented patent protection and whether the next stage of patent law internationalization should be limited to these solutions. There is no doubt that countries' preference for private international law solutions stems from their resistance to patent law harmonization or unification of patent rights; experts turn to private international law as an avenue for enhancing the international legal order without requiring countries to confront deeper substantive patent law harmonization. Although countries failed to negotiate a general convention on jurisdiction, recognition, and enforcement, experts envision that countries will be more likely to agree on a convention that would deal with those issues in the specific area of intellectual property.

Private international law solutions will not shield patent law from further harmonization; some degree of harmonization will inevitably occur through judicial interpretation as courts adjudicate the validity and scope of foreign patents. Court decisions will be impacted by countries' own notions of patentability and will tend to align, gradually, in the interpretation of patent laws. Even if decisions are limited so that they formally apply only inter partes, their effects are likely to transcend the particular litigation; the decisions will affect the particular patent being litigated and possibly impact the interpretation of related patent law provisions. Using the jurisdictional flexibility contained in the existing proposals, patent holders may be able to return to the courts that have adopted a preferred interpretation of foreign patent laws, a practice that would contribute to the shaping of laws through foreign judicial interpretation.

If a certain degree of patent law harmonization is unavoidable, the next stage of patent law internationalization should not retreat from substantive law harmonization but address it directly, together with procedural solutions. Recent developments in the European Union, where a proposal for a mechanism for centralization of patent litigation has been discussed together with a proposal for a European Union patent,[13] suggest that this is indeed where the next stage of patent law internationalization might lie.

A conclusion that harmonization is inevitable should not be interpreted to mean that the next stage of patent law internationalization must consist of a large-scale international treaty binding many countries and result in an increased uniform level of patent protection or unitary patent protection for all patentable subject matters. The statistics in this book show that, at least in the short term, countries could seek solutions with only the few countries that are most often represented as the domiciles of foreign defendants. The fact that the most important countries in cross-border enforcement are also the countries from which many foreign holders of patents issued by the country of litigation originate may simplify the opening of negotiations of bilateral or limited multilateral solutions. Initially, an international treaty could be limited to subject matters on which countries disagree the least; for example, starting with gene or software patents would clearly not be the best course of action.

[13] *See* Chapter 2, Section 2.2, for the European Union proposals.

In the long term, countries should revisit the idea of a global patent. The creation of a uniform patent would be an opportunity to adjust the incentives and exclusive rights of a uniform system; changing to the international exhaustion of patent rights could be one of the principles used to recalibrate the scale. A uniform patent would assure that whatever incentives the patent system should provide would be accessible to all inventors. Currently, the patchwork of national systems pushes individual inventors and SMEs to sell or license their patents to the largest corporations, who are the only entities that can actually afford to secure patents in multiple countries and enforce such patents by parallel litigation when necessary. Unless we actually wish inventing activity or administration of patent rights to be channeled primarily to such entities, we should consider substantially revising the existing patent system and revisiting the idea of a global patent.

Of course, the creation of global rights is only one part of the solution to the cross-border enforcement problem; a litigation mechanism would have to be designed in parallel with the establishment of the rights. However, the existence of uniform rights would support the creation of a litigation mechanism and overcome the primary hurdle to the adoption of private international law solutions—the act of state doctrine. The introduction of uniform rights would also support an institutional solution—a solution that would centralize litigation in a unified court. It could centralize appellate-level proceedings only, or alternatively, create a new unified court system with first-instance regional divisions in addition to appellate courts. Current patent litigation practice has already identified specific courts that might serve as important regional centers, and modern communications technologies could aid in the implementation of one multinational appellate court.

The push for deeper harmonization of patent laws must overcome the objections of a number of critics who emphasize the need for experimentation in various jurisdictions or specially-tailored legislation for certain parts of the world. However, the value of experimentation does not exceed the value of enforceability; patent laws can only be effective and serve underlying policies if they provide enforceable rights. Since patent policies cannot be promoted without effective cross-border enforcement, and since cross-border enforcement inevitably results in an increased harmonization of patent rights, it appears that the effective promotion of national patent policies will require the creation of uniform multinational or global patent rights.

Bibliography

Benjamin Vaughan Abbott, The Patent Laws of All Nations: Algeria–Turkey (2009).

Frederick M. Abbott, *Seizure of Generic Pharmaceuticals in Transit Based on Allegations of Patent Infringement: A Threat to International Trade, Development and Public Welfare*, 1 World Intell. Prop. Org. J. 43 (2009).

Edward B. "Teddy" Adams, Jr., *Personal Jurisdiction over Foreign Parties*, *in* International Litigation: Defending and Suing Foreign Parties in U.S. Federal Courts 113 (David J. Levy ed., 2003).

Jens Adolphsen, *Das Territorialitätsprinzip im europäischen Patentrecht*, 11 Zeitschrift für Zivilprozess International 137 (2006).

Jens Adolphsen, Europäisches und internationals Zivilprozessrecht in Patentsachen (2nd ed. 2009).

Jens Adolphsen, *Renationalisierung von Patentstreitigkeiten in Europa*, 2007 IPRax 15.

John R. Allison, Mark A. Lemley, and Joshua Walker, *Extreme Value or Trolls on Top? The Characteristics of the Most-Litigated Patents*, 158 U. Pa. L. Rev. 1 (2009).

J. Jonas Anderson, *Hiding Behind Nationality: The Temporary Presence Exception and Patent Infringement Avoidance*, 15 Mich. Telecomm. & Tech. L. Rev. 1 (2008).

Robert Aronoff, *The State of the US IP Marketplace 2009–2010*, 1004 PLI/Pat 477 (2010).

Gordon Asher, *International Patent Cooperation*, 11 J. Chemical Documentation 14 (1971).

Heinz W. Auerswald, *Können Ansprüche wegen Verletzung eines ausländischen Patents vor deutschen Gerichten verfolgt werden?*, *in* Festschrift Werner von Stein 8 (1961).

Cláudio R. Barbosa, *From Brussels to The Hague—The Ongoing Process Towards Effective Multinational Patent Enforcement*, 32 IIC 729 (2001).

Alessandro Barzaghi, *Recognition and Enforcement of United States Judgments in Italy*, 18 N.Y. Int'l L. Rev. 61 (2005).

Samuel P. Baumgartner, *Is Transnational Litigation Different?*, 25 U. PA. J. INT'L ECON. L. 1297 (2004).

Samuel P. Baumgartner, *How Well Do U.S. Judgments Fare in Europe?*, 40 GEO. WASH. INT'L L. REV. 173 (2008).

Joseph H. Beale, *The Jurisdiction of a Sovereign State*, 36 HARV. L. REV. 241 (1922–1923).

Ryan Beard, *Reciprocity and Comity: Politically Manipulative Tools for Protection of Intellectual Property Rights in the Global Economy*, 30 TEX. TECH L. REV. 155 (1999).

Paul von Beck-Mannagetta, Das österreichische Patentrecht (1893).

Volker Behr, *Punitive Damages in American and German Law—Tendencies Towards Approximation of Apparently Irreconcilable Concepts*, 78 CHI.-KENT L. REV. 105 (2003).

F.-K. Beier, *Stand und Aussichten der europäischen Rechtsvereinheitlichung auf dem Gebiete des gewerblichen Rechtsschutzes*, 1969 GRUR INT. 145.

Friedrich-Karl Beier and Dieter Stauder, *Weltraumstationen und das Recht des geistigen Eigentums*, 1985 GRUR INT. 6.

Gretchen Ann Benden, *Clash of the Titans: The Territoriality of Patent Law vs. The European Union*, 40 IDEA 49 (2000).

Geord Benkard and Claus Dietrich Asendorf, Patentgesetz (10th ed. 2006).

Robert J. Benson, *Beyond Borders: How U.S. Patent and Copyright Laws Can Reach Transactions That Occur Entirely Outside U.S. Borders*, 18 INTELL. PROP. & TECH. L.J. 15 (2008).

George Bermann, *Provisional Relief in Transnational Litigation*, 35 COLUM. J. TRANSNAT'L L. 553 (1997).

Heleen Bertrams, *The Cross-Border Prohibitory Injunction in Dutch Patent Law*, 26 IIC 618 (1995).

Robert Blackburn, *Extraterritorial Enforcement: Practical Considerations for Lawyers*, *in* RETHINKING INTERNATIONAL INTELLECTUAL PROPERTY: BIODIVERSITY & DEVELOPING COUNTRIES, EXTRATERRITORIAL ENFORCEMENT, THE GRACE PERIOD, AND OTHER ISSUES 63 (Kraig M. Hill, Toshiko Takenaka, and Kevin Takeuchi eds., 2000).

Todd P. Blakely, *Extraterritorial Infringement of a United States Utility Patent*, *in* GEWERBLICHE SCHUTZRECHTE UND IHRE DURCHSETZUNG—FESTSCHRIFT FÜR TILMAN SCHILLING 13 (Marcus Grosch and Eike Ullmann eds., 2007).

Bas de Blank and Bing Cheng, *Where Is the ITC Going After Kyocera?*, 25 SANTA CLARA COMPUTER & HIGH TECH. L.J. 701 (2009).

Knut Blind, Katrin Cremers, and Elisabeth Mueller, *The Influence of Strategic Patenting on Companies' Patent Portfolios*, Centre for European Economic Research, Discussion Paper No. 07-013, *available at* ftp://ftp.zew.de/pub/zew-docs/dp/dp07013.pdf.

Fritz Blumer, *Jurisdiction and Recognition in Transatlantic Patent Litigation*, 9 TEX. INTELL. PROP. L.J. 329 (2001).

Karl-Heinz Böckstiegel, Paul Michael Krämer, and Isabel Polley, *Kann der Betrieb von Satelliten im Weltraum patentrechtlich geschützt werden?*, 1999 GRUR 1.

Georg Hendrik Christiaan Bodenhausen, Guide to the Application of the Paris Convention for the Protection of Industrial Property as Revised at Stockholm in 1967 (WIPO 2004) (1969).

A. du Bois-Reymond, *Das Weltpatent*, in Studien zur Förderung des gewerblichen Rechtsschutzes 465 (1909).

Thomas Borecki, *Moving Towards Regional Patent Systems*, in RETHINKING INTERNATIONAL INTELLECTUAL PROPERTY: BIODIVERSITY & DEVELOPING COUNTRIES, EXTRATERRITORIAL

ENFORCEMENT, THE GRACE PERIOD, AND OTHER ISSUES 58 (Kraig M. Hill, Toshiko Takenaka, and Kevin Takeuchi eds., 2000).

Joachim Bornkamm, *Intellectual Property Litigation under the Civil Law Legal System; Experience in Germany*, WIPO/ACE/2/3 (June 4, 2004).

Otto Bossung, *Nachtrag zu "Unionspatent statt Gemeinschaftspatent,"* 2002 GRUR INT. 575.

Otto Bossung, *Unionspatent statt Gemeinschaftspatent—Entwicklung des europäischen Patents zu einem Patent der Europäischen Union*, 2002 GRUR INT. 463.

Curtis A. Bradley, *Territorial Intellectual Property in an Age of Globalism*, 37 VA. J. INT'L L. 505 (1997).

Ronald A. Brand, Punitive Damages Revisited: Taking the Rationale for Non-Recognition of Foreign Judgments Too Far (2005), University of Pittsburgh School of Law Working Paper Series, Paper 26.

Dieter Brändle, *Kann und darf Auslegung und Ermittlung des Schutzbereichs eines europäischen Patents in verschiedenen Ländern zu unterschiedlichen Ergebnissen führen*, 1998 GRUR 854.

Jan J. Brinkhoff, *Between Speed and Thoroughness: The Dutch "Kort Geding" Procedure in Patent Cases*, 18 EUR. INTELL. PROP. REV. 499 (1996).

Jan J. Brinkhoff, *Could the President of the District Court of the Hague Take Measures Concerning the Infringement of Foreign Patents?*, 16 EUR. INTELL. PROP. REV. 360 (1994).

Jan J. Brinkhoff, *The Desirability, Necessity and Feasibility of Co-Operation Between Courts in the Field of European Patent Law*, 19 EUR. INTELL. PROP. REV. 226 (1997).

Jan J. Brinkhof, *The Enforcement of Patent Rights in the Netherlands*, 31 IIC 706 (2000).

Jan J. Brinkhof, *Geht das grenzüberschreitende Verletzungsverbot im niederländischen einstweiligen Verfügungsverfahren zu weit?*, 1997 GRUR INT. 489.

Jan Brinkhof, *Pure Coffee? On Indirect Infringement*, in FESTSCHRIFT FÜR JOCHEN PAGENBERG 9 (Dietrich Beier, Laurence Brüning-Petit, and Christopher Heath eds., 2006).

Jan Brinkhof, *Wish List in the Area of Patent Law*, 35 IIC 407 (2004).

Bart J. Van den Broek, *Netherlands: Patents—Belgian Torpedo—Equivalence*, 23 EUR. INTELL. PROP. REV. N121 (2001).

Bart J. Van den Broek, *Netherlands: Patents—Cross-Border Injunctions*, 20 EUR. INTELL. PROP. REV. N132 (1998).

Bart Van den Broeak, *Netherlands: Patents—Preliminary Injunction—Cross Border Relief Refused But Relief Granted in Netherlands*, 22 EUR. INTELL. PROP. REV. N111 (2000).

Jochen Bühling, *Cross-Border Injunctions in Patent Infringement Cases: Paradise Lost?*, *in* BUILDING AND ENFORCING INTELLECTUAL PROPERTY VALUE (Krieger Mes and Grad v. der Groeben, 2007), 172–75.

Johannes Bukon, *Die Entscheidung GAT/LUK und ihre Konsequenzen*, *in* GEWERBLICHE SCHUTZRECHTE UND IHRE DURCHSETZUNG—FESTSCHRIFT FÜR TILMAN SCHILLING 59 (Marcus Grosch and Eike Ullmann eds., 2007).

Dan L. Burk, *Patents in Cyberspace: Territoriality and Infringement on Global Computer Networks*, 68 TUL. L. REV. 1 (1993).

Dan L. Burk and Mark A. Lemley, *Policy Levers in Patent Law*, 89 VA. L. REV. 1575 (2003).

Jan Busche, *Mittelbare Patentverletzung—zu den dogmatischen Grundlagen eines Rechtsinstituts*, 2009 GRUR 236.

Rudolf Busse, Patentgesetz (1999).

Ingemar Carl, Einstweiliger Rechtsschutz bei Torpedoklagen (2007).

Shigeki Chaen, Toshiyuki Kono, and Dai Yokomizo, *Jurisdiction in Intellectual Property Cases: The Transparency Proposal*, *in* INTELLECTUAL PROPERTY IN THE GLOBAL ARENA 77 (Jürgen Basedow, Toshiyuki Kono, and Axel Metzger eds., Mohr Siebeck 2010).

Eric Chan, *Asserting Foreign Patent Claims in U.S. Federal Courts: What's Left After* Voda v. Cordis?, 18 ALB. L.J. SCI. & TECH. 1 (2007).

Bernard H. Chao, *After* eBay, Inc. v. MercExchange: *The Challenging Landscape for Patent Remedies*, 9 MINN. J. L. SCI. & TECH. 543 (2008).

Colleen Chien, *Patently Protectionist? An Empirical Analysis of Patent Cases at the International Trade Commission*, 50 WM. & MARY L. REV. 63 (2008).

Donald S. Chisum, *Normative and Empirical Territoriality in Intellectual Property: Lessons from Patent Law*, 37 VA. J. INT'L L. 603 (1997).

Dongwook Chun and Minwook Kang, *Patent Law Harmonization in an Open Economy: How Should the Patent System React in the International Arena?*, 2 ASIAN JOURNAL OF LAW AND ECONOMICS 1 (2010).

Laurence J. Cohen, *Intellectual Property and the Brussels Convention: An English Perspective*, 19 EUR. INTELL. PROP. REV. 379 (1997).

Shlomo Cohen, *Jurisdiction over Cross-Border Internet Infringements*, 20 EUR. INTELL. PROP. REV. 294 (1998).

Avern Cohn, *A Federal Court Perspective on Extraterritorial Enforcement of Intellectual Property*, *in* RETHINKING INTERNATIONAL INTELLECTUAL PROPERTY: BIODIVERSITY & DEVELOPING COUNTRIES, EXTRATERRITORIAL ENFORCEMENT, THE GRACE PERIOD, AND OTHER ISSUES 31 (Kraig M. Hill, Toshiko Takenaka, and Kevin Takeuchi eds., 2000).

Lawrence Collins, *Provisional and Protective Measures in International Litigation*, *in* ESSAYS IN INTERNATIONAL LITIGATION AND THE CONFLICT OF LAWS 1 (1994).

W. R. Cornish, *Intellectual Property Infringement and Private International Law: Changing the Common Law Approach*, 1996 GRUR INT. 285.

Masato Dogauchi, *Private International Law on Intellectual Property: A Civil Law Overview*, WIPO/PIL/01/8 (Jan. 24, 2001).

Jens Dammann and Henry Hansmann, A Global Market for Judicial Services, *available at* http://ssrn.com/abstract=976115.

Felix Damme, Das deutsche Patentrecht (1906).

Denise W. DeFranco and Adrienne N. Smith, *Technology and The Global Economy: Progress Challenges the Federal Circuit to Define the Extraterritorial Scope of U.S. Patent Law*, 34 AIPLA Q. J. 373 (2006).

Philippe De Jong, *The Belgian Torpedo: From Self-Propelled Armament to Jaded Sandwich*, 27 EUR. INTELL. PROP. REV. 75 (2005).

Remco E. P. De Ranitz, *Jan Brinkhof in Conversation with Remco De Ranitz*, 21 EUR. INTELL. PROP. REV. 142 (1999).

Remco De Ranitz, *Mr. Justice Laddie in Conversation with Remco De Ranitz*, 25 EUR. INTELL. PROP. REV. 528 (2003).

François Dessemontet, *The ALI Principles: Intellectual Property in Transborder Litigation*, *in* INTELLECTUAL PROPERTY IN THE GLOBAL ARENA (Jürgen Basedow, Toshiyuki Kono, and Axel Metzger eds., Mohr Siebeck 2010), 31.

Alan Devlin, *The Misunderstood Function of Disclosure in Patent Law*, 23 HARV. J.L. & TECH. 401 (2010).

Alan Devlin and Neel Sukhatme, *Self-Realizing Inventions and the Utilitarian Foundation of Patent Law*, 51 WM. & MARY L. REV. 897 (2009).

Graeme B. Dinwoodie, *Affirmation of Territorial Limits of US Copyright Protection: Two Recent Decisions*, 14 EUR. INTELL. PROP. REV. 136 (1992).

Graeme B. Dinwoodie, *Developing a Private International Intellectual Property Law: The Demise of Territoriality?*, 51 WM. & MARY L. REV. 713 (2009).

Graeme B. Dinwoodie, *International Intellectual Property Litigation: A Vehicle for Resurgent Comparativist Thought?*, 49 AM. J. COMP. L. 429 (2001).

Graeme B. Dinwoodie, Rochelle Dreyfuss, and Annette Kur, The Law Applicable to Secondary Liability in Intellectual Property Cases, University of Oxford Legal Research Paper Series, Paper No. 51 (2009).

Masato Dogauchi, *Private International Law on Intellectual Property: A Civil Law Overview*, WIPO/PIL/01/8 (Jan. 24, 2001).

Marc Döring and Francis van Velsen, *Is Cross-Border Relief in European Patent Litigation at an End?*, 1 J. INTELL. PROP. L. & PRAC. 858 (2006).

Rochelle C. Dreyfuss and Jane C. Ginsburg, *Draft Convention on Jurisdiction and Recognition of Judgments in Intellectual Property Matters*, 77 CHI.-KENT L. REV. 1065 (2001–2002).

Rochelle C. Dreyfuss, *Resolving Patent Disputes in a Global Economy*, *in* PATENT LAW AND THEORY: A HANDBOOK OF CONTEMPORARY RESEARCH (Toshiko Takenaka and Rainer Moufang eds., 2007), *available at* http://papers.ssrn.com/sol3/papers.cfm?abstract_id=1226562.

John F. Duffy, *Harmony and Diversity in Global Patent Law*, 17 BERKELEY TECH. L.J. 685 (2002).

Richard Ebbink, *A Fire-Side Chat on Cross-Border Issues (before the ECJ in GAT v. LuK)*, *in* FESTSCHRIFT FÜR JOCHEN PAGENBERG 255 (Dietrich Beier, Laurence Brüning-Petit, and Christopher Heath eds., 2006).

Richard Ebbink and Charles Gielen, *First Europe-Wide Biotech Patent Injunction*, 16 EUR. INTELL. PROP. REV. 243 (1994).

Jochen Ehlers, Soenke Fock, Philipp Harlfinger, Stefan Horstmann, Gerd Jaekel, Karsten Königer, Anja Lunze, Johann Pitz, Christoph Schober, and Stefan Schohe, *Haftung für die mittelbare Verletzung von Rechten des Geistigen Eigentums (Q 204)*, 2008 GRUR INT. 935.

Douglas Ellis, John Jarosz, Michael Chapman, and L. Scott Oliver, *The Economic Implications (and Uncertainties) of Obtaining Permanent Injunctive Relief After eBay v. MercExchange*, 17 FED. CIR. B.J. 437 (2008).

Assafa Endeshaw, *Free Trade Agreements as Surrogates for TRIPs-Plus*, 28 EUR. INTELL. PROP. REV. 374 (2006).

Enforcement of Intellectual Property Rights Through Border Measures (Olivier Vrins and Marius Schneider eds., 2006).

Bernd Fabry, *Die Harmonisierung der europäischen Patentrechtsprechung—Notwendiges Übel—oder üble Notwendigkeit?*, 2008 GRUR 7.

Bernd Fabry and Michael Trimborn, *Die mittelbare Patentverletzung—Das unterschätzte Geschäftsrisiko*, 2008 GRUR 861.

Martin Fähndrich and Arne Ibbeken, *Gerichtzuständigkeit und anwendbares Recht im Falle grenzüberschreitender Verletzungen (Verletzungshandlungen) der Rechte des geistigen Eigentums (Q174)—Bericht für die deutsche Landesgruppe*, 2003 GRUR INT. 616.

Josine Fasseur-van Santen and R. A. Grootoonk, *Court of Appeal of The Hague—Some Recent Developments in Dutch Patent Law*, 14th European Patent Judges' Symposium, European Patent Office, O.J. 1/2009, Spec. ed., 157.

James J. Fawcett and Paul Torremans, Intellectual Property and Private International Law (1998).

Jonathan A. Franklin and Roberta J. Morris, *Symposium on Constructing International Intellectual Property Law: The Role of National Courts: International Jurisdiction and Enforcement of Judgments in the Era of Global Networks: Irrelevance of, Goals for, and Comments on the Current Proposals*, 77 Chi.-Kent. L. Rev. 1213 (2001–2002).

Mario Franzosi, *Germany: Patents—Unitary Character of a European Patent*, 22 Eur. Intell. Prop. Rev. N173 (2000).

Mario Franzosi, *Italy: Patents—Cross-Border Declaration of Non-Infringement—Italian Torpedo—German Torpedo*, 22 Eur. Intell. Prop. Rev. N142 (2000).

Mario Franzosi, *Torpedoes Are Here to Stay*, 33 IIC 154 (2002).

Mario Franzosi, *Worldwide Patent Litigation and the Italian Torpedo*, 19 Eur. Intell. Prop. Rev. 382 (1997).

Joe Fricker and Richard A. Kempner, *Can UK Courts Face the Dutch Challenge on Cross-Border Injunctions in Intellectual Property Cases*, 18 Eur. Intell. Prop. Rev. 377 (1996).

Jörg Fritzsche, Unterlassungsanspruch und Unterlassungsklage (2000).

Margot Fröhlinger, *Patent Litigation in Europe*, 14th European Patent Judges' Symposium, European Patent Office, O.J. 1/2009, Spec. ed., 157.

J. Rodrigo Fuentes, *Patent Insurance: Towards a More Affordable, Mandatory Scheme?*, 10 Colum. Sci. & Tech. L. Rev. 267 (2009).

Otto-Friedrich Frhr. von Gamm, *Die internationale und örtliche Zuständigkeit im gewerblichen Rechtsschutz*, 50 Mitteilungen der deutschen Patentanwälte 212 (1959).

Edwin D. Garlepp, *An Analysis of the Patentee's New Exclusive Right to "Offer to Sell,"* 81 J. Pat. & Trademark Off. Soc'y 315 (1999).

Richard Garnett, *Cross-Border Internet Trade Mark Litigation: Towards a Model of Co-Existence and Parallel Use*, 28 Eur. Intell. Prop. Rev. 213 (2006).

Reinhold Geimer, Internationales Zivilprozeßrecht (5th ed. 2005).

Reinhold Geimer, *Rechtsschutz in Deutschland künftig nur bei Inlandsbezug?*, 1991 Neue Juristische Wochenschrift 3072.

Michael Geist, *The Shift Toward "Targeting" for Internet Jurisdiction*, *in* Who Rules the Net? 91 (Adam Thierer and Clyde Wayne Crews, Jr. eds., 2003).

Edward Geller, *International Intellectual Property, Conflicts of Laws and Internet Remedies*, 22 Eur. Intell. Prop. Rev. 125 (2000).

Paul Edward Geller, *An International Patent Utopia?*, 85 J. Pat. & Trademark Off. Soc'y 582 (2003).

Olaf Giebe, *Gedränge im Vorfeld—Mittelbare Patentverletzung, Verwendungsschutz und unfertiger Gegenstand*, *in* Gewerbliche Schutzrechte und ihre Durchsetzung—Festschrift für Tilman Schilling 143 (Marcus Grosch and Eike Ullmann eds., 2007).

Jane C. Ginsburg, *Extraterritoriality and Multiterritoriality in Copyright Infringement*, 37 Va. J. Int'l L. 587 (1996–1997).

Richard Godson, A Practical Treatise on the Law of Patents for Inventions and of Copyright (1840).

Marc J. Goldstein, *Interpreting the New York Convention: When Should an Interlocutory Arbitral "Order" Be Treated as an "Award"?*, *in* HANDBOOK ON INTERNATIONAL ARBITRATION AND ADR 177 (Thomas E. Carbonneau ed., 2006).

Paul Goldstein, International Intellectual Property Law (2nd ed. 2008).

John Y. Gotanda, *Charting Developments Concerning Punitive Damages: Is the Tide Changing?*, 45 COLUM. J. TRANSNAT'L L. 507 (2007).

Klaus Grabinski, *Cross-Border Injunctions in Patent Litigations Following the ECJ Decision in* GAT v. LuK—*Life After Death?*, *in* PATENTS AND TECHNOLOGICAL PROGRESS IN A GLOBALIZED WORLD—LIBER AMICORUM JOSEPH STRAUS 565 (Wolrad Prinz zu Waldeck und Pyrmont, Martin J. Adelman, Robert Brauneis, Josef Drexl, and Ralph Nack eds., 2009).

Klaus Grabinski, *Kann und darf die Bestimmung des Schutzbereichs eines europäischen Patents in verschiedenen Ländern zu unterschiedlichen Ergebnissen führen?*, 1998 GRUR 857.

Klaus Grabinski, *Zur Bedeutung des Europäischen Gerichtsstands- und Vollstreckungsübereinkommens (Brüssels Übereinkommens) und des Lugano-Übereinkommens in Rechtsstreitigkeiten über Patentverletzungen*, 2001 GRUR INT. 199.

Clive Gringras and Andrew Inglis, *Conflict of Intellectual Property Laws: A UK Perspective on Europe*, 19 EUR. INTELL. PROP. REV. 396 (1997).

Sebastian Gronstedt, Grenzüberschreitender einstweiliger Rechtsschutz (1994).

Friedrich Groß, *Wie mache ich im Inland Ansprüche aus Schutzrechten geltend, deren Verletzung im Ausland erfolgt ist?*, 1957 GRUR INT. 346.

Hennig Grosse Ruse-Khan, *Protecting Intellectual Property under BITs, FTAs, and TRIPs: Conflicting Regimes or Mutual Coherence?*, *in* EVOLUTION IN INVESTMENT TREATY LAW AND ARBITRATION (K. Miles and C. Brown, eds., Cambridge University Press 2011).

Maximilian Haedicke, *Schutzrechtsverletzende Importe in die USA, das Verfahren nach "Section 337" und TRIPS—Zum Gebot der effektiven Rechtsdurchsetzung im internationalen Immaterialgüterrecht*, 1999 GRUR INT. 497.

Dietmar Harhoff, Economic Cost-Benefit Analysis of a Unified and Integrated European Patent Litigation System, *available at* http://ec.europa.eu/internal_market/indprop/docs/patent/studies/litigation_system_en.pdf (Feb. 26, 2009).

Dietmar Harhoff, Karin Hoisl, and Bruno van Pottelsberghe de la Potterie, *Languages, Fees and the International Scope of Patenting*, Discussion Paper 2009-06, *available at* http://ideas.repec.org/p/cpr/ceprdp/7241.html.

LTC Harms, The Enforcement of Intellectual Property Rights: A Case Book (2005).

Iris Haupt, *Territorialitätsprinzip im Patent- und Gebrauchsmusterrecht bei grenzüberschreitenden Fallgestaltungen*, 2007 GRUR 187.

Christopher Heath, *Harmonisation of International Patent Law?—A Reply to Straus and Klunker*, 39 IIC 210 (2008).

Christopher Heath, *Methods of Industrial Property Harmonisation—The Example of Europe*, *in* INTELLECTUAL PROPERTY HARMONISATION WITHIN ASEAN AND APEC 39 (Christopher Antons, Michael Blakeney, and Christopher Heath eds., 2004).

Christian Heinze, *Choice of Court Agreements, Coordination of Proceedings and Provisional Measures in the Reform of the Brussels I Regulation*, Max Planck Private Law Research Paper No. 11/5, *available at* http://ssrn.com/abstract=1804111.

Christian A. Heinze and Esther Roffael, *Internationale Zuständigkeit für Entscheidungen über die Gültigkeit ausländischer Immaterialgüterrechte*, 2006 GRUR INT. 787.

Timothy R. Holbrook, *Territoriality Waning? Patent Infringement for Offering in the United States to Sell an Invention Abroad*, 37 U.C. Davis L. Rev. 701 (2003–2004).

Timothy R. Holbrook, *Extraterritoriality in U.S. Patent Law*, 49 Wm. & Mary L. Rev. 2119 (2008).

Per von Holstein, *International Co-operation in the Field of Patent Law with Special Reference to the Activities of the Council of Europe*, 16 Int'l & Comp. L.Q. 191 (1967).

Cameron Hutchison and Moin A. Yahya, *Infringement & the International Reach of U.S. Patent Law*, 17 Fed. Cir. B.J. 241 (2008).

Tony Huydecoper, *Netherlands: Extra-Territoriality: French Appeal Court Recognises and Enforces Netherlands Decision Having Extra-Territorial Effect*, 17 Eur. Intell. Prop. Rev. D73 (1995).

Rebekka Hye-Knudsen, Marken-, Patent- und Urheberrechtsverletzungen im europäischen internationalen Zivilprozessrecht (2005).

Robin Jacob, Patents and Pharmaceuticals—A Paper Given on 29th November at the Presentation of the Directorate-General of Competition's Preliminary Report of the Pharma-Sector Inquiry, 2008, *available at* http://ec.europa.eu/competition/sectors/pharmaceuticals/inquiry/jacob.pdf.

Robin Jacob, *The Judge's Perspective—A Speech Given at the EPLA Munich Conference*, July 2007.

Christian Friedrich Jaeger, Ueber Erfindungs-Patente (1840).

Vincenzo Jandoli, *The "Italian Torpedo,"* 31 IIC 783 (2000).

Paul Joseph, *The Rise and Fall of Cross-Border Jurisdiction and Remedies in IP Disputes*, 1 J. Intell. Prop. L. & Prac. 850 (2006).

Ian Karet, *Cross-Border Skirmishing in* Fort Dodge v. Akzo, 20 Eur. Intell. Prop. Rev. 76 (1998).

Erhard Keller, *Patentverletzungen durch Handlungen im patentfreien Ausland*, *in* Festschrift für Eike Ullmann 449 (Hans-Juergen Ahrens, Joachim Bornkamm, and Hans Peter Kunz-Hallstein eds., 2006).

Konstantionos Kerameus, *Provisional Remedies in Transnational Litigation, 2nd Part, International Aspects*, in Trans-National Aspects of Procedural Law 1169 (1998).

Jay P. Kesan, *Taking Stock of the U.S. Patent System*, *in* Intellectual Property and Information Wealth: Patents and Trade Secrets (Peter K. Yu, 2007), 227–47.

Dariush Keyhani, *U.S. Patent Law and Extraterritorial Reach*, 7 Tul. J. Tech. & Intell. Prop. 51 (2005).

Eva-Maria Kieninger, *Internationale Zuständigkeit bei der Verletzung ausländischer Immaterialgütterrechte: Common Law auf dem Prüfstand des EuGVÜ—Zugleich Anmerkung zu Pearce v. Ove Arup Partnership Ltd. and Others (Chancery Division) und Coin Controls Ltd. v. Szo International (UK) Ltd. and Others (Chancery Division)*, 1998 GRUR Int. 280.

Carl Theodor von Kleinschrod, Die internationale Patentgesetzgebung nach ihren Prinzipien nebst Vorschlägen für ein künftiges gemeines deutsches Patentrecht (1855).

Jan Klink, *Cherry Picking in Cross-Border Patent Infringement Actions: A Comparative Overview of German and UK Procedure and Practice*, 26 Eur. Intell. Prop. Rev. 493 (2004).

Simon Klopschinski and Wolrad Prinz zu Waldeck und Pyrmont, *Der Schutz geistigen Eigentums in einer globalisierten Welt—Bericht über ein internationales Fachhearing der Bayerischen Staatsregierung und des Munich Intellectual Property Law Center (MIPLC) am 29. Februar 2008 in München*, 2008 GRUR Int. 393.

Rudolf Klostermann, Das Patentgesetz für das deutsche Reich vom 25. Mai 1877 (1877).

von Knieriem, *Europäisches Patent*, 1942 GRUR 449.

Oliver L. Knöfel, *Kein "konzernübergreifender" europäischer Mehrparteiengerichtsstand für Patentverletzungsklagen!*, 2006 MEDIEN UND RECHT INTERNATIONAL 127.

Louise Knudsen and Nicolai Lindgreen, *Danish High Court Rejects Pan European Injunctions in Patent Cases*, 26 EUR. INTELL. PROP. REV. 182 (2004).

Iouri Kobiako, *Durchfuhr als Patentverletzungshandlung?—Zugleich Anmerkung zum Urteil des LG Hamburg vom 2. April 2004*, 2004 GRUR INT. 832.

Toshiyuki Kono, *Intellectual Property Rights, Conflict of Laws and International Jurisdiction: Applicability of ALI Principles in Japan?*, 30 BROOK. J. INT'L L. 865 (2005).

Xandra E. Kramer, The Dutch Kort Geding Procedure in an International Perspective: A Comparative View on Provisional Measures and Private International Law, *available at* http://papers.ssrn.com/sol3/papers.cfm?abstract_id=1122344.

Rudolf Kraßer, Patentrecht (2004).

Rudolf Kraßer, Patentrecht (6th ed. 2009).

Layne E. Kruse and Rebecca H. Benavides, *Subject Matter Jurisdiction in Federal Court in International Cases*, *in* INTERNATIONAL LITIGATION: DEFENDING AND SUING FOREIGN PARTIES IN U.S. FEDERAL COURTS 133 (David J. Levy ed., 2003).

Thomas Kühnen, *What Becomes of Judgments on Infringement When the Patents in Suit Are Revoked: The Legal Situation in Germany*, 14th European Patent Judges' Symposium, European Patent Office, O.J. 1/2009, Spec. ed., 56.

Thomas Kühnen and Eva Geschke, Die Durchsetzung von Patenten in der Praxis (2008).

Annette Kur, *Immaterialgüterrechte in einem weltweiten Vollstreckungs- und Gerichtsstandsübereinkommen—Auf der Suche nach dem Ausweg aus der Sackgasse*, 2001 GRUR INT. 908.

Annette Kur, *International Hague Convention on Jurisdiction and Foreign Judgments: A Way Forward for I.P.*, 24 EUR. INTELL. PROP. REV. 175 (2002).

Annette Kur, *Jurisdiction and Choice of Law in Intellectual Property Matters—Perspectives for the Future*, 2004 GRUR INT. 306.

Julius Küster, Patent-, Muster- und Marken-Schutz in der Motoren- und Fahrzeug-Industrie (1908).

Stephen Pericles Ladas, Patents, Trademarks, and Related Rights (1975).

Mario Leitzen, *Comeback des "Torpedo"?*, 2004 GRUR INT. 1010.

Mark A. Lemley, *Are Universities Patent Trolls?*, 18 FORDHAM INTELL. PROP. MEDIA & ENT. L. J. 611, 621 (2008).

Mark Lemley, *Inducing Patent Infringement*, 39 U.C. DAVIS L. REV. 225 (2005).

Mark A. Lemley, David O'Brien, Ryan M. Kent, Ashok Ramani, and Robert Van Nest, *Divided Infringement Claims*, 33 AIPLA Q. J. 255 (2005).

Mark A. Lemley and Philip J. Weiser, *Should Property or Liability Rules Govern Information?*, 85 TEX. L. REV. 783 (2007).

David J. Levy, *Antisuit Injunctions in Multinational Cases*, *in* INTERNATIONAL LITIGATION: DEFENDING AND SUING FOREIGN PARTIES IN U.S. FEDERAL COURTS 163 (David J. Levy ed., 2003).

Dr. Lindenmaier, *Die Vereinheitlichung des Materiellen Europäischen Patentrechts*, 1942 GRUR 485.

Beatrice Lindstrom, *Scaling Back TRIPs-Plus: An Analysis of Intellectual Property Provisions in Trade Agreements and Implications for Asia and the Pacific*, 42 INTL. L. & POLITICS 917 (2010).

Andreas F. Lowenfeld, *Recognition and Enforcement of Judgments*, in INTERNATIONAL LITIGATION AND THE QUEST FOR REASONABLENESS 109 (1996).

Stefan Luginbuehl, *A Stone's Throw Away from a European Patent Court: The European Patent Litigation Agreement*, 25 EUR. INTELL. PROP. REV. 256 (2003).

Stefan Luginbuehl and Heike Wollgast, *IP Rights in The Hague Convention on Choice of Court Agreements, in* FESTSCHRIFT FÜR JOCHEN PAGENBERG 321 (Dietrich Beier, Laurence Brüning-Petit, and Christopher Heath eds., 2006).

Stefan Luginbühl, *Streitregelungsübereinkommen vs. Gemeinschaftspatent?*, 2004 GRUR INT. 357.

Lydia Lundstedt, *Gerichtliche Zuständigkeit und Territorialitätsprinzip im Immaterialgüterrecht—Geht der Pendelschlag zu weit?*, 2001 GRUR INT. 103.

H. Geoffrey Lynfield, *Patent Infringement on British and American Ships*, 37 J. PAT. OFF. SOC'Y 389 (1955).

Robert Andrew Macfie, John Maclaurin Dreghorn, and Michel Chevalier et al., Recent Discussions on the Abolition of Patents for Inventions in the United Kingdom, France, Germany, and the Netherlands (1869).

Fritz Machlup and Edith Penrose, *The Patent Controversy in the Nineteenth Century*, J. ECON. HIST., May 1950, at 1.

Vito Mangini, *Die rechtliche Regelung des Verletzungs- und Nichtigkeitsverfahrens in Patentsachen in den Vertragstaaten des Münchner Patentübereinkommens*, 1983 GRUR INT. 226.

William Martin, The English Patent System (1904).

Arthur T. von Mehren and Donald T. Trautman, *Recognition of Foreign Adjudications: A Survey and a Suggested Approach*, 81 HARV. L. REV. 1601 (1967–1968).

Wolfgang von Meibom and Johann Pitz, *Die europäische "Transborderrechtsprechung" stößt an ihre Grenzen*, 1998 GRUR INT. 765.

Peter Meier-Beck, *Aktuelle Fragen des Patentverletzungsverfahrens*, 1999 GRUR 379.

Peter Mes, *Reflections on the German Patent Litigation System, available at* http://www.springerlink.com/content/t71311177w294105/fulltext.pdf.

Tomoko Miyamoto, *International Treaties and Patent Law Harmonization: Today and Beyond, in* PATENT LAW AND THEORY: A HANDBOOK OF CONTEMPORARY RESEARCH 154 (Toshiko Takenaka ed., 2009).

Kimberly A. Moore, *Xenophobia in American Courts*, 97 NW. U. L. REV. 1497 (2003).

Robert Ryan Morishita, *Patent Infringement After GATT: What Is an Offer to Sell?*, 1997 UTAH L. REV. 905.

R. Moser v. Filseck, *Patentverletzendes Feilhalten und erlaubter Vertragsschluß bei Auslandsgeschäften (Bemerkungen Zum BGH-Urteil "Kreuzbodenventilsäcke" in GRUR 1960, 423)*, 1961 GRUR 178.

R. Moser v. Filseck, *Verletzung deutscher Patente durch Handlungen, die im Verkehr mit dem Ausland vorgenommen werden*, 1961 GRUR 613.

Rainer Moufang, *The Extraterritorial Reach of Patent Law, in* PATENTS AND TECHNOLOGICAL PROGRESS IN A GLOBALIZED WORLD—LIBER AMICORUM JOSEPH STRAUS 601 (Wolrad Prinz zu Waldeck und Pyrmont, Martin J. Adelman, Robert Brauneis, Josef Drexl, and Ralph Nack eds., 2009).

Jean-Marc Mousseron, Jacques Raynard, and Pierre Véron, *Cross-Border Injunctions—A French Perspective*, 29 IIC 884 (1998).

Alexander von Mühlendahl and Dieter Stauder, *Territorial Intellectual Property Rights in a Global Economy—Transit and Other "Free Zones," in* PATENTS AND TECHNOLOGICAL PROGESS IN A GLOBALIZED WORLD—LIBER AMICORUM JOSEPH STRAUS 653 (Wolrad Prinz zu Waldeck und Pyrmont, Martin J. Adelman, Robert Brauneis, Josef Drexl, and Ralph Nack eds., 2009).

Heinrich Nagel and Peter Gottwald, Internationales Zivilprozessrecht (6th ed. 2007).

George M. Newcombe, Jeffrey E. Ostrow, Patrick E. King, and Gabriel N. Rubin, *Prospective Relief for Patent Infringement in a Post-eBay World*, 4 N.Y.U. J. L. & BUS. 549 (2008).

Lawrence W. Newman and Michael Burrows, *Enforcement of Foreign Provisional Remedies*, 212 INTERNATIONAL LITIGATION (1994).

Lawrence W. Newman, *Orders in Support of Foreign Proceedings*, 226 INTERNATIONAL LITIGATION (2001).

Michael Nieder, Die Patentverletzung (2004).

Michael Nieder, *Die mittelbare Patentverletzung—eine Bestandsaufnahme*, 2006 GRUR 977.

Rudolf Nirk, *Grundfragen des deutschen Internationalen Privat- und Zivilprozeßrechts im Patent- und Lizenzrecht*, 60 MITTEILUNGEN DER DEUTSCHEN PATENTANWÄLTE 328 (1969).

Rudolf Nirk, *Zum Anwendungsbereich des Territorialitätsprinzip und der Lex Rei (Sitae) im internationalen Patent- und Lizenzrecht*, in EHRENGABE FÜR BRUNO HEUSINGER 217 (1968).

Gearoid O'Sullivan, *Cross-Border Jurisdiction in Patent Infringement Proceedings in Europe*, 18 EUR. INTELL. PROP. REV. 654 (1996).

Yoav Oestreicher, Recognition and Enforcement of Foreign Intellectual Property Judgments: Analysis and Guidelines for a New International Convention (2004) (unpublished S.J.D. dissertation, Duke University School of Law), *available at* http://scholarship.law.duke.edu/faculty_scholarship/700/.

Albert Ohl, *Der Sitz des Rechtsinhabers als Gerichtsstand der unerlaubten Handlung bei Streitigkeiten wegen Verletzung gewerblicher Schutzrechte*, 1961 GRUR 521.

Covey T. Oliver, Edwin B. Firmage, Christopher L. Blakesley, Richard F. Scott, and Sharon A. Williams, Cases and Materials on the International Legal System (1995).

Nicholas Oros, *Infringement Twice Removed: Inducement of Patent Infringement for Overseas Manufacture of Infringing Products Imported by Another*, 10 COMPUTER L. REV. & TECH J. 163 (2006).

Lucas S. Osborn, *Deconstructing an "Offer to Sell" in the Patent Infringement Context,* draft paper, on file with the author.

Andreas Oser, *The European Patent Litigation Agreement—Admissibility and Future of a Dispute Resolution for Europe*, 37 IIC 520 (2006).

Christian Osterrieth and Klaus Haft, *Grenzüberschreitende Patentverletzungsverfahren in Europa, in* FESTSCHRIFT ZU 50 JAHRE VPP 372 (Rolf W. Einsele and Erich R. Franke eds., 2005).

Jochen Pagenberg, *Another Year of Debates on Patent Jurisdiction in Europe and No End in Sight?*, 38 IIC 805 (2007).

Jochen Pagenberg, *Ausstellen und Anbieten auf internationalen Messen—eine Verletzung inländischer gewerblicher Schutzrechte?*, 1983 GRUR INT. 560.

Jochen Pagenberg, *Streitprotokoll für Patentverletzungen und Gemeinschaftspatent—Tagung der Untergruppe der Working Party on Litigation in München am 19. und 20.5.2003*, 2003 GRUR INT. 718.

Jochen Pagenberg, *Die Zukunft nationaler Patentgerichte im System einer künftigen europäischen Gerichtsbarkeit*, 2009 GRUR 314.

Jinseok Park, *Interpretation of Patent Claims in the EPO, USPTO and JPO—In the Context of the Doctrine of Equivalents and Functional Claims*, 27 EUR. INTELL. PROP. REV. 237 (2005).

Donald F. Parsons, Jack B. Blumenfeld, Mary B. Graham, and Leslie A. Polizoti, *Explaining Venue Choice and Litigant Preferences: Solving the Delaware "Mystery," in* ECONOMIC DAMAGES IN INTELLECTUAL PROPERTY—A HANDS-ON GUIDE TO LITIGATION 67 (Daniel Slottje, ed. 2006).

Andrew D. Patterson, *The Act of State Doctrine Is Alive and Well: Why Critics of the Doctrine Are Wrong*, 15 U.C. DAVIS J. INT'L L. & POL'Y 111 (2008).

Carine Peeters and Bruno van Pottelsberghe de la Potterie, *Innovation Strategy and the Patenting Behavior of Firms*, 2006 J. EVOL. ECON. 109.

Marta Pertegás Sender, Cross-Border Enforcement of Patent Rights (2002).

Marta Pertegas, *EC: Patents—Cross-Border Injunctions*, 28 EUR. INTELL. PROP. REV. N193 (2006).

Alexander Peukert, *Territoriality and Extraterritoriality in Intellectual Property Law*, in BEYOND TERRITORIALITY: TRANSNATIONAL LEGAL AUTHORITY IN THE AGE OF GLOBALIZATION (Gunther Handl and Joachim Zekoll eds., 2011).

Jeremy Phillips, *Should Forum-Shopping Be a Basket Case?*, 1 J. INTELL. PROP. L. & PRAC. 683 (2006).

Yves P. Piantino, *Switzerland's Treatment of U.S. Money Judgments*, 46 AM. J. COMP. L. 181 (1998).

Stephen G. A. Pitel, *Enforcement of Foreign Non-Monetary Judgments in Canada (and Beyond)*, J. PRIVATE INT'L L. 241 (October 2007).

Johann Pitz and Wolfgang V. Meibom, *Cross-Border Injunctions in International Patent Infringement Proceedings*, 19 EUR. INTELL. PROP. REV. 469 (1997).

Johann Pitz, Patentverletzungsverfahren (2003).

Johann Pitz, *Torpedos unter Beschuss*, 2001 GRUR INT. 32.

Bruno van Pottelsberghe de la Potterie and Didier Francois, *The Cost Factor in Patent Systems*, CEB Working Paper No. 06/002, *available at* http://ideas.repec.org/p/sol/wpaper/06-002.html.

Bruno van Pottelsberghe de la Potterie, *Innovation Strategy and the Patenting Behavior of Firms*, 2006 J. EVOL. ECON. 109.

Bruno van Pottelsberghe de la Potterie and Malwina Mejer, *The London Agreement and the Cost of Patenting in Europe*, Bruegel Working Paper No. 2008/05, *available at* http://ideas.repec.org/p/cpr/ceprdp/7033.html.

Laurence H. Pretty, *Going for a Patent Preliminary Injunction*, THE IP LITIGATOR 19 (January/February 2006).

Alingh Prins, *Ein internationals Büro zur Vorprüfung von Patentanmeldungen*, 1931 GRUR 1240.

Iain Purvis and Christopher Floyd, *Can an English Court Restrain Infringement of a Foreign Patent?*, 17 EUR. INTELL. PROP. REV. 110 (1995).

Jonathan Radcliffe, *Patent and Trademark Issues in the United Kingdom*, THE IP LITIGATOR 37 (May/June 2006).

Michael N. Rader, *Toward a Coherent Law of Inducement to Infringe: Why the Federal Circuit Should Adopt the Hewlett-Packard Standard for Intent Under §271(B)*, 10 FED. CIR. B.J. 299 (2000).

Gaétan de Rassenfosse and Bruno van Pottelsberghe, *The Role of Fees in Patent Systems: Theory and Evidence*, Intellectual Property Research Institute of Australia, Working Paper No. 7/10, November 2010.

Franz Redies, *Zur Frage der Vereinheitlichung des Patenterteilungsverfahrens*, 1942 GRUR 450.
Sascha Reichardt, *Die Auswirkung des Nichtigkeitseinwands auf die internationale Zuständigkeit in Patentstreitigkeiten*, 2008 GRUR Int. 574.
Sascha Reichardt, Internationale Zuständigkeit im Gerichtsstand der unerlaubten Handlung bei Verletzung europäischer Patente (2006).
Jerome H. Reichman and Rochelle Cooper Dreyfuss, *Harmonization Without Consensus: Critical Reflections on Drafting a Substantive Patent Law Treaty*, 57 Duke L.J. 85 (2007).
Eduard Reimer, *Die europäische Idee im Patentrecht*, 1955 GRUR Int. 473.
Eduard Reimer, Europäisierung des Patentrechts (1955).
Eduard Reimer, *Patentverletzung durch Lieferung ins Ausland*, 31 Mitteilungen vom Verband deutscher Patentanwälte 85 (1931).
Bradley D. Riel and Paul T. Meiklejohn, *A Correlation Between the State of the US Economy and Patent Litigation Activity*, 92 J. Pat. & Trademark Off. Soc'y 71, 103 (2010).
Cyrill P. Rigamonti, *Theorie und Praxis der mittelbaren Patentverletzung*, 2009 Mitteilungen der deutschen Patentanwälte 57.
Michiel Rijsdijk, *Patent Cases: 1994 to the Present*, 22 Eur. Intell. Prop. Rev. 120 (2000).
Kendra Robins, *Extraterritorial Patent Enforcement and Multinational Patent Litigation: Proposed Guidelines for U.S. Courts*, 93 Va. L. Rev. 1259 (2007).
Anne M. Rodgers, *Forum Non Conveniens in International Cases*, *in* International Litigation: Defending and Suing Foreign Parties in U.S. Federal Courts 205 (David J. Levy ed., 2003).
Rüdiger Rogges and Klaus Grabinski, Patentgesetz (10th ed. 2006).
Maximilian von Rospatt, *Grenzüberschreitender Rechtsschutz für europäische Patente—III. Diskussion*, 1997 GRUR Int. 863.
Peter von Rospatt, *Grenzüberschreitender Rechtsschutz für europäische Patente—II. Teil: Entscheidungen deutscher Gerichte in Patentverletzungsprozessen mit grenzüberschreitender Wirkung*, 1997 GRUR Int. 861.
Francisco Rossi, *Free Trade Agreements and TRIPS-Plus Measures*, 1 Int'l J. Intell. Prop. Mgmt. 150 (2006).
Matthias Rößler, *The Court of Jurisdiction for Joint Parties in International Patent Disputes*, 38 IIC 380 (2007).
Haimo Schack, *Internationale Urheber-, Marken- und Wettbewerbsrechtsverletzungen im Internet—Internationales Privatrecht*, 2000 Multimedia und Recht 59.
Marko Schauwecker, *Die Entscheidung GAT gegen LuK und drittstaatliche Patente*, 2009 GRUR Int. 187.
Marko Schauwecker, *Europäische Union/EFTA—Revidiertes Lugano-Übereinkommen kodifiziert umstrittene EuGH-Rechtsprechung zur internationalen Zuständigkeit bei grenzüberschreitenden Patentverletzungsklagen*, 2007 GRUR Int. 552.
Marko Schauwecker, *Der Fall Voda v. Cordis im Lichte europäischer und internationaler Entwicklungen*, 2008 GRUR Int. 96.
Daniel Schimmel and Ila Kapoor, *Resolving International Intellectual Property Disputes in Arbitration*, Intell. Prop. & Tech L. J. 5 (February 2009).
Michael Schneider, Die Patentgerichtsbarkeit in Europa—Satus quo und Reform (2005).
Paul M. Schoenhard, *Who Took My IP? Defending the Availability of Injunctive Relief for Patent Owners*, 16 Tex. Intell. Prop. L.J. 187 (2008).

Gerhard Schricker, *Anbieten als Verletzungstatbestand im Patent- und Urheberrecht*, 2004 GRUR INT. 786.

Jacob A. Schroeder, *So Long as You Live Under My Roof, You'll Live By . . . Whose Rules?: Ending the Extraterritorial Application of Patent Law*, 18 TEX. INTELL. PROP. L.J. 55 (2009).

Andrea Schulz, *The Hague Conference Project for a Global Convention on Jurisdiction, Recognition and Enforcement in Civil and Commercial Matters—An Update*, *in* INTELLECTUAL PROPERTY AND PRIVATE INTERNATIONAL LAW—HEADING FOR THE FUTURE 5 (Josef Drexl and Annette Kur eds., 2005).

Reinhardt Schuster, *Das Gebot der Anpassung an die konkrete Verletzungsform im Patentrecht—eine unendliche Geschichte*, *in* FESTSCHRIFT FÜR JOCHEN PAGENBERG 57 (Dietrich Beier, Laurence Brüning-Petit, and Christopher Heath eds., 2006).

Rolf A. Schütze, Ausgewählte Probleme des internationalen Zivilprozessrecht (2006).

Steffen Schwarz, *Freezing Orders in the Context of the Lugano Convention and the TRIPs Agreement* (2004) (MAS-IP Diploma Papers & Research Reports, No. 13).

Torsten Schwarze, *"Das Ende des Schreckens?"—Beschränkung der punitive damages durch den US-Supreme Court*, 2003 NEUE ZEITSCHRIFT FÜR GESELLSCHAFTSRECHT 804.

Margrit Seckelman, *Industrial Engineering and the Struggle for the Protection of Patents in Germany, 1856–1877*, 5 QUADERNS D'HISTÒRIA DE L'ENGINYERIA 234 (2002–2003).

Rajita Sharma and Heather Forrest, *A Lifeline for Infringing Ships?*, 25 EUR. INTELL. PROP. REV. 430 (2003).

George M. Sirilla, William P. Atkins, and Stephanie F. Goeller, *Will* eBay *Bring Down the Curtain on Automatic Injunctions in Patent Cases?*, 15 FED. CIR. B.J. 587 (2005–2006).

Patrick Smith, *Harmonisation, Regional Collaboration and Small Patent Offices*, *in* INTELLECTUAL PROPERTY HARMONISATION WITHIN ASEAN AND APEC 227 (Christopher Antons, Michael Blakeney, and Christopher Heath eds., 2004).

Richard Spencer, *A European Patent: An Old and Vexing Problem*, 42 J. PAT. OFF. SOC'Y 371 (1960).

Dieter Stauder, *Die Anwendung des EWG-Gerichtsstands- und Vollstreckungsübereinkommens auf Klagen im gewerblichen Rechtsschutz und Urheberrecht*, 1976 GRUR INT. 465.

Dieter Stauder, *Cross-Border Protection of European Patents, Part One: A Stocktaking*, 29 IIC 497 (1998).

Dieter Stauder and Annette Kur, *Extraterritoriale Jurisdiktion und Streitbeilegung*, *in* GEISTIGES EIGENTUM IM DIENST DER INNOVATION 151 (Gerhard Schricker, Thomas Dreier, and Annette Kur eds., 2001).

Dieter Stauder, *Patent Infringement in Export Trade—The Vulnerable Combination Patent*, 3 IIC 491 (1972).

Dieter Stauder, *Patent Protection in Extraterritorial Areas (Continental Shelf, High Seas, Air Space, and Outer Space)*, 7 IIC 470 (1976).

Dieter Stauder, Patentverletzung im grenzüberschreitenden Wirtschaftsverkehr (1975).

Friedrich Stein and Martin Jonas, Kommentar zur Zivilprozessordnung (22nd ed. 2003).

Charlene A. Stern-Dombal, *Tripping Over TRIPs: Is Compulsory Licensing Under* eBay *at Odds With U.S. Statutory Requirements and TRIPs?*, 41 SUFFOLK U. L. REV. 249 (2007).

Mitchell G. Stockwell, *Implementing* eBay: *New Problems in Guiding Judicial Discretion and Enforcing Patent Rights*, 88 J. PAT. & TRADEMARK OFF. SOC'Y 747 (2006).

Eduard Stolle, Die einheimische und ausländische Patentgesetzgebung zum Shutze gewerblicher Erfindungen (1855).

Joseph Straus, *Patent Litigation in Europe—A Glimmer of Hope? Present Status and Future Perspectives*, 2 WASH. U. J.L. & POL'Y 403 (2000).

Dan Jerker B. Svantesson, *Geo-Location Technologies and Other Means of Placing Borders on the "Borderless" Internet*, 23 MARSHALL J. COMPUTER & INFO. L. 101 (2004).

Symeon C. Symeonides, *Choice of Law in the American Courts in 2008: Twenty-Second Annual Survey*, 57 AM. J. COMP. L. 269 (2009).

Symeon C. Symeonides, *Resolving Punitive-Damages Conflicts*, 5 Y.B. PRIVATE INT'L L. 3 (2003).

Louise Ellen Teitz, *Both Sides of the Coin: A Decade of Parallel Proceedings and Enforcement of Foreign Judgments in Transnational Litigation*, 10 ROGER WILLIAMS U. L. REV. 1 (2004–2005).

Volkmar Tetzner, *Die Verfolgung der Verletzung ausländischer Patente vor deutschen Gerichten unter Berücksichtigung des EWG-Gerichtsstands und Vollstreckungs-Abkommens*, 1976 GRUR 669.

Volkmar Tetzner, *Verletzung deutscher Patente bei Auslandsgeschäften*, 1980 GRUR 882.

Theobald, *Englische Gedanken über ein britisches Reichspatent*, 1920 GRUR 29.

John R. Thomas, *Litigation Beyond the Technological Frontier: Comparative Approaches to Multinational Patent Enforcement*, 27 LAW & POL'Y INT'L BUS. 277 (1996).

Hans Christian Thomsen, *Recent Developments in Denmark Since 2006*, 14th European Patent Judges' Symposium, European Patent Office, O.J. 1/2009, Spec. ed., 127.

Winfried Tilmann and Andreas von Falck, *EU-Patentrechtsharmonisierung II: Forum-Shopping und Torpedo*, 2000 GRUR 579.

Winfried Tilmann, *Harmonization of Invalidity and Scope-of-Protection Practice of National Courts of EPC Member States*, 28 EUR. INTELL. PROP. REV. 169 (2006).

Winfried Tilmann, *Gemeinschaftspatent mit einem zentralen Gericht*, 2003 GRUR INT. 381.

Winfried Tilmann, *Neue Überlegungen im Patentrecht (Teil III)*, 2008 GRUR 312.

Andrew W. Torrance and Bill Tomlinson, *Patents and the Regress of Useful Arts*, 10 COLUM. SCI. & TECH. L. REV. 130 (2009).

Marketa Trimble, *Cross-Border Injunctions in U.S. Patent Cases and Their Enforcement Abroad*, 13 MARQ. INTELL. PROP. L. REV. 331 (2009).

Marketa Trimble, *The Future of Cybertravel: Legal Implications of the Evasion of Geolocation*, manuscript, on file with the author.

Marketa Trimble, *When Foreigners Infringe Patents: An Empirical Look at the Involvement of Foreign Defendants in Patent Litigation in the U.S.*, 27 SANTA CLARA COMPUTER & HIGH TECH. L.J. 499 (2011).

Marketa Trimble Landova, *Public Policy Exception to Recognition and Enforcement of Judgments in Cases of Copyright Infringement*, 40 IIC 642 (2009).

Clare Tritton and Guy Tritton, *The Brussels Convention and Intellectual Property*, 9 EUR. INTELL. PROP. REV. 349 (1987).

Alois Troller, *Europäisierung des Patentrechts und Gerichtsstand*, 1955 GRUR INT. 529.

Alois Troller, *Vorschlag für den Abschluß eines Gerichtsstands- und Vollstreckungsabkommens zwischen einzelnen Mitgliedstaaten der PVÜ in Form einer Union restreinte*, 1956 GRUR INT. 521.

John E. Tsavaris II, *Proceedings After KSM: Has the Federal Circuit Infringed Patentee's Rights*, 54 FORDHAM L. REV. 1005 (1985–1986).

Bruno Vandermeulen, *Harmonization of IP Litigation Practice—Still a Long Road Ahead*, 1 J. INTELL. PROP. L. & PRAC. 30 (2005).

Pierre Véron, *ECJ Restores Torpedo Power*, 35 IIC 638 (2004).

Pierre Véron, *Thirty Years of Experience with the Brussels Convention in Patent Infringement Litigation*, 84 J. PAT. & TRADEMARK OFF. SOC'Y 431 (2002).

Peirre and Margerie Véron, *The Internet: A Fourth Procedural Dimension for Patent Infringement Litigation*, in FESTSCHRIFT FÜR JOCHEN PAGENBERG 363 (Dietrich Beier, Laurence Brüning-Petit, and Christopher Heath eds., 2006).

Fernand De Visscher, *Belgium: Patents—International Jursidiction*, 24 EUR. INTELL. PROP. REV. N30 (2002).

Christopher Wadlow, *Strasbourg, the Forgotten Patent Convention, and the Origins of the European Patents Jurisdiction*, 41 IIC 123 (2010).

David E. Wagoner, *Interim Relief in International Arbitration—Enforcement Is a Substantial Problem, in* HANDBOOK ON INTERNATIONAL ARBITRATION AND ADR 145 (Thomas E. Carbonneau ed., 2006).

Wolrad Prinz zu Waldeck und Pyrmont, *Patent Infringement in Europe*, 2005 GRUR INT. 32.

Albert Henry Walker, Text-Book of the Patent Laws of the United States of America (1904).

Steven Warner and Susie Middlemiss, *Patent Litigation in Multiple Jurisdictions: An End to Cross Border Relief in Europe*, 28 EUR. INTELL. PROP. REV. 580 (2006).

Melissa Feeney Wasserman, *Divided Infringement: Expanding the Extraterritorial Scope of Patent Law*, 82 N.Y.U. L. REV. 281 (2007).

Kimberlee Weatherall, *Can Substantive Law Harmonisation and Technology Provide Genuine Alternatives to Conflict Rules in Intellectual Property?*, 11 MEDIA & ARTS L. REV. 393 (2006).

Arnulf Weigel, Gerichtsbarkeit, internationale Zuständigkeit und Territorialitäts-Prinzip im deutschen gewerblichen Rechtsschutz (1973).

Randall B. Weill, *The Internet and Personal Jurisdiction in the United States, in* INTERNATIONAL JUDICIAL ASSISTANCE IN CIVIL MATTERS 209 (Dennis Campbell ed., 1999).

David Westin and Peter Chrocziel, *Interim Relief Awarded by U.S. and German Courts in Support of Foreign Proceedings*, 28 COLUM. J. TRANSNAT'L L. 723 (1990).

Friedrich Georg Wieck, Grundsätze des Patentwesens (1839).

Paul Wiegand, *Die europäische Vereinheitlichung auf dem Gebiet der Rechtsprechung in Patentangelegenheiten*, 1942 GRUR 468.

Dirk Wüstenberg, *Die Haftung der Veranstalter von Teleshopping-Programmen wegen Patentrechtsverletzungen durch Verkauf*, 2002 GRUR 649.

Larry S. Zelson, *The Illusion of "Offer to Sell" Patent Infringement: When an Offer Is an Offer But Is Not an Offer*, 154 U. PA. L. REV. 1283 (2006).

Matthias Zigann, Entscheidungen inländischer Gerichte über ausländische gewerbliche Schutzrechte und Urheberrechte (2002).

DOCUMENTS—U.S.

ALI/UNIDROIT Principles and Rules of Transnational Civil Procedure, Proposed Final Draft (ALI 2004).

Intellectual Property: Principles Governing Jurisdiction, Choice of Law, and Judgments in Transnational Disputes (ALI 2008).

Restatement (Third) of Foreign Relations Law.
Restatement (Second) of Conflict of Laws.
2000 Special 301 Report, *available at* http://www.keionline.org/ustr/2000special301.
2001 Special 301 Report, *available at* http://www.keionline.org/sites/default/files/ustr_special301_2001.pdf.
2002 Special 301 Report, *available at* http://www.keionline.org/sites/default/files/ustr_special301_2002.pdf.
2003 Special 301 Report, May 1, 2003, *available at* http://www.keionline.org/sites/default/files/ustr_special301_2003.pdf.
2004 Special 301 Report *available at* http://www.keionline.org/sites/default/files/ustr_special301_2004.pdf.
2005 Special 301 Report, *available at* http://www.ustraderep.gov/assets/Document_Library/Reports_Publications/2005/2005_Special_301/asset_upload_file195_7636.pdf.
2006 Special 301 Report, *available at* http://www.ustraderep.gov/assets/Document_Library/Reports_Publications/2006/2006_Special_301_Review/asset_upload_file473_9336.pdf.
2007 Special 301 Report, *available at* http://www.ustr.gov/sites/default/files/asset_upload_file230_11122.pdf.
2008 Special 301 Report, *available at* http://www.ustr.gov/sites/default/files/asset_upload_file553_14869.pdf.
2009 Special 301 Report, Apr. 30, 2009, *available at* http://www.ustr.gov/sites/default/files/Full%20Version%20of%20the%202009%20SPECIAL%20301%20REPORT.pdf.
2010 Special 301 Report, Apr. 30, 2010, *available at* http://www.ustr.gov/webfm_send/1906.
2011 Special 301 Report, April 2011, *available at* http://www.ustr.gov/webfm_send/2841.
Trilateral Statistical Report, 2007 Edition, *available at* http://www.trilateral.net/statistics/tsr/2007/TSR.pdf.

DOCUMENTS—EU

Report on the Convention on Jurisdiction and the Enforcement of Judgments in Civil and Commercial Matters, P. Jenard, 1979 O.J. (C 59) 1.
Green Paper on the Community Patent and the Patent System in Europe, COM(97) 314 final (June 24, 1997).
General Affairs Council Meeting, 5455/99 (Jan. 25, 1999).
Proposal for a Council Regulation on the Community Patent, COM(2000) 412 final (Aug. 1, 2000).
Proposal for a Directive of the European Parliament and of the Council on Measures and Procedures to Ensure the Enforcement of Intellectual Property Rights, COM(2003) 46 final (Jan. 30, 2003).
Proposal for a Council Decision Conferring Jurisdiction on the Court of Justice in Disputes Relating to the Community Patent, COM(2003) 827 final (Dec. 13, 2003).
Proposal for a Council Decision Establishing the Community Patent Court and Concerning Appeals Before the Court of First Instance, COM(2003) 828 final (Dec. 13, 2003).
Proposal for a European Parliament and Council Directive on Criminal Measures Aimed at Ensuring the Enforcement of Intellectual Property Rights, COM(2005) 276-1 (July 12, 2005).
Proposal for a Council Framework Decision to Strengthen the Criminal Law Framework to Combat Intellectual Property Offences, COM(2005) 276-2 (July 12, 2005).

Amended Proposal for a Directive of the European Parliament and of the Council on Criminal Measures Aimed at Ensuring the Enforcement of Intellectual Property Rights, COM(2006) 168 final (April 26, 2006).

Communication from the Commission to the European Parliament and the Council—Enhancing the Patent System in Europe, 8302/07 (Apr. 4, 2007).

An Industrial Property Rights Strategy for Europe, Communication from the Commission to the European Parliament, the Council and the European Economic and Social Committee, COM(2008) 465 final (July 16, 2008).

Draft Agreement on the European Union Patent Court and Draft Statute, Council of the European Union, 14970/08 (Nov. 4, 2008).

Recommendation from the Commission to the Council, To Authorise the Commission to Open Negotiations for the Adoption of an Agreement Creating a Unified Patent Litigation System, SEC (2009) 330 final (Mar. 20, 2009).

Green Paper on the Review of Council Regulation (EC) No 44/2001 on Jurisdiction and the Recognition and Enforcement of Judgments in Civil and Commercial Matters, COM(2009) 175 final (Apr. 21, 2009).

Convention on Jurisdiction and the Recognition and Enforcement of Judgments in Civil and Commercial Matters, 2009 O.J. (L 147) 5.

Towards an Enhanced Partnership between Patent Offices under the Community Patent—European Standard for Searches, 12342/09 (July 30, 2009).

Explanatory Report, Fausto Pocar, 2009 O.J. (C319) 1.

Conclusions on an Enhanced Patent System in Europe, Council of the European Union (Dec. 4, 2009), *available at* http://www.consilium.europa.eu/uedocs/cms_data/docs/pressdata/en/intm/111744.pdf.

Report on EU Customs Enforcement of Intellectual Property Rights—Results at the EU Border—2009, 2 and 17, *available at* http://ec.europa.eu/taxation_customs/resources/documents/customs/customs_controls/counterfeit_piracy/statistics/statistics_2009.pdf.

Proposal for a Regulation of the European Parliament and of the Council on Jurisdiction and the Recognition and Enforcement of Judgments in Civil and Commercial Matters (Recast), COM(2010) 748 final, Dec. 14, 2010.

Draft Agreement on the Creation of a European and Community Patent Court Is Not Compatible with European Union Law, Court of Justice of the European Union, Press Release No. 17/11, Mar. 8, 2011.

Proposal for a Regulation of the European Parliament and of the Council Implementing Enhanced Cooperation in the Area of Creation of Unitary Patent Protection, COM(2011) 215/3.

Impact Assessment, Accompanying Document to the Proposal for a Regulation of the European Parliament and of the Council Implementing Enhanced Cooperation in the Area of Creation of Unitary Patent Protection, SEC(2011) 482/2.

DOCUMENTS—EPO

The Structure Paper of the Working Party on Litigation Mandated by the Intergovernmental Conference of the Member States of the European Patent Organisation on the Reform of the Patent System in Europe, *in The First Steps Towards an Optional Protocol under the European*

Patent Convention on the Settlement of Litigation Concerning European Patents, 22 EUR. INTELL. PROP. REV. 2 (2000).
Assessment of the Impact of the European Patent Litigation Agreement (EPLA) on Litigation of European Patents (European Patent Office 2006), *available at* http://www.eplaw.org/Downloads/EPLA_Impact_Assessment_2006_.pdf.
EPO Annual Report, 2008, *available at* http://documents.epo.org/projects/babylon/eponet.nsf/0/79435870 24b8e445c12575a00056831b/$FILE/epo_annual_report_2008.pdf.
EPO Annual Report, 2009, *available at* http://documents.epo.org/projects/babylon/eponet.nsf/0/afbc07d9e3b95f12c125770d0055a883/$FILE/epo_annual_report_2009.pdf.

DOCUMENTS—OTHER

Annual Report of the Eurasian Patent Organization, 2008, *available at* http://www.eapo.org/rus/ea/reports/eapo_2008.pdf.
Annual Report of the Eurasian Patent Organization, 2009, *available at* http://www.eapo.org/rus/ea/reports/eapo_2009.pdf.
Annual Report of the Eurasian Patent Organization, 2010, *available at* http://www.eapo.org/rus/ea/reports/eapo_2010.pdf (last visited Sept. 2, 2011).
Compendium of Patent Statistics, OECD, 2008, *available at* http://www.oecd.org/dataoecd/5/19/37569377.pdf.
Compendium of Patent Statistics, OECD, 2009, *available at* http://www.oecd.org/dataoecd/5/19/37569377.pdf.
Draft Substantive Patent Law Treaty, WIPO, SCP/10/4, September 30, 2003.
The International Patent System, Yearly Review, WIPO, 2007, *available at* http://www.wipo.int/export/sites/www/pct/en/activity/pct_2007.pdf.
The International Patent System, Yearly Review, WIPO, 2008, *available at* http://www.wipo.int/export/sites/www/ipstats/en/statistics/pct/pdf/yearly_review_09.pdf.
The International Patent System, Yearly Review, WIPO, 2009, *available at* http://www.wipo.int/export/sites/www/ipstats/en/statistics/pct/pdf/901e_2009.pdf.
The International Patent System, Yearly Review, WIPO, 2010, *available at* http://www.wipo.int/export/sites/www/pct/en/activity/pct_2010.pdf.
World Intellectual Property Indicators 2009, WIPO, *available at* http://www.wipo.int/freepublications/en/intproperty/941/wipo_pub_941.pdf.
World Intellectual Property Indicators 2010, WIPO, *available at* http://www.wipo.int/export/sites/www/ipstats/en/statistics/patents/pdf/941_2010.pdf.
World Patent Report, WIPO, 2008, *available at* http://www.wipo.int/export/sites/www/ipstats/en/statistics/patents/pdf/wipo_pub_931.pdf.
Declaration on the TRIPS Agreement and Public Health, WTO, WT/MIN(01)/DEC/2 (Nov. 20, 2001).
Least-Developed Country Members—Obligations under Article 70.9 of the TRIPs Agreement with Respect to Pharmaceutical Products, Decision of July 8, 2002, WTO, WT/L/478 (July 12, 2002).
Extension of the Transition Period under Article 66.1 of the TRIPs Agreement for Least-Developed Country Members for Certain Obligations with Respect to Pharmaceutical

Products, Decision of the Council for TRIPs of June 27, 2002, WTO, IP/C/25 (July 1, 2002).
Implementation of Paragraph 6 of the Doha Declaration on the TRIPs Agreement and Public Health, Decision of August 30, 2002, WTO, WT/L/540 (Sept. 2, 2003).
Exclusive Jurisdiction and Cross Border IP (Patent) Infringement-Suggestions for Amendment of the Brussels I Regulation, European Max Planck Group for Conflict of Laws in Intellectual Property (Dec. 20, 2006), *available at* http://www.ip.mpg.de/shared/data/pdf/clip_brussels_i_dec_06_final.pdf.
Principles for Conflict of Laws in Intellectual Property, the European Max Planck Group on Conflict of Laws in Intellectual Property, Draft, March 25, 2011.
Explanatory Report on the preliminary draft Convention on exclusive choice of court agreements, drawn up by Trevor C. Hartley and Masato Dogauchi (Dec. 26, 2004).
National Patent Development Strategy (2011–2020), the State Intellectual Property Office, *available at* http://graphics8.nytimes.com/packages/pdf/business/SIPONatPatentDevStrategy.pdf.
The U.S. 2011 Global Patent & IP Trends Indicator, inovia, February 2001, *available at* http://www.inovia.com/survey/inovia_2011_US_IP_Trends_Report.pdf (last visited Apr. 19, 2011).

INTERNATIONAL, MULTILATERAL, AND BILATERAL TREATIES

Paris Convention for the Protection of Industrial Property, Mar. 20, 1883, revised in 1911, 1925, 1934, 1958, and 1967, and amended in 1979.
Convention Relating to the Regulation of Aerial Navigation, 1919.
Convention on International Civil Aviation, Dec. 7, 1944.
General Agreement on Tariffs and Trade, Oct. 30, 1947.
European Convention Relating to Formalities Required for Patent Applications, 1953.
European Convention on the International Classification of Patents of Invention, 1954.
Convention on the Recognition and Enforcement of Foreign Arbitral Awards, 1958.
Convention on the Unification of Certain Points of Substantive Law on Patents for Invention, 1963.
Patent Cooperation Treaty, June 19, 1970.
Convention on the Grant of European Patents, Oct. 5, 1973.
North American Free Trade Agreement, Dec. 17, 1992.
Agreement on Trade-Related Aspects of Intellectual Property Rights, Annex 1C of the Marrakesh Agreement Establishing the World Trade Organization, (Apr. 15, 1994).
U.S.-Australia Free Trade Agreement, May 18, 2004.
Amendment of the TRIPs Agreement, Decision of 6 December 2005, WTO, WT/L/641 (Dec. 8, 2005).
Convention on Choice of Court Agreements, June 30, 2005.
Agreement on the Establishing of the Nordic Patent Institute, July 5, 2006.
Anti-Counterfeiting Trade Agreement, Dec. 3, 2010.

LEGISLATION AND CONVENTIONS—EU

Convention of 27 September 1968 on Jurisdiction and the Enforcement of Judgments in Civil and Commercial Matters, 1978 O.J. (L 304) 36.
Convention for the European Patent for the Common Market, 1976 O.J. (L 17) 1.

Convention of 16 September 1988 on Jurisdiction and the Enforcement of Judgments in Civil and Commercial Matters, 1988 O.J. (L319) 9.
Council Regulation (EC) No. 40/94 of 20 December 1993 on the Community trade mark, 1994 O.J. (L 11) 1.
Council Regulation (EC) No 3295/94 of 22 December 1994 laying down measures to prohibit the release for free circulation, export, re-export or entry for a suspensive procedure of counterfeit and pirated goods, 1994 O.J. (L 341) 8.
Council Regulation (EC) No 44/2001 of 22 December 2000 on jurisdiction and the recognition and enforcement of judgments in civil and commercial matters, 2001 O.J. (L 12) 1.
Treaty Establishing the European Community, Consolidated Version, 2002 O.J. (C 325) 33.
Council Regulation (EC) No 1383/2003 of 22 July 2003 concerning customs actions against goods suspected of infringing certain intellectual property rights and the measures to be taken against goods found to have infringed such rights, 2003 O.J. (L 196) 7.
Directive 2004/48/EC of the European Parliament and of the Council of 29 April 2004 on the enforcement of intellectual property rights, 2004 O.J. (L 157) 45.
Regulation (EC) No 864/2007 of the European Parliament and of the Council of 11 July 2007 on the law applicable to noncontractual obligations (Rome II), 2007 O.J. (L 199) 40.
Council Regulation (EC) No 207/2009 of 26 February 2009 on the Community trademark, 2009 O.J. (L 78) 1.

Table of Cases

UNITED STATES

EUROPEAN UNION

GERMANY

Index